KU-307-276

Naming the Rose

Naming the Rose

ECO, MEDIEVAL SIGNS, AND MODERN THEORY

Theresa Coletti

Cornell University Press

ITHACA AND LONDON

This book has been published with the aid of a grant from the Office of Graduate Studies and Research of the University of Maryland, College Park.

First published 1988 by Cornell University Press.

International Standard Book Number 0-8014-2114-4
Library of Congress Catalog Card Number 87-47872
Printed in the United States of America
Librarians: Library of Congress cataloging information appears on the last page of the book.

The paper in this book is acid-free and meets the guidelines for permanence and durability of the Committee on Production Guidelines for Book Longevity of the Council on Library Resources.

For my father
and for the memory of my mother

Contents

Acknowledgments

I have received much support throughout the making of this book, and I am happy to have the opportunity to acknowledge it here. Nikhilesh Banerjee, William Munson, Pamela Sheingorn, and Peter Travis responded enthusiastically when this project was in its earliest phases. Richard Gilbert supported my efforts at the eleventh hour. Maurice Bennett, Phillip Berk, Vincent Marsicano, and Sheryl Stevenson brought to my attention materials that helped shape my discussion in critical ways. Annabel Patterson showed me how to turn a cumbersome rough draft into a book. Richard K. Emmerson generously and painstakingly commented on nearly every page of that draft, providing me with a virtual blueprint for revisions. Leopold Damrosch, Jr., gave good advice at every stage from script to print. As a critic, colleague, and friend, Heather Dubrow offered inestimable guidance and encouragement. Manju Suri graciously helped me keep my professional life in order on a daily basis. A grant from the Graduate School of the University of Maryland helped support the publication of this book. I have felt privileged to have Bernhard Kendler superintend the fortunes of this book at Cornell University Press.

I am especially grateful to the women whose friendship and forbearance have sustained me through the writing of this book and much else: Deborah Fox, Donna Hamilton, Joyce Reiser

Kornblatt, Katharine Kravetz, Marian Coletti Roberts, Carol Urban, Valerie Wilbur, Elizabeth Williamson, and Patricia Yeager.

Finally, I thank Umberto Eco for writing the novel that filled several years of my life with immense labor and pleasure and taught me to rethink my own idea of the Middle Ages.

THERESA COLETTI

Washington D.C.

Abbreviations of Works by Umberto Eco

AC	*Aesthetics of Chaosmos*
FF	"Frames of Comic Freedom" (in *Carnival!* ed. Thomas Sebeok)
PS	*Postscript to "The Name of the Rose"*
RR	*The Role of the Reader*
SP	*Semiotics and the Philosophy of Language*
SA	*La structure absente*
TS	*A Theory of Semiotics*

Naming the Rose

An ideological bias can lead a critical reader to make a given text say more than it apparently says, that is, to find out what in that text is ideologically presupposed, untold. In this movement from the ideological subcodes of the interpreter to the ideological subcodes tentatively attributed to the author . . . fiction is transformed into document and the innocence of fancy is translated into the disturbing evidence of a philosophical statement.

Umberto Eco, *The Role of the Reader*

The fact is that everyone has his own idea, usually corrupt, of the Middle Ages.

Umberto Eco, *Postscript to "The Name of the Rose"*

Introduction

The remarkable success of Umberto Eco's *The Name of the Rose* bears witness equally to the infectious appeal of a good story and the marketing strategies that have made this sophisticated novel appealing to mass culture. But this success has also puzzled observers of the literary scene, who have wondered how many copies of the novel purchased have actually been read. Massive hardcover and paperback sales in various languages have made *The Name of the Rose* what the trade calls a "phenomenon." The novel has held different meanings for its different readers: the Conference on Christianity and Literature has given it the Book of the Year award for the work that "has contributed most to the dialogue between literature and the Christian faith"; Hollywood has graced it with its secular imprimatur, "a major motion picture." Clearly *The Name of the Rose* has struck a dominant chord in academic circles and in the popular imagination and public taste.

The novel's broad appeal is partly attributable to its unusual treatment of a genre favored by its author and the reading public: the detective narrative. As detective fiction *The Name of the Rose* evidences the recent trend among so-called "serious" authors to use the material and techniques of genre writing such as the mystery to probe the nature of narrative itself.[1] In his engaging account of the creation of his novel, Eco describes how, wishing to make his reader a "prey" of the text, he chose among model plots "the most metaphysical and philosophical."[2] Though he disingenuously suggests that his model plot deceives the ingenuous reader ("this is a mystery in which very little is discovered and the detective is defeated"), Eco also intimates that his formula fiction serves a larger purpose:

> The fact is that the crime novel represents a kind of conjecture, pure and simple. . . . The fundamental question of philosophy . . . is the same as the question of the detective novel: who is guilty? To know this (to think you know this), you have to conjecture that all the events have a logic, the logic that the guilty party has imposed on them. . . . It is clear why my basic story (whodunit?) ramifies into so many other stories, all stories of other conjectures, all linked with the structure of conjecture as such. (*PS* 54, 57)

The philosophical appeal of detective fiction's "structure of conjecture" has recently won for the genre both an authorship and an audience among intellectuals and the "oppressively bookish."[3] Eco's long-time interest in the genre is reflected in his work on the James Bond novels of Ian Fleming and a recent collection of essays on Sherlock Holmes, a book whose stated gen-

1. Michiko Kakutani, "Mysteries Join the Mainstream," *New York Times Book Review,* 15 Jan. 1984. John Updike makes a similar point in his review of the *Rose;* "Baggy Monsters," *New Yorker,* 14 Nov. 1983, 190. On the recent theory of detective fiction see Robert Champigny, *What Will Have Happened: A Philosophical and Technical Essay on Mystery Stories* (Bloomington: Indiana University Press, 1977). My study is not concerned with the relation of the novel to detective fiction as a genre nor to its obvious borrowings from Conan Doyle; on the particular narrative strategies of the *Rose* as detective fiction, see Robert F. Yeager, "Fear of Writing, or Adso and the Poisoned Text," *SubStance* 14 (1985): 40–45.

2. *Postscript to "The Name of the Rose,"* trans. William Weaver (San Diego: Harcourt Brace Jovanovich, 1984), p. 53. This work was originally published in Italian as *Postille a "Il nome della rosa"* (1983). Hereafter, references to the *Postscript* are cited as *PS* plus page number.

3. Michael Holquist, "Whodunit and Other Questions: Metaphysical Detective Stories in Post-War Fiction," *New Literary History* 3 (1971): 143–44. Holquist mentions, for instance, Lacan's work on Poe's "The Purloined Letter" in his *Ecrits.*

eral purpose—to demonstrate the overlap of scientific method, detection, and semiotics—resembles the grand narrative strategy of *The Name of the Rose.* In his own contribution to this volume, Eco more pointedly elaborates the connection between detection and semiotics: "The sequence of events investigated by a detective can be defined as a text. Not only because it can be reduced to a sequence of propositions . . . but also because verbal and pictorial texts, as well as criminal cases, require . . . an 'idiolectal rule,' a code of their own."[4]

The philosophical purpose of the *Rose*'s detective narrative is remarkably compatible with the historical period and culture in which the novel is set. Though I do not think the *Rose* has inspired new groundswells of interest in Joachite apocalypticism, the Franciscan preaching of poverty, or monastic scriptoria, its popularity is surely attributable in part to the fascination with a vision of the medieval past which in recent years has swelled the sales of Tuchman's *A Distant Mirror,* revitalized the mythology of Arthuriana, and ushered in such pastimes as the Society for Creative Anachronism and "Dungeons and Dragons." With its gothic illustrations and its burnished tones, the *Rose*'s paperback cover was obviously meant to appeal to the audience attracted to this exotic medieval past. In the summer of 1984 promotions for the novel even found a place among the advertisements on New York subway cars.

Eco himself maintains that "we are witnessing, both in Europe and America, a period of renewed interest in the Middle Ages." This return should not surprise us, Eco says, for "modern ages have revisited the Middle Ages from the moment when, according to historical handbooks, they came to an end."[5] These contemporary revisitations have taken many forms, ranging from "wash-and-wear sorcery and Holy Grail frappé" to "re-

4. "Horns, Hooves, Insteps: Some Hypotheses on Three Types of Abduction," in *The Sign of Three: Dupin, Holmes, Peirce,* ed. Umberto Eco and Thomas A. Sebeok (Bloomington: Indiana University Press, 1983), pp. 204–5; see also the preface by Eco and Sebeok, and the essays by Sebeok and Jean Umiker-Sebeok, Carlo Ginzberg, and Gian Paolo Carettini.

5. These remarks are from Eco's essay "Dreaming of the Middle Ages," in his *Travels in Hyper Reality,* trans. William Weaver (San Diego: Harcourt Brace Jovanovich, 1986), pp. 63, 65.

sponsible philological examination."[6] But what they hold in common is a search for origin, a "quest for our roots" and for a "reliable" past about which we can be assured that "'it really happened like that.'"[7] However outlandish some of these cultural expressions may be—and Eco wittily recounts them—they may, according to Paul Zumthor, nonetheless constitute "for professional medievalists the sociological foundations for their activities."[8] It is, then, in the broad context of a medievalism ranging from the pop-cultish to the scholarly that the reception of *The Name of the Rose,* as well as its own appropriation of the Middle Ages, must be viewed.[9]

Thus the medievalism of *The Name of the Rose* is more than a picturesque backdrop for a quaintly arcane tale of mystery and murder. So too the novel's multifaceted reception signals more than a pleasant literary oddity. In this book I entertain both these large subjects. Taking seriously the intellectual complexity perceived by both casual and initiated readers, this book approaches *The Name of the Rose* as a novel of ideas. Specifically, I address the relationship between the novel's medievalism and its preoccupation with signs, focusing on the thorough ground-

6. Ibid., pp. 62–63. On the recent growth of medieval studies as an academic discipline see Cullen Murphy, "Nostalgia for the Dark Ages," *Atlantic,* May 1984, 12; Francis G. Gentry and Christopher Kleinhenz, eds., *Medieval Studies in North America* (Kalamazoo: Medieval Institute Publications, 1982).

7. Eco, "Dreaming of the Middle Ages," p. 65; Paul Zumthor, *Speaking of the Middle Ages,* trans. Sarah White (Lincoln: University of Nebraska Press, 1986), p. 10, and see Zumthor's general discussion of the modern reading of the Middle Ages, pp. 8–13.

8. *Speaking of the Middle Ages,* p. 11.

9. Medieval scholars have been awed by the extraordinary accuracy of the novel's many details, by its casual reference, for example, to influential though hardly well-known exegetes such as Hugh of Newcastle or by its description of manuscripts that clearly can be identified as Beatus Apocalypses. On Hugh of Newcastle see Richard K. Emmerson, *Antichrist in the Middle Ages: A Study of Medieval Apocalypticism, Art, and Literature* (Seattle: University of Washington Press, 1981), pp. 77–79. Eco's book on the Beatus Apocalypses, *Beato di Liebana,* was published in 1973. The novel's rich representation of medieval history and culture has even begun to impinge upon traditional scholarly discourse not primarily devoted to the *Rose.* Thus Charles T. Davis in a recent article on Ubertino di Casale mentions "one important error" in Eco's otherwise accurate portrait of the Spiritual Franciscan; see "Ubertino da Casale and His Conception of 'altissima paupertas,'" *Studi Medievali* 22 (1981): 1–2.

ing of its semiotic concerns in its representation of medieval culture. Though I devote my attention to the accuracy and precision of that representation, my concern is not primarily with accuracy per se but with the way the novel employs historical details to reflect on the uses of the past and on history itself. My general thesis is this: out of a concrete rendering of medieval social and intellectual life Eco substantively crafts a distinctly contemporary statement about language and meaning, responsible intellectual activity, and the nature of critical discourse.

My secondary aim is to consider what this mingling of medieval and modern means in light of the novel's reception. At the end of this book I consider the relationship between the *Rose* as a novel of ideas and as a best-seller, a relationship that is further complicated by the academic position of its philosopher/theoretician author. I see the *Rose*'s hybrid status in the public imagination as not simply peculiar but as a theoretical issue inseparable from the novel's attention to the conditions of discourse and its representation of a multiplicity of cohabiting languages. I maintain that *The Name of the Rose* lays a strong claim to our attention precisely because it is both a serious and a popular work.

The *Rose*'s semiotics, its modernity, its medievalism, and its relation to its author's other work have been addressed in reviews and commentaries on the novel, even that by Eco himself, but no study has considered these subjects in the context of a sustained reading of the entire novel.[10] A medievalist by training, I have inevitably employed the tools of my trade in the reading presented here, but my larger purpose has been to reflect on the obvious contemporary issues raised by the novel and on the very manner and spirit in which we study the past. Hence, I do not claim to offer primary scholarship or new findings on medieval culture for its own sake. Rather, I am interested in delineating the ways in which *The Name of the Rose* illuminates how we moderns might read the Middle Ages. Developments in the human sciences in recent decades have increasingly im-

10. The most substantive considerations of the novel I have encountered are Walter E. Stephens, "Ec[h]o in Fabula," *Diacritics* 13 (1983): 51–64, and the essays in *SubStance* 14 (1985), an issue devoted to Eco as novelist.

pressed upon us the importance of reflecting on our hermeneutic procedures. Declaring that our readings of the past cannot be innocent, scholars have reminded us that our object of study—the Middle Ages—"is produced by the discourse upon it." It is, in fact, no object at all, but rather "a practice, a process, and a work" constituted out of our prior interpretations and our present interests.[11] This book investigates the way Eco's novel self-consciously bears witness to the modern critical confrontation with the Middle Ages.

As I have told people about my work on Eco's novel, I have frequently been asked for whom I was writing this book. Though I entertain the fantasy that my audience might be as various as the audiences for the novel itself, I more realistically expect to find my readers among medievalists and persons interested in contemporary theory. Though these two groups increasingly overlap, the dialogue between students of the medieval past and of modern theory is still in its preliminary stages.[12] This book is a gesture toward the furthering of that dialogue. With this end in view, I have tried to anticipate the knowledge and expectations of these different audiences, assuming neither too much nor too little. Throughout this book, I have dealt with important medieval and theoretical matters in summary form, attempting to walk the fine line between adequacy and excess. Readers wishing to pursue matters unfamiliar to them will find guidance in the notes. The first chapter is intended to acquaint the reader with the general medieval and theoretical issues of the novel.

From its appearance in 1980 Eco's novel has provoked many inquiries about what it "means," to which he has responded elusively. These queries were ostensibly pressing enough to elicit

11. Zumthor, *Speaking of the Middle Ages*, p. 23.

12. See the remarks of Eugene Vance in his "Foreword" to Zumthor's *Speaking of the Middle Ages*, p. ix. Of course, medievalists are increasingly incorporating contemporary theoretical perspectives into their work; I refer to many of them in this book. An entire journal, *Assays*, is now devoted to "critical approaches to medieval and renaissance texts." One recent example of the overlap of medieval studies and contemporary theory is the collection of essays *Medieval Texts and Contemporary Readers*, ed. Laurie A. Finke and Martin B. Shichtman (Ithaca: Cornell University Press, 1987).

from him a little "poetics" about the making of the work, his *Postscript to "The Name of the Rose,"* in which he would have us believe that he decided to write a novel set in the Middle Ages for the simple reason that he wished to put to use the voluminous notes and files about the period he had been accumulating since 1952 (*PS* 14). Eco maintains that this largely anecdotal account of the genesis of the novel is not an interpretation of it; interpretation of this sort is proscribed ("The author should die once he has finished writing"). In fact, because the "material . . . reveals natural laws of its own," interpretation is impossible (7, 11).

The *Postscript* shows Eco backing off from interpretation in the most engaging ways. He claims, for instance, that the title of his novel came to him by chance, "and I liked it because the rose is a symbolic figure so rich in meanings that by now it hardly has any meaning left" (3). This statement reflects the characteristic manner and tone of many of Eco's pronouncements about his novel and, indeed, about all his work: it purports to give the eager reader an explanation for "the way things are" yet undercuts that explanation at the very moment of tendering it. Such statements, in fact, give to Eco's commenting voice a quality reminiscent of his detective hero William, who "laughed only when he said serious things, and remained very serious when he was presumably joking."[13]

Whatever frustration these noninterpretive disclaimers might pose to Eco's reader, such posturing is in fact related to the novel's central issues. Eco's glosses on his novel, as well as his attempts to disengage himself from any authoritative perspective on the interpretation of his own fictional discourse, must be seen in light of that novel's manifest concern with matters of interpretation, with the authorizing of discourse, with the certainties and uncertainties of meaning. His gesture of disowning his text, as recent theory has increasingly reminded us, humorously

13. *The Name of the Rose*, trans. William Weaver (San Diego: Harcourt Brace Jovanovich, 1983), p. 425. All quotations from the novel, hereafter cited parenthetically, refer to this edition. On the mixing of voices as a constitutive aspect of Eco's work, see Reginaldo Frascisco, "Un romanzo-saggio di U. Eco: 'Il nome della rosa,'" *Idea: Rivista di cultura* 37 (1981): 138.

questions the codification of ownership with which texts—and meaning in general—are associated.

Eco's disclaimers confound and humble an interpreter of *The Name of the Rose*, as does his consciousness of its readership. The *Postscript* describes the novel's creation, in part, as the creation of a particular kind of reader (47–53). Asked why the first hundred pages of the *Rose* are so demanding, Eco explains they are intended as "a penance or an initiation, and if someone does not like them, so much the worse for him. He can stay at the foot of the hill" (*PS* 41).[14] The interpreter thus modeled into the author's "accomplice" must then confront Eco's abiding concern with the constitutive "role of the reader" in all interpretive endeavors, and indeed the entire body of his theoretical work—would-be guides to the reading of the novel from which Eco playfully distanced himself with the work's initial publication. On the dust jacket of the first Italian edition he anticipates that the novel may be read in three ways. The first group of readers, involved with the plot, will tolerate the novel's bookishness and philosophizing because "it will sense that the signs, the traces, and the revelatory symptoms are nesting precisely in those inattentive pages." The second group "will attempt to establish connections (which the author refuses to authorize) with the present." The third category "will realize that this text is a textile of other texts, a 'whodunit' of quotations, a book built of books." To all of these the "author refuses to reveal . . . what the book means. If he had wanted to advance a thesis, he would have written an essay (like so many others he has written). If he has written a novel, it is because he has discovered, upon reaching maturity, that those things which we cannot theorize about, we must narrate."[15]

In distinguishing his theoretical work from a different, "narrative" discourse, Eco in fact calls attention to the connections,

14. Eco describes the "value of interpretive labor" in relation to medieval and modern texts in *The Aesthetics of Chaosmos: The Middle Ages of James Joyce*, trans. Ellen Esrock, University of Tulsa Monograph Series 18 (Tulsa, Okla.: University of Tulsa Press, 1982), p. 81; hereafter cited as *AC*.

15. Translated from the Italian in Stephens, "Ec[h]o in Fabula," p. 51.

simple and complex, between the two. They are simple, in that many of the texts that make up the "textile" of his novel are his own essays that "advance a thesis": as Eco observes in his *Postscript,* a writer's material will inevitably contain "the recollection of the culture with which it is loaded" (11). But the intertextuality of Eco's own theory and his narrative is subsumed in the novel's larger interrogation of the aim, authority, and reception of theory and narrative as distinct modes of discourse.

The would-be interpreter of *The Name of the Rose* can nonetheless approach these complexities with a sense of exhilaration. "Nothing is of greater consolation to the author of a novel," Eco states, "than the discovery of readings he had not conceived but which are then prompted by his readers. . . . For that matter, the large majority of readings reveal effects of sense that one had not thought of. But what does not having thought of them mean?" (*PS* 3–4). Borrowing the idiom of Eco's theoretical discourse, I offer here a system of interpretants in what is inevitably a "process of unlimited semiosis."[16] I have tried to keep in mind a comment Eco makes in his *Postscript*: "I wanted the reader to enjoy himself, at least as much as I was enjoying myself. This is a very important point, which seems to conflict with the more thoughtful ideas we believe we have about the novel" (59). The dialectic of enjoyment and "thoughtful ideas" recalls the familiar medieval distinction, usually associated with Augustine, between *uti* and *frui,* things to be used and things to be enjoyed. This distinction not only informs the novel's discussion of laughter, but it also corresponds to the contemporary Janus-face of Eco's own novel of ideas that has found a popular audience. Hence medieval and modern mingle fully in the enjoyment and use of *The Name of the Rose.*

Within the general framework of the approach I have outlined here, my discussion of *The Name of the Rose* is nearly as eclectic as the novel itself. I have appealed to history and semiotics, biblical exegesis and anthropology, medieval studies and literary

16. Umberto Eco, *A Theory of Semiotics* (Bloomington: Indiana University Press, 1976), p. 68; hereafter cited as *TS.*

theory. In weaving together these disparate discourses, I, like Adso, have often thought that "everything looked the same as everything else" (191). Exploring that sameness is largely what the novel—and this book—are about.

In the body of my text I have quoted from the English version of the *Rose*. I have checked my readings throughout against the Italian, and in places where the Italian has offered something different or enabled me to further my point, I have noted it. But I am also aware that the different versions of the novel themselves constitute a theoretical issue: translations are a version of intertextuality, and opinions about them in fact reflect notions about "the modes of existence of significant texts."[17] In the foreword to his *Theory of Semiotics* Eco speaks of the perils and pleasures of translation. He explains that the *Theory* had its genesis in an Italian work, *La struttura assente* (1968), which was corrected, enlarged, and rearranged as it was translated into various modern European vernaculars. After two unsuccessful attempts to translate the book into English, Eco decided in 1973 to give up the idea of translation and to write the book directly in English: "To re-write in another language means *to re-think*: and the result of this truly semiotic experience . . . is that this book no longer has anything to do with *La struttura assente* —so that I have now retranslated it into Italian as a brand-new work" (*TS* vii–viii). Eco has said elsewhere that a "translation is an actualized and manifested interpretation."[18] That means that my book is an interpretation of an interpretation of a work already presented as a transcript and translation of a version of an earlier translation. Into the labyrinth, then.

17. Jeffrey Mehlman, "Portnoy in Paris," *Diacritics* 2 (1972): 21. On intertextuality and translation see also Gayatri Chakravorty Spivak's "Translator's Preface" to Jacques Derrida, *Of Grammatology* (Baltimore: Johns Hopkins University Press, 1976), pp. lxxxvi–lxxxvii.

18. Umberto Eco, *Role of the Reader: Explorations in the Semiotics of Texts* (Bloomington: Indiana University Press, 1979), p. 35; hereafter cited as *RR*.

[1]

Eco, Sign Theory, and the Middle Ages

The Name of the Rose is the work of a distinguished semiotician, language theorist, and literary critic who has devoted much study to the Middle Ages. His unusual combination of vocations has thrown into relief both novel and author as avatars of intellectual fashion. More important, Eco's unique mix of interests has drawn attention to his novel as the meeting ground for his modern theoretical and his medieval concerns, provoking questions about the relationships between theory and practice, modernity and medievalism.

This chapter sketches in broad strokes the general character of these relationships. It is intended as a general prologue to the following discussion of how *The Name of the Rose* constitutes its fictional narrative out of both the Middle Ages and modern theory. Fiction, theory, and medievalism necessarily overlap at all points of *The Name of the Rose*, but the mingling of discourses and of medieval and modern concerns predominates in the three aspects of the novel I have singled out for discussion here. Part one of this chapter considers assumptions about Eco's novel and theory as parts of a single enterprise. Part two examines the relationship between medieval and modern language theory; it indicates how basic features of Eco's novel and modern theory are allied to medieval thinking about the linguistic sign. Building on this section, part three shows how the novel translates a contemporary preoccupation with language and sign theory into detailed portraits of medieval monasticism and apocalypticism.

I

Early reviews called *The Name of the Rose* "semiotic," observing that the novel consistently addresses the nature and interpretation of signs. But these observations served mainly to give notice to Eco's academic interests. Recently, the novel's theoretical implications have received more thorough attention: one theory-oriented American journal has devoted an entire issue to Eco as novelist.[1] Even a casual acquaintance with Eco's theory suggests how situation and character in the novel may profitably be read against the background provided by his other works. For example, Adso's gradual education as a reader of texts illustrates a basic point of Eco's semiotic theory: the encoded form and circumstances of a message, as well as the situation of its addressee, make it something "to which various possible senses can be attributed." The novel's representation of conflicting interpretations of Scripture and the Franciscan *Rule* on poverty aptly illustrates Eco's observations on the inevitable ideological bias of all reading. And the entire novel is a monument to what Eco elsewhere terms "the treasury of intertextuality" (*RR* 5, 22, 21). But *The Name of the Rose* epitomizes Eco's theoretical interests in a larger sense, for the novel's very fictiveness enhances Eco's effort to set forth in it an accessible yet comprehensive version of his semiotic and literary theory and to locate that novelization of theory in the context of current critical discourse.[2]

1. *SubStance* 14 (1985).

2. On the relation of Eco's theory and practice, see Walter E. Stephens, "Ec[h]o in Fabula," *Diacritics* 13 (1983): 51 and 64; and the remarks of Teresa De Lauretis, who calls the *Rose* a novel "built in the vast laboratory" of Eco's critical studies and politico-cultural activities; see "Gaudy Rose: Eco and Narcissism," *SubStance* 14 (1985): 15–16. This essay is adapted from her earlier work, *Umberto Eco* (Florence: La nuova Italia, 1981), pp. 81–90.

This commingling of fiction and theory can be approached first from the perspective provided by Eco's comments on the aesthetic text, which he deems "a sort of summary and laboratory model of all the aspects of sign function" and thus as paradigmatic of his semiotic concerns (*TS* 261). According to Eco, aesthetic messages are ambiguous, encouraging interpretive efforts that lead to the discovery of the flexibility of language; they are also self-focusing, drawing attention to their own shape. Aesthetic texts function semiotically to produce knowledge because they introduce new semiotic possibilities, compelling their addressee "to rethink the whole language, the entire inheritance of what has been said, can be said, and could or should be said." By both increasing the addressee's knowledge of codes and "training" semiosis, aesthetic texts challenge the organization of the semantic system. They offer the potential for change because they acknowledge that the world could be defined and organized by, and known through, other models (*TS* 274).

Eco's account of the workings of ambiguous "aesthetic" texts is broadly applicable to *The Name of the Rose*, which incorporates the processes of decoding and interpretation that the *Theory of Semiotics* describes. The novel raises the decoding implicit in the reading of aesthetic texts to the level of narrative activity, as William and Adso set out to crack the code that holds the key to the identity of the mysterious book. In the terms of contemporary critical discourse, *The Name of the Rose* thematizes decoding, which is also a preeminent feature of the mystery story's epistemology. But the novel also probes ambiguity and ambivalence as themes that in their own right serve as organizing motifs for its multiple plots, each raising questions about the models by which knowledge is organized. Thus, while the *Rose* as fiction must inevitably signify in the manner of an aesthetic text, the novel also addresses the process of signification itself.

The novel's densely semiotic theme is incarnated in a structure that iterates these concerns in its overall design. Eco deems this repetition an inevitable feature of aesthetic texts, in which multiple meanings and interacting codes produce "an underlying system of mutual correlations" that is realized in a work's "aesthetic idiolect": the systematic rule by which its many messages are consolidated (*TS* 271).[3] If his description of the manner in which aesthetic texts communicate corresponds to the narrative preoccupations of his novel, Eco's notion of the aesthetic idiolect likewise presents a fitting gloss to its structure and strategy. Because all its levels are interconnected, "the aesthetic text continuously transforms its denotations into new connotations; none of its items stop[s] at their first interpretant, contents are never received for their own sake but rather as the sign-vehicle for something else" (*TS* 274). The *Rose*'s overlapping multiple narratives might be referred to as the novel's "aesthetic idiolect," which, Eco maintains, will never be fully recovered by a critical process that can only "constitute continuous and unfinished approximations" of the idiolectal definition of a work (*TS* 273). From the general perspective offered by Eco's theory, then, *The Name of the Rose* emerges as an aesthetic text that epitomizes the structure and the experience of reading aesthetic texts.

Eco's observations on the semiotic workings of aesthetic texts are but a portion of a body of theoretical work that might be applied to *The Name of the Rose*. The novel in fact realizes some of Eco's best-known theoretical concepts, for instance, his ideas of closed and open texts, limited and unlimited semiosis, and the model or implied reader.[4] It is possible to read the *Rose* consistently in terms of Eco's own systematic categories, though these are often confusing in themselves.[5] But the character of

3. The definition of aesthetic idiolect is from William Ray, *Literary Meaning: From Phenomenology to Deconstruction* (Oxford: Blackwell, 1984), p. 128. The discussion of aesthetic texts is a summary of *TS*, 261–76.

4. For a discussion of these concepts, see Eco's "Introduction" to *RR*, 3–43, and, in the same collection, "The Poetics of the Open Work," pp. 47–66, and "*Lector in Fabula*," pp. 200–260. The idea of limited and unlimited semiosis pervades Eco's semiotic writings, but see especially *TS*, 68–83, and the recent *Semiotics and the Philosophy of Language* (London: Macmillan, 1984); hereafter cited as *SP*. For comments on Eco's notions of semiosis see Michael McCanles, "Conventions of the Natural and the Naturalness of Conventions," *Diacritics* 7 (1977): 54–63; and Kaja Silverman, *The Subject of Semiotics* (New York: Oxford University Press, 1983), p. 15.

5. See, for example, Eco's description of "closed" and "open" texts in *RR*, 8–10. Stephens offers an illuminating discussion of the novel in light of this and Eco's other categories; see "Ec[h]o in Fabula," pp. 52–54.

Eco's theory itself discourages such a reductive reading, for several reasons. First, with its encompassing interest in the structure of language and the sign, Eco's theory participates in the larger theoretical debate of recent decades, coinciding with, complementing, and challenging some of the major ideas in that debate. Second, Eco's theory is itself very eclectic: it ranges from the highly technical semiotic models of his *Theory of Semiotics*, through historical reflections on the structure of metaphor and symbol, to broad meditations on such diverse subjects as carnival, the avant-garde, and cultural criticism. In what follows I make regular appeals to Eco's own theory, taking advantage of its wide-ranging method and scope; yet I also use the work of other recent theorists to illuminate *The Name of the Rose*, underscoring how the novel incorporates the terms of recent theoretical debate. The novel itself calls for such an approach, for it is semiotic not simply or even mainly in terms of its author's own systems but rather in terms of the broader reflections on a philosophy of language and culture which, Eco maintains, a "general semiotics" will embrace (*SP* 4).

The complex interplay of theory and practice is illustrated by Eco's use of the labyrinth as the focal point for his novel's mystery and for its discussion of signs. In describing the monastery's library, Eco invokes his favorite metaphor for the aesthetic text: "Like a large labyrinthine garden, a work of art permits one to take many different routes, whose number is increased by the criss-cross of its paths" (*TS* 275). For Eco, the labyrinth is also a model for the "universe of semiosis," which "is structured according to a *network of interpretants*" and "is virtually *infinite*" (*SP* 83).[6] As such, it explains in part his attraction to Joyce's *Ulysses*, which he calls "a labyrinthic territory where it is possible to move in many directions" (*AC* 54). As structure and metaphor, the labyrinth is also signal evidence of Eco's large debt to Jorge Luis Borges.[7] The semiotic and intertextual implications of the structure of the *Rose*'s library are underscored by appeals to the metaphor of the labyrinth in recent theoretical discus-

6. Eco describes the semiotic resonances of three types of labyrinths in *SP*, 80–84, and in *PS*, 57–58.

7. On the Borgesian presence in the novel, see Stephens, "Ec[h]o in Fabula."

sions of narrative form.[8] The structure of Eco's narrative is itself labyrinthine; so, he maintains, is the world that its hero William inhabits.

The semiotic significance of the labyrinth as structure and metaphor in Eco's fictional and theoretical discourse underlines the difficulty of reading one in light of the other and cautions against equating Eco's novel solely with his other work. The relation of theory and practice is complicated further by what seems to be Eco's deliberate criss-crossing of his discourses, often with amusing effects. His recent *Semiotics and the Philosophy of Language* (1984) illustrates this criss-crossing well. The reader who comes to these essays after reading the *Rose* and encounters Eco's comments on distorting mirrors or his description of a code for labeling books in a library by which "the form of the expression maps . . . the spatial organization of the content" may very well think of Adso's first nocturnal visit to the novel's code-structured library (*SP* 176). It is in fact difficult to dismiss the likelihood that, in some instances at least, the theoretical discourse includes purposive and playful references to the fictional. For example, Eco inevitably recalls the central metaphor of his novel when, to explain how metaphors work, he submits two "genuine metaphors: *She was a rose* and . . . *Et rose elle a veçu ce que vivent les roses, l'espace d'un matin.*" "She was a rose," Eco asserts, is a "poor metaphor" (*SP* 121). But it is precisely the one Adso employs when he attempts to understand the meaning of the girl of his erotic encounter. Appealing to monastic theology's definition of the universe as metaphor, he expresses her significance in terms of the "humblest rose" (279). Adso's strenuous intellectual effort to fix the girl's meaning, as well as his emotional confusion, are hardly the result of a "poor metaphor," as Eco's comments on the working of metaphor suggest:

> The "deadest" trope can work "like new" for . . . any "virgin" subject, approaching for the first time the complexity of the semiosis. . . . Imagine a subject who has never heard of comparing a girl to a rose, who ig-

8. J. Hillis Miller, "Ariadne's Thread: Repetition and the Narrative Line," *Critical Inquiry* 3 (1976): 57–77.

nores the intertextual institutionalizations, and who responds even to the most worn-out metaphors as though discovering for the first time the relations between a woman's face and a flower (*SP* 128).

Adso's interpretation of the girl's meaning illustrates perfectly the "virgin" subject's encounter with a "dead" metaphor, just as Eco's theorizing about the freshness of such a reading experience seems inspired by the Benedictine novice himself. Such interpenetration of the modes of discourse may attest, in part, to the speaking of books among themselves, the "susurri di libri" in which William instructs Adso. But they also bespeak the purposive narrating of theory which is *The Name of the Rose.*

II

The semiotic self-consciousness that securely establishes the modernity of *The Name of the Rose* also reflects the intellectual preoccupations of the medieval period in which the novel is set. Indeed, it is hardly surprising that when one of Europe's foremost semioticians determined to write a novel about signs and interpretation, he should set it in the Middle Ages. Though some contemporary readers may think that sign theory began with C. S. Peirce or that the current fashion for regarding culture as a text is a modern conception, semiotics in fact flourished in the Middle Ages. In the "autobiographical" preface to his edition of the Beatus Apocalypse manuscripts, Eco explains how he came to study signs, "which the Abbot Beatus of Liebana had greatly appreciated," and how he began to unravel "the strands of the most ancient discipline of semiotics (which foolish people believe was invented only yesterday by the sycophants of structuralism, and which in fact was begun over two thousand years ago)."[9] Sign theory, as another critic puts it, is "the most singular feature of the intellectual coherence of the Middle Ages, seen as a phase of Western culture."[10]

9. The preface is reprinted in De Lauretis, *Umberto Eco*, pp. 5–8; the translation is my own.

10. Eugene Vance, "Mervelous Signals: Poetics, Sign Theory, and Politics in Chaucer's *Troilus*," *New Literary History* 10 (1979): 293.

Critics who accept the radical involvement with language as a distinguishing feature of contemporary culture have only recently discovered the medieval preoccupation with the nature and function of language as a system of signs.[11] The current interest in medieval sign theory has increasingly focused on its similarities to and departures from contemporary thinking about language.[12] But every age is conscious of the sign in distinctive ways. Hence we cannot easily equate medieval and modern perceptions of language; nor can we unquestioningly assume absolute differences between them. In this book I intend to illuminate the intricacies of these relationships, which constitute one of the primary subjects of *The Name of the Rose*. My concern is less with locating in the novel one-to-one correspondences between medieval and modern language theory than it is with identifying families of resemblances and analogous preoccupations. This procedure will enable us to see how the medieval absorption in language and its systems illuminates Eco's choice of setting for his modern "semiotic" novel.

When William addresses the gathering of imperial supporters and papal representatives who have come to the abbey to discuss

11. Brian Stock suggests that modern semiotics has resurrected a good portion of medieval language theory; see "The Middle Ages as Subject and Object," *New Literary History* 5 (1974): 535, n. 27.

12. R. Howard Bloch, *Etymologies and Genealogies: A Literary Anthropology of the French Middle Ages* (Chicago: University of Chicago Press, 1983); Margaret W. Ferguson, "Saint Augustine's Region of Unlikeness: The Crossing of Exile and Language," *Georgia Review* 29 (1975): 842–64; Jesse Gellrich, *The Idea of the Book in the Middle Ages* (Ithaca: Cornell University Press, 1985), and "Deconstructing Allegory," *Genre* 18 (1985): 197–213; Stephen G. Nichols, Jr., *Romanesque Signs: Early Medieval Narrative and Iconography* (New Haven: Yale University Press, 1983); Eugene Vance, "Augustine's *Confessions* and the Grammar of Selfhood," *Genre* 6 (1973): 1–28, "Augustine's *Confessions* and the Poetics of the Law," *MLN* 93 (1978): 618–34, "Désir, rhétorique et texte—Semences de la différence: Brunet Latin chez Dante," *Poétique* 42 (1980): 137– 55, "Mervelous Signals," pp. 293–337, "Roland and the Poetics of Memory," in *Textual Strategies: Perspectives in Post-Structuralist Criticism*, ed. Josué V. Harari (Ithaca: Cornell University Press, 1979), pp. 374–403, "Saint Augustine: Language as Temporality," in *Mimesis: From Mirror to Method*, ed. John D. Lyons and Stephen G. Nichols, Jr. (Hanover, N.H.: University Press of New England, 1982), pp. 20–35. Many of Vance's essays on this topic are collected in his recent book, *Mervelous Signals: Poetics and Sign Theory in the Middle Ages* (Lincoln: University of Nebraska Press, 1986).

competing interpretations of Franciscan claims to poverty, Adso describes how William refers his discussion of earthly and divine law to a consideration of language. Citing God's instruction to Adam "to give things names," William observes:

> though some in our times say that nomina sunt consequentia rerum, the book of Genesis is actually quite explicit on this point: God brought all the animals unto Adam to see what he would call them: and whatsoever Adam called every living creature, that was the name thereof. And though surely the first man had been clever enough to call, in his Adamic language, every thing and animal according to its nature, nevertheless he was exercising a kind of sovereign right in imagining the name that in his opinion best corresponded to that nature. Because, in fact, it is now known that men impose different names to designate concepts, though only the concepts, signs of things, are the same for all. (353)

William here addresses a fundamental topic of medieval language theory dating back to Plato's *Cratylus*: the problem of the origin of language in nature or convention.[13] Although the medieval period is customarily characterized as one in which a natural or "realist" view of the relation between words and things eventually gave way to an anti-Cratylistic or "nominalist" view of the conventionality of that relationship, medieval language theory in fact presents a range of attitudes toward the status of the verbal sign and the nature of language as a referential system. William's statement invokes both theories of linguistic origin. He refers to the naturalist view that "names are the consequence of things," which was represented by the medieval emphasis on etymologies. Yet he also elaborates on the idea that however naturally motivated Adam's chosen names may have been, they were nonetheless his choices. Even Isidore of Seville, whose *Etymologies* influenced medieval language theory for centuries, conceded that "not all names were imposed from the

13. See Marcia Colish, *The Mirror of Language: A Study in the Medieval Theory of Knowledge*, rev. ed. (1968; Lincoln: University of Nebraska Press, 1983), pp. 8–15. On Cratylism in general, see Gérard Genette, "Valéry and the Poetics of Language," in Harari, *Textual Strategies*, pp. 359–61, and his "Avatars du Cratylisme," *Poétique* 11 (1972): 367–94; 13 (1973): 111–33; 15 (1973): 265–91.

beginning according to nature, but some according to pleasure."[14] William's statement identifies an aspect of medieval language theory to which the attention of modern students has increasingly been drawn, the "split between what medieval writers *knew* about verbal signs and what they *desired* to believe about them—a split evident in the easy copresence of what seem like mutually exclusive explanations of linguistic origin."[15]

Medieval language theory was far from simple. It was the product of centuries of commentary on the language arts—grammar, rhetoric, logic; it intersected in fundamental ways with theology and philosophy; it was central to medieval epistemology. In the Middle Ages, as in our own time, thinking about language both reflected and contributed to a changing intellectual and social environment. For all these reasons, the language theory of the Middle Ages does not lend itself easily, if at all, to summary or schematization, though it has often necessitated such treatment. The discussion that follows does not pretend to be an overview of so vast and rich a subject. Rather, it offers a selective treatment of some major thinkers and issues in the medieval reflection on the linguistic sign, chosen both for their centrality to that reflection and for their relevance to Eco's novel.[16]

14. *Etymologiarum sive originum* 1.29.2, ed. W. M. Lindsay, 2 vols. (Oxford: Clarendon Press, 1911). On Isidore, see Ernst Curtius, *European Literature and the Latin Middle Ages*, trans. Willard R. Trask (New York: Harper and Row, 1963), pp. 450–57.

15. Bloch, *Etymologies and Genealogies*, p. 44. John Alford expresses a similar view in "The Grammatical Metaphor: A Survey of Its Use in the Middle Ages," *Speculum* 57 (1982): 736–37.

16. For an excellent discussion of the recent study of medieval language theory, the challenges it faces, and questions it needs to address, see G. L. Bursill-Hall's "Introduction" to the collection of essays by R. W. Hunt, *The History of Grammar in the Middle Ages*, Studies in the History of Linguistics 5, Amsterdam Studies in the Theory and History of Linguistic Science 3 (Amsterdam: John Benjamins, 1980), pp. ix–xxiv. Bursill-Hall provides an extensive bibliography of recent editions of texts and studies in medieval language theory, pp. xxvii–xxxvi. For another up-to-date bibliography on this subject, see Jan Ziolkowski, *Alan of Lille's Grammar of Sex: The Meaning of Grammar to a Twelfth-Century Intellectual*, Speculum Anniversary Monographs 10 (Cambridge, Mass.: Medieval Academy of America, 1985), pp. 145–71. Contemporary students of medieval language theory still acknowledge their debt to Charles Thurot's compila-

Any discussion of medieval language theory must take into account the work of Augustine, whose interest in signs in many of his major writings marks him as the first and most influential Christian theoretician of language. The preoccupations of Augustine's sign theory—its notion of the epistemological centrality of the sign, its attention to techniques and variability of interpretation—have made his work the starting point for the contemporary probing of medieval views of language, which has found therein a detailed and often passionate approach to the linguistic sign that corresponds to the concerns of our own time.

Augustine wholeheartedly accepts the conventionality of the linguistic sign. His *De magistro*, a dialogue with his son, Adeodatus, offers a commentary on signs manifested in words and things, looking closely, and often playfully, at this subject. For instance, Augustine explains to Adeodatus how the word "nihil" (nothing) is not identical with what it signifies, since "something" is meant by it. The non-identity of sign and referent is also intended by Adeodatus's assertion that the word "'filth' [*coenum*] . . . far excels the reality it signifies."[17] This acknowledgment of the sign's conventionality undergirds Augustine's exploration of multiple meanings in scriptural interpretation. In *De doctrina christiana* he explains how words may signify not only contrary or two diverse things "but sometimes many different things in accordance with the meaning of passages in which they are found."[18] He elaborates on this multiplicity in his discussion of Genesis in book twelve of the *Confessions*, where he anchors the variability of the scriptural sign to the internal disposition of the reader or hearer and to the intentionality of revealed truth.[19]

---

tion of excerpts from manuscripts from the Carolingian period to the Renaissance: *Notices et extraits de divers manuscrits latins pour servir à l'histoire des doctrines grammaticales au moyen âge* (Paris, 1869; rpt. Frankfurt: Minerva, 1964).

17. *The Teacher*, trans. Robert B. Russell, *Fathers of the Church*, vol. 59 (Washington, D.C.: Catholic University of America Press, 1968), pp. 10–11, 38.

18. *On Christian Doctrine* 3.25.37, trans. D. W. Robertson, Jr. (Indianapolis: Bobbs-Merrill, 1958), p. 101.

19. *The Confessions of St. Augustine*, 12.18–32, trans. John K. Ryan (Garden City, N.Y.: Doubleday, 1960), pp. 319–33.

At times in the *Confessions* Augustine underscores the radical contingency even of scriptural signs, comparing the words of God spoken by a creature in time to the "eternal Word in its silence": "'It is far different; it is far different.'" God reveals himself to natural man "in signs and in times, in days and in years" that are the necessary condition of mortal communication with divinity.[20] Acknowledging the inevitable ruptures in this communication in his *Confessions*, Augustine expresses his desire for a recovery of univocal signification and for a consensus of meaning. He longs to "catch hold" of Moses, to lay his "body's ears to the sounds breaking forth from his mouth" and "beseech him to make these things plain to me." At another moment he wishes for "a power of eloquence" like that of Moses so that his words might be embraced equally by those who do and do not understand them, the divine authorizing of his voice resolving variability of interpretation.[21]

Though verbal signs and the humans who must use them are limited by their very natures, Augustine accepts the multiplicity, even the opacity, of meaning because he is confident that reference does occur. As he states in *De doctrina*, "Now when I am discussing signs I wish it understood that no one should consider them for what they are but rather for their value as signs which signify something else. A sign is a thing which causes us to think of something beyond the impression the thing itself makes upon the senses."[22] The *De magistro* may revel in the implications of the sign's conventionality, but Augustine makes clear that the linguistic games he plays with his son are only preliminary to the serious apprehension that "will enable us not only to endure, but also to love the warmth and light of that region wherein is found the happy life." That illumination of "truth which presides over the mind itself from within," comes from God, "the Wisdom which every rational soul does indeed consult" when faced with the multiplicity of signs or confusion about their referents.[23] Ultimately, then, Augustine's sign the-

20. Ibid., 11.6.8, 13.18.23, 13.23.24, 13.29.44; pp. 282, 350, 357, 364.
21. Ibid., 11.3.5, 12.26.36; pp. 279–80, 327–28.
22. *On Christian Doctrine* 2.1.1; p. 34.
23. *The Teacher*, pp. 33, 51.

ory is thoroughly informed by a belief in God's stable truth. His wishful thinking about trading places with or seizing hold of Moses bespeaks a faith in the sign's divine origin and endpoint.

Augustine's dramatic linguistic fantasies convey, with slightly different emphases, the same impulse inherent in the medieval preoccupation with an originating moment of signification, a "founding linguistic gesture," generally seen as the Edenic Adam's bestowal of names.[24] A belief in the existence of an ultimate reference and in the myth of the founding moment indicates that signs are "not merely . . . intramental entities but . . . indices of realities that exist outside of and prior to the knowing subject."[25] As an epistemological structure, the sign was thought to mediate between the knower and the object known. Augustine maintained that all "things are learned by signs"; the goal of that learning was love of God. In the twelfth century Hugh of St. Victor summed up centuries of tradition when in his *Didascalicon* he expressed his reverence for the profound "understanding to be sought in the Sacred Writings, in which we come through the word to a concept, through the concept to a thing, through the thing to its idea, and through its idea arrive at Truth."[26]

Thus the early medieval study of signs was inseparable from a theory of divine knowledge. Semiotics was a theological discipline; language was to be studied because verbal signs were considered essential in acquiring knowledge of God. This view of the sign's relation to religious epistemology characterized the "mental universe" of the Latin West from the patristic period until the high Middle Ages, when the effects of the study of formal logic begun in the twelfth century produced "a decisive split between reality, thought, and language."[27] Intellectual historians, perhaps too schematically, customarily register the

24. Bloch, *Etymologies and Genealogies*, pp. 37–53; Colish, *Mirror of Language*, pp. 176–77. Vance notes other instances of the medieval ontological privileging of the moment of origin; see "Roland and the Poetics of Memory," p. 375.

25. Colish, *Mirror of Language*, p. vii.

26. *The Didascalicon of Hugh of St. Victor: A Medieval Guide to the Arts* 5.3, trans. Jerome Taylor (New York: Columbia University Press, 1961), p. 122.

27. Colish, *Mirror of Language*, p. 5.

changes that occurred during this period in a dramatic terminology of disruption, speaking of the "divorce between faith and reason," "the breakdown of the medieval synthesis," or "the dissolution of the medieval outlook." Though some recent students of medieval language theory would revise this model in the direction of more precise periodization, it is nonetheless important to note that the high Middle Ages witnessed the breakdown of a certain "community of assumptions" regarding the bases of philosophical and theological truth and the investigation of natural phenomena.[28]

This shift in intellectual orientation is often traced to Abelard, whose twelfth-century innovations in logic resulted in a "radicalized sign theory" that relegated "to the realm of the contigent, relative, and historically determined that which once partook of the necessary, absolute, and eternal."[29] Abelard proposed a language theory independent of theology, advancing positions on linguistic signification that emphasized the constitutive role of the intellect rather than the realm of a prior signified. Particularly in his commentaries on Porphyry's *Isagoge*, Abelard explored the abstraction of universals, concluding universals are not found in things but, rather, are ascribable "to words alone."[30] The view of the linguistic sign that emerged

28. See, for example, Gordon Leff, *The Dissolution of the Medieval Outlook* (New York: Harper and Row, 1975), pp. 6–9. For a revised assessment of this characterization of the later Middle Ages, see Steven Ozment, *The Age of Reform 1250–1550: An Intellectual and Religious History of Late Medieval and Reformation Europe* (New Haven: Yale University Press, 1980), pp. 8–20. Bursill-Hall comments on misunderstandings of twelfth-century developments in language theory, and urges a concept of periodization not strictly chronological; see his "Introduction" to Hunt, *History of Grammar in the Middle Ages*, pp. x–xi, xv–xvi.

29. Bloch, *Etymologies and Genealogies*, p. 146, and, in general, pp. 141–49. On the change in medieval language theory around 1100, see G. L. Bursill-Hall, "Toward a History of Linguistics in the Middle Ages, 1100–1450," in *Studies in the History of Linguistics: Traditions and Paradigms*, ed. Dell Hymes (Bloomington: Indiana University Press, 1974), p. 80; R. H. Robins, *Ancient and Medieval Grammatical Theory in Europe* (London: G. Bell and Sons, 1951), p. 70. On the impact of Abelard, see D. E. Luscombe, *The School of Peter Abelard: The Influence of Abelard's Thought in the Early Scholastic Period* (Cambridge: Cambridge University Press, 1969), especially chaps. 2 and 3.

30. *The Glosses of Peter Abailard on Porphyry*, in *Philosophy in the Middle Ages: The Christian, Islamic, and Jewish Traditions*, ed. Arthur Hyman and

from the interaction of dialectic, logic, and philosophy was extended in the thirteenth and fourteenth centuries by the speculative grammarians and the nominalists, who opened out the assumptions of an earlier sign theory that focused on a fixed, universal, prior object of knowledge in the direction of a logically based grammar that was "transformed into an energetic tool of analysis, constitutive as well as reflective of reality."[31] The fourteenth century saw considerations of the linguistic sign displaced from the realm of metaphysics to that of logic.

The prominence of sign theory in medieval intellectual culture is also expressed in an elaborate imagery of signification. Latin and vernacular writers alike consolidated the period's semiological preoccupations in a metaphorics of reading, writing, and the book. As Curtius's famous survey of the *topos* has shown, figures of the book and of writing appear throughout world literature, but Christianity gave the book its "highest consecration": its belief in the Bible's absolute totality of divinely inspired meaning sanctioned the use of the book as metaphor for

---

James J. Walsh (New York: Harper and Row, 1967), p. 177. Abelard's commentary on Porphyry is one source of Eco's playful Latin quotation regarding "the name of the rose" (Hyman and Walsh, p. 187). On Abelard's language theory and philosophy, see Brian Stock, *The Implications of Literacy: Written Language and Models of Interpretation in the Eleventh and Twelfth Centuries* (Princeton: Princeton University Press, 1983), pp. 362–403; Jean Jolivet, *Arts du langage et théologie chez Abelard*, Etudes de philosophie médiévale 57, 2d ed. (Paris: J. Vrin, 1982); Martin M. Tweedale, *Abailard on Universals* (Amsterdam: North-Holland, 1976).

31. Bloch, *Etymologies and Genealogies*, p. 157. On early and late strains of nominalism, the one associated with Abelard, the other with William of Occam, see Paul Vignaux, "Nominalisme," *Dictionnaire de théologie catholique* (Paris: Librairie Letouzey et Ané, 1931), 11.1:717–84. Occam also wrote a commentary on Porphyry: see Jean Jolivet, "Abélard et Guillaume d'Ockham, Lecteurs de Porphyre," *Abélard: Le dialogue*, Cahiers de la Revue de Théologie et de Philosophie 6 (Geneva, 1981): 31–57. On the speculative grammarians see Robins, *Ancient and Medieval Grammatical Theory*, pp. 75–90. Michael A. Covington provides an outline of medieval speculative grammar and an annotated bibliography in "Grammatical Theory in the Middle Ages," *Studies in the History of Western Linguistics*, ed. Theodora Bynon and F. R. Palmer (Cambridge: Cambridge University Press, 1986), pp. 23–42. On developments in language theory in the high and later Middle Ages, see the essays in part four of the *Cambridge History of Later Medieval Philosophy*, ed. Norman Kretzmann, Anthony Kenny, and Jan Pinborg (Cambridge: Cambridge University Press, 1982), pp. 161–269.

signifying systems.[32] Medieval theologians and philosophers distinguished between the book of God's word and the book of his works, employing book metaphors to talk about the nature of meaning in epistemological, religious, and literary contexts.

The Name of the Rose represents these medieval semiotic preoccupations in minute detail, appropriating touchstones of medieval sign theory and the metaphorics of the book. The opening of Adso's narrative invokes the medieval preoccupation with origins: "In the beginning was the Word" (12). He incorporates into his story many examples—from Isidore of Seville, Alan of Lille, Hugh of St. Victor—that illustrate the popularity of figures of the book and writing in the Middle Ages. Adso and William's discussion of signs, language, and referentiality reproduces the theoretical positions just outlined. Whereas Adso's initial understanding of language coincides with the view of signification propounded by early medieval sign theory, William's critical stance in the debate on language is thoroughly grounded in the intellectual culture whose shifting semiotic alliances displaced metaphysics by logic. His linguistic positions are commonplaces of nominalist theory. Eco explains in his *Postscript* that William's character is made possible by the new conceptions of language and signs advanced by nominalist thinkers. William must postdate Occam because, as an investigator "with a great gift of observation and a special sensitivity in interpreting evidence," he must have at his disposal the idea that "signs are used to acquire knowledge of individuals" (*PS* 26).

Yet in its treatment of medieval sign theory *The Name of the Rose* does more than simply incorporate historically verifiable positions and figures prominent in the debate on language. The novel's medieval semiotics is just as appropriately located in the context of Eco's lifelong preoccupation with the Middle Ages, which is attested not only by his work on medieval apocalypse manuscripts and aesthetics but also by his regular appeals to classical and medieval language theory in his exploration of sig-

32. Curtius, *European Literature*, pp. 303–19; Gellrich, *The Idea of the Book*, pp. 17–28; Gabriel Josipovici, *The World and the Book: A Study of Modern Fiction*, 2d ed. (London: Macmillan, 1979), pp. 25–51.

nifying systems and the rules governing their interpretation. In his *Semiotics and the Philosophy of Language*, for instance, Eco explores the same aspects of language theory that drew Abelard's attention to Porphyry (*SP* 57–68). Eco's semiotic theory has been directly likened to the nominalism of William of Occam by one critic who finds it an "atavistic throwback to a medieval concern."[33] The work of James Joyce has attracted Eco's attention because it is "the node where the Middle Ages and the avant-garde meet" (*AC* vii).

In the *Postscript* to his novel Eco speaks humorously of his preoccupation with the Middle Ages. Calling himself a "medievalist in hibernation," he claims that, since the Middle Ages were his "day-to-day fantasy," he decided to write a medieval novel: "I know the present only through the television screen, whereas I have a direct knowledge of the Middle Ages" (14). Eco's playful distinction here between the modes of knowing past and present hints at more than a casual relationship between these temporally distant ages. When he calls the Middle Ages a "constant temptation," and says, "I see the period everywhere, transparently overlaying my daily concerns, which do not look medieval, though they are" (*PS* 18), he refers not simply to a charming but arcane interest in the medieval past.[34] Rather, he intimates the intellectual coherence between his contemporary semiotic project and the Middle Ages, a coherence that subsumes the preoccupations of his own career as well as the highly articulated probing of medieval sign theory and epistemology foregrounded in *The Name of the Rose*. The complementarity of medieval and modern sign theory does indeed account in part for Eco's densely semiotic contemporary narrative set in the Middle Ages. But in terms of the intellectual project of

33. McCanles, "Conventions of the Natural," p. 62.

34. Eco indicates some of the ways the medieval period "overlays" contemporary times in "Towards a New Middle Ages," in *On Signs*, ed. Marshall Blonsky (Baltimore: Johns Hopkins University Press, 1985), pp. 488–504; this essay appears in a slightly different version in Eco's *Travels in Hyper Reality*, trans. William Weaver (San Diego: Harcourt Brace Jovanovich, 1986), pp. 73–85. Eco's work as a medievalist needs no legitimation, but it would nonetheless seem to be entering the mainstream with his contribution to the forthcoming *Cambridge History of Literary Criticism*, vol. 2, *The Middle Ages*, ed. Alaistair Minnis.

The Name of the Rose, this relationship is further illuminated by the contexts in which medieval and modern sign theory have flourished and by the cultural import of the "two" semiotics.

Far from being an isolated intellectual phenomenon, the medieval debate on verbal signs affected nearly every mode of formal inquiry. From the fifth to the fifteenth century, the discussion of signs was central to discussions about the order of the universe. Speculation about the structure of language, the status of the sign, and the nature of reference informed such diverse disciplines as history, philosophy, and theology.[35] The traditional subordination of all learning to the arts of language, which was inherent in the structure of the medieval curriculum, was carried further by the schoolmen's efforts to formulate a unified system of knowledge. In the thirteenth and fourteenth centuries, the *modistae*, or speculative grammarians, reoriented language study toward a grammar based on universal rules of language and general linguistic laws. They conceived of grammar as a comprehensive metalanguage that, through logic and eternal laws, makes itself an abstract and immaterial science that parallels cognition.[36]

The centering of medieval intellectual discourse in language brings to mind what Fredric Jameson has said about structuralism: that it is an attempt to "rethink everything through once again in terms of linguistics."[37] Contemporary intellectual discourse shares with that of the Middle Ages what theorists customarily refer to as a "language paradigm," a concept that implies that language is not simply a subject matter of inquiry but has become instead "the starting point and orienting model" for the "methodological self-understanding" of the major disciplines.[38] Shaped by structuralist and poststructuralist theories

35. Bloch, *Etymologies and Genealogies*, p. 12.

36. Ibid., pp. 149–58; Gellrich, *The Idea of the Book*, pp. 105–9; Bursill-Hall, "Toward a History of Linguistics in the Middle Ages," pp. 80, 87; Robins, *Ancient and Medieval Grammatical Theory*, pp. 77–90.

37. Fredric Jameson, *The Prison-House of Language: A Critical Account of Structuralism and Russian Formalism* (Princeton: Princeton University Press, 1972), p. vii.

38. I borrow these phrases from György Márkus, "The Paradigm of Language: Wittgenstein, Lévi-Strauss, Gadamer," in *The Structural Allegory: Reconstruc-*

of recent decades, the contemporary "language paradigm" now constitutes a "structural allegory" whose organizing concepts have eroded "traditional disciplinary foundations and . . . [repatterned] the field of intellectual attention."[39]

Medieval and modern realizations of the "language paradigm" manifest interesting resemblances. For instance, the speculative grammarians' distinction between the immutable rules governing all language and the particular, diverse uses of specific languages seems remotely anticipatory of the now familiar Saussurian distinction between *langue* and *parole*. Similarly, the homology between linguistic and psychological categories which they posited bears a resemblance to Lévi-Strauss's identification of the fundamental structures of language and the human mind.[40] But more important, the emphasis on language in both medieval and modern intellectual culture invites an assessment of the relationship of the study of the past to the present. R. Howard Bloch notes that recent advances in historical studies, the consolidation of the "human sciences," and consequent blur-

---

tive Encounters with the New French Thought, ed. John Fekete, Theory and History of Literature 11 (Minneapolis: University of Minnesota Press, 1984), p. 105.

39. John Fekete, "Descent into the New Maelstrom: Introduction," in *Structural Allegory*, p. xii.

40. On the speculative grammarians' view of language usage and linguistic rules, see Alford, "Grammatical Metaphor," p. 739. For a characterization of the structuralist positions, see Markus, "Paradigm of Language," pp. 112–17; and T. K. Seung, *Structuralism and Hermeneutics* (New York: Columbia University Press, 1982), pp. 1–20. G. L. Bursill-Hall notes the relevance of the *modistae* to modern linguistics in terms of their concern for a comprehensive theory of language; he advises restraint, however, in posing such similarities; see his *Speculative Grammars of the Middle Ages: The Doctrine of "Partes Orationis" of the Modistae* (The Hague: Mouton, 1971), pp. 12 and 327–41; see also his "Introduction" to Hunt, *History of Grammar in the Middle Ages*, p. ix. Robins suggests connections between Saussure and the medieval grammarian Siger de Courtrai (*Ancient and Medieval Grammatical Theory*, pp. 82–83). Eco comments on connections between the Middle Ages and "many kinds of formal and logical thinking in contemporary secular philosophers": "there is a lot of hidden medievalism in some speculative and systematic approaches of our time, such as structuralism" ("Dreaming of the Middle Ages," in *Travels in Hyper Reality*, p. 70). On the general relationship between medieval and contemporary linguistic philosophy, see Desmond Paul Henry, *That Most Subtle Question (Quaestio Subtilissima): The Metaphysical Bearing of Medieval and Contemporary Linguistic Disciplines* (Manchester: Manchester University Press, 1984), pp. vii–ix.

ring of distinctions among academic disciplines are all "appropriate to the universalizing culture of the Middle Ages." They point "in the direction of a dialogue between the past and the present. . . . More precisely, the issues that define our own intellectual temper were sufficiently crucial to the period we designate as our 'historical other' as to render such a dialogue compelling. . . . This temporally distant and logically inaccessible era speaks directly to our time as a kind of challenge to many of the burning issues of the day."[41]

The interplay of medieval and modern sign theory provides a reference point for considering the intellectual and historical dimensions of *The Name of the Rose*, the cultural motivation for the making of the novel, its adoption by intellectuals as a favored text, and even perhaps, through some process of semiotic "trickle down," its popularity on the respectable fringes of mass culture. For it is, I believe, as part of a "dialogue between the past and the present" that the medieval semiotics of *The Name of the Rose* is most appropriately viewed. In order to pose the possibility of such a dialogue, we must first acknowledge what we have come to know as the "alterity" of the irrevocably distant medieval past as well as the inescapable cultural determinism that shapes our readings of that past.[42] Eco's own remarks on the relation of past to present in the making of his novel are also pertinent, for they constitute a pointed critique of one-dimensional conceptions of the *Rose*'s "relevance": "Of all idle questions the most idle has been the one raised by those who suggest that writing about the past is a way of eluding the present. 'Is that true?' they ask me. It is quite likely, I answer: if

41. Bloch, *Etymologies and Genealogies*, pp. 16–17. Bloch singles out three areas in which the medieval intellectual temper is particularly relevant to our own: the centrality of semiotics, the status of the subject, and the coincidence of the linguistic and the social (pp. 17–18). All three areas are critical to the relation of medieval and modern in *The Name of the Rose*. On the medieval creation of the various discourses "that give form to our instincts and thoughts," see Paul Zumthor, *Speaking of the Middle Ages*, trans. Sarah White (Lincoln: University of Nebraska Press, 1986), p. 13.

42. H. R. Jauss, "The Alterity and Modernity of Medieval Literature," *New Literary History* 10 (1979): 181–229; Alexandre Leupin, "The Middle Ages, the Other," *Diacritics* 13 (1983): 22–31.

Manzoni wrote about the seventeenth century, that means the nineteenth century did not interest him. Shakespeare rewrote medieval subjects and was not concerned with his time" (*PS* 73). Eco ironically addresses the problem of relevance: as if writing about the past necessarily precludes an interest in the present; as if writing *about* the present necessarily means speaking *in* or *of* the present. The narrator/presenter of the manuscript from which the novel is supposedly transcribed echoes Eco when he protests a similar detachment from questions of relevance:

> I transcribe my text with no concern for timeliness. In the years when I discovered the Abbé Vallet volume, there was a widespread conviction that one should write only out of a commitment to the present, in order to change the world. Now, after ten years and more, the man of letters (restored to his loftiest dignity) can happily write out of pure love of writing. And so I now feel free to tell, for sheer narrative pleasure, the story of Adso of Melk, and I am comforted and consoled in finding it immeasurably remote in time . . . gloriously lacking in any relevance for our day, atemporally alien to our hopes and our certainties. (5)

Despite this protestation of the story's glorious irrelevance, the novel that this voice introduces is in fact inevitably connected to the present from within which it speaks. The import of its medieval sign theory resides in the embodiment of an "intellectual temper" that also informs the contemporary inquiry into the orders of knowledge. Through its representation of the Middle Ages, *The Name of the Rose* emerges as a novel of grand interdisciplinary proportions, the "blurring of the borders" between its subjects and themes necessarily manifesting their common tie to its consideration of verbal signs. It is, I believe, from the perspective offered by the current perception of the orders of knowledge that the most profound commingling of medieval and modern in *The Name of the Rose* occurs.

III

If *The Name of the Rose* aligns the philosophical persuasions of medieval semiotics with its modern concerns, the novel also realizes the medieval preoccupation with the sign in far more local ways. Its probing of how signs mean is inseparable from two preeminent features of its setting and structure and the patterning of its plot: its portrait of Benedictine monasticism and its saturation with apocalyptic themes and images. The monasticism and apocalypticism of *The Name of the Rose* broaden its semiotic concerns into the wider compass of medieval cultural behaviors and beliefs, showing how its consideration of the linguistic sign pertains to medieval versions of the sign's use, interpretation, and value.

Monasticism, particularly under the institution of the Benedictine *Rule*, included as one of its fundamental observances the *lectio divina*, a term that referred both to the scriptural text and the act of reading itself. The Benedictine *Rule* prescribed fixed hours of the day for sacred reading, thus requiring "that each monastery possess a library and that each monk be literate."[43] Monastic life, to borrow Jean Leclercq's famous phrase, was devoted to the love of learning and the desire for God. The life of letters—of reading, interpreting, and making books—was so central to monasticism, that from the early to the high Middle Ages monasticism took over the "transmission—not only of the truths of the faith and of Christian history, but also of both profane and sacred learning. It became one of the chief supports —and from the eighth century onwards the only support—of writing and the book."[44]

By no means undertaken for its own sake, the pursuit of learning in monastic life was purposively directed toward the second of Leclercq's terms. If monks preserved texts, they "did so in . . . the interests of their religious life, the cult and the culture." The "desire for God" spiritualized all monastic literary endeavors, which were fundamentally sanctioned by worship of the god

43. John Baldwin, *The Scholastic Culture of the Middle Ages 1000–1300* (Lexington, Mass.: D. C. Heath, 1971), p. 35; Jean Leclercq, *The Love of Learning and the Desire for God*, trans. Catharine Misrahi (1961; New York: Fordham University Press, 1974), p. 89. Marc Drogin notes Benedictine statutes that required monks not otherwise employed to help with book production; see *Anathema! Medieval Scribes and the History of Book Curses* (Totowa, N.J.: Allanheld and Schram, 1983), p. 5.

44. Curtius, *European Literature*, p. 312; see also Leclercq, *Love of Learning*, pp. 153–55.

who was the Word and whose Word had been set down in a sacred book. The total interpenetration of divinity and monastic letters is beautifully imaged in Peter Damian's affirmation: "Mea grammatica Christus est."[45]

The Name of the Rose evokes the bookish and literate character of monastic life and culture on every page, most obviously through its representation of the library. Most monastic libraries were far more modest than that featured in the *Rose,* for they did not usually involve a separate room or structure; neither did the scriptoria, which were frequently located in the archways of the cloister. Certain crucial features of the novel's library nonetheless do correspond to the structure of historical monastic libraries. For instance, though it housed both in a portion of the abbey church adjacent to the north transept and not in a tower, the Plan of St. Gall calls for a library directly above a scriptorium, just as the *Rose*'s library crowns the tower in which the scriptorium sits directly beneath it.[46] This tower is reminiscent of those built by early monastic communities to protect both monks and books, such as the one that provided the model for an illustration in a thirteenth-century Beatus Apocalypse produced at the Cistercian convent near Burgos, Spain.[47]

The novel carefully represents monastic attachment to books and the life of letters, showing how the "love of learning" is shaped by "desire for God." In his first appearance in the novel the abbot speaks to William about the Benedictine propagation and preservation of learning:

> "And our order, growing up under the double command of work and prayer, was light to the whole known world, depository of knowledge,

45. Leclercq, *Love of Learning,* pp. 311, 316.

46. Drogin, *Anathema!* p. 10; Joan Evans, *Monastic Life at Cluny 910–1157* (1931; Archon Books, 1968), pp. 114–15; Lorna Price, *The Plan of St. Gall in Brief* (Berkeley: University of California Press, 1982), pp. 10–11.

47. The illustration is reproduced in Drogin, *Anathema!* p. 38. The monastic tower building, according to Drogin, was under "maximum security"; it called for bells that could signal an alarm at the appearance of an enemy and ladders that could be pulled up to deter access. Given Eco's familiarity with the Beatus manuscripts, the resemblance between the protected tower in the thirteenth-century manuscript and the forbidden library of his novel hardly seems coincidental.

salvation of an ancient learning that threatened to disappear. . . . It is up to us to defend the treasure of the Christian world, and the very word of God, as he dictated it to the prophets and to the apostles, as the fathers repeated it without changing a syllable. . . . And as long as these walls stand, we shall be custodians of the divine Word." (36–37)

The province of monastic learning serves as a focal point for many of the novel's intellectual debates; it is also the central issue in the mystery William is enlisted to solve.

In the history of Benedictine bookishness, Adso finds his order's highest claim to excellence and its greatest vulnerability. He observes how the monastic commitment to sustaining tradition inevitably brings about that tradition's own demise, as the monastic ideal of preserving knowledge becomes inextricably bound up with the desire to pursue it, to create and make it new (184). Caught up in this internal paradox, monasticism as an institution is also vulnerable externally to the very forces whose rise to prominence accompanied the consolidation of monastic power. Thus learning, once undertaken as a form of prayer, becomes a form of capital. To maintain their conservative hegemony in the intellectual marketplace, the monasteries must compete with "cathedral schools, urban corporations, universities." The paradox of monastic learning is realized in the paradox of the abbey library, which is, for the monks, "at once the celestial Jerusalem and an underground world on the border between terra incognita and Hades," the greatest collection of books in the West that gives access to no one. With narrative hindsight Adso sees the threats hidden in such paradoxes: that the pursuit of learning and the love of books bring about change; that the library, when it is used, is a "living thing" and as such is open to the "risk of knowledge" (185–86).

Adso's meditations on the intellectual activity of his order distill the novel's major issues and suggest another reason why the twilight years of medieval monasticism provide such an evocative setting for Eco's thematic concerns. The shifting contours of monastic bookishness are tied to much larger questions about the creation and institutionalization of meaning: is learning simply something to be preserved in a single, unalterable form, or is it made new, "like a very handsome dress . . . worn out through use and ostentation" (185)? As the novel's several stories unfold, monasticism's institutional control over cultural meanings also proves central to Adso's personal dilemma and to the much grander social and political conflicts in which his tale is implicated. Monastic hegemony in the production of texts is represented by the narrative itself, which is significantly put under the control of Benedictine Adso, not Franciscan William. As such it is shaped at every turn by the monastic culture of the book: Adso's idiom is that of Scripture and its exegesis.

Equally bookish as the novel's monasticism is its elaboration of apocalyptic themes and images. The semiotic character of apocalypticism is grounded in its principal text—Revelation—the book, according to the *Dies Irae*, "in which the total is contained."[48] Signs and books are intimately connected to the manner in which apocalypticism as a form of eschatology proclaims its message, which is characteristically learned and scribal.[49] Distinguished from general eschatology by its sense of the imminence of the "last things," apocalypticism also "involves an unveiling of the 'divine secrets which God made known to certain elect individuals . . . initiated into an understanding of the secrets of heaven.'" It is "essentially secretive; it develops strange and fantastic symbols that are a special language for the initiated."[50] The fundamentally semiotic character of apocalypticism is forcefully articulated in the figure of its messenger, the Antichrist. Created by exegetes out of the interpretation of difficult scriptural passages, the Antichrist will be known by his signs.[51]

These aspects of apocalypticism figure prominently in *The Name of the Rose*. The novel invokes the Antichrist to lend a

48. Curtius, *European Literature*, p. 318.

49. Bernard McGinn, "Introduction" to *Apocalyptic Spirituality* (New York: Paulist Press, 1979), p. 5; see also his "Apocalypticism in the Middle Ages: An Historiographical Sketch," *Medieval Studies* 37 (1975): 252–86.

50. Richard K. Emmerson, *Antichrist in the Middle Ages: A Study of Medieval Apocalypticism, Art, and Literature* (Seattle: University of Washington Press, 1981), p. 13. Emmerson quotes here from D. S. Russell, *Between the Testaments*, 2d ed. (Philadelphia, 1965).

51. Emmerson, *Antichrist in the Middle Ages*, pp. 35–37, 84.

moral and universal historical dimension to events in the abbey, the frequency of these invocations epitomizing the appeal of the Antichrist figure to a variety of cacophonous interpretive voices. Thus Ubertino sees manifestations of the Antichrist in the line of papal succession and finds his minister in Fra Dolcino, whereas Jorge casts himself as a John the Baptist to the Antichrist whose coming he announces. Jorge himself, of course, is also identified with the Antichrist. Apocalyptic prophecies of the imminence of the end are crucial to the mystery plot and poignantly realized on a smaller scale in the character of Salvatore, for whom the world is always ending. The novel recreates an historical moment in which apocalyptic prophecy informed the politics of both Church and state, particularly as these affected and were influenced by those elements in the Franciscan order that had embraced Joachite teachings.[52]

The representation of medieval apocalyptic traditions in the *Rose* also accounts for many details whose significance is not as obvious as those deriving from the book of Revelation. Narrator Adso, as Jorge tells him, bears the "great and very beautiful name" of Adso of Montier-en-Der, the tenth-century writer of the *Libellus de Antichristo*, one of the most popular medieval lives of the Antichrist.[53] The novel's apocalypse manuscripts, which incite fear and confusion in Adso, highlight a notable feature of the medieval transmission of the Antichrist tradition: though it appears in various media, it occurs most frequently in illustrated manuscripts—Bibles, encyclopedias, Apocalypse books.[54] The abbey library is said to contain the largest collection of copies of Revelation in Christendom, most of these

52. On apocalyptic literature and politics, see McGinn, *Apocalyptic Spirituality*, p. 9. For an overview of the novel's apocalypticism, see Lois Zamora, "Umberto Eco's Revelation: *The Name of the Rose*," *Humanities in the South* 61 (1985): 3–5.

53. Richard K. Emmerson, "Antichrist as Anti-Saint: The Significance of Abbot Adso's *Libellus de Antichristo*," *American Benedictine Review* 30 (1979): 175–90.

54. Emmerson, *Antichrist in the Middle Ages*, p. 109. For an indication of the importance of apocalypse manuscripts in the Middle Ages, see the first installment of the census by Richard K. Emmerson and Suzanne Lewis, "Census and Bibliography of Medieval Manuscripts Containing Apocalypse Illustrations, ca. 800–1500," *Traditio* 40 (1984): 337–79.

housed in the area designated "Yspania," the home of the celebrated apocalyptic commentator, Beatus of Liebana. The shelf plan of the library conflates the Apocalypse and the map of the world, while its final episodes seem shaped by the Antichrist legends which say that, bringing fire from heaven, he will be a book burner.[55]

Just as the novel's monastic setting provides a fitting context for its heady discussion of the making and meaning of books, its mystery narrative lends itself perfectly to apocalypticism's preoccupation with signs and secret codes. Though in the end he finds out he was mistaken in assuming the deaths were evidence of a premeditated, apocalyptic "code," William is nonetheless compelled to see in the pattern of murders an articulation of the signs of the last days. The entire narrative of *The Name of the Rose* is symbolically shaped by a conflation of the two fundamentally historical patterns of Apocalypse and liturgy, which impose on the murder mystery expectations of order, closure, and correspondence that are not borne out. Like the (non)-patterning of the murders, these subversions of structured forms of history and cosmos defy the very premises of teleological order on which the narrative is ostensibly based. Thus the novel's foregrounding of apocalyptic narrative ultimately directs attention to the structured appeal of narrative itself.[56]

The novel's portraits of monastic life and letters and apocalyptic thought and imagery provide elaborate contexts for exploring how meanings are constructed. The representations of monasticism and apocalypticism give shape and purpose to the three major narrative threads of the novel: the intellectual and emotional education of the Benedictine novice and narrator Adso;

55. Stephens, "Ec[h]o in Fabula," p. 58; Emmerson, *Antichrist in the Middle Ages*, pp. 93–94, 131.

56. Stephens, "Ec[h]o in Fabula," pp. 56–57. Louis Mackey takes a slightly different view, maintaining that the novel is a "cacophony of mutually interfering and reciprocally frustrating sign systems" in which "the principal line of signification—the tale of detection—is blocked and misdirected by the tangle of semiotic coordinates" ("The Name of the Book," *SubStance* 14 [1985]: 37). My intention is to show the homology of these coordinates, not their reciprocal frustration of each other, and to demonstrate, rather, the redundancy of the novel's sign systems.

the theological and political discussion of heresy and Franciscan activity and belief; and the murder mystery linked to the library, the discussion of laughter, and the search for the unknown book. These strands overlap and interweave to create a narrative structure as labyrinthine as the library that serves as the novel's presiding symbol. But just as William and Adso find order in the library when they discover it is planned as a *speculum mundi*, so too there is a rigorous pattern of correspondence among these several narrative threads. These several stories are presented in precisely the same language; further, each is a story about language, a discourse on certainty and doubt, identity and difference.

The following chapters discuss each of these narratives. I maintain that each centers on a hermeneutic question, on the problems of reading and meaning occasioned by Adso's experience of love and the confrontation of the Church with heresy. The semiotic dimensions of these narratives are analogous to the more overtly interpretive and bookish issues raised by the mystery plot. Since these issues cluster around the treatment of laughter, my consideration of the mystery concentrates on what laughter means in the novel. In the case of each narrative I have based my discussion on its medieval "authenticity"; that is, I have tried to show how the interpretive questions they raise may be seen as part of a postmodern reading of medieval history and culture. I then situate the novel's multileveled inquiry into signs and the creation of meaning within the context of the larger debate on interpretation conducted by William and Jorge. I am interested in the semiotic and ideological resonances of each character, in William's Franciscanism and Jorge's Benedictinism. Finally, since their fundamental conflict centers on a work of literary criticism written by a philosopher, I consider the philosophical opposition between William and Jorge in light of recent literary theory.

[2]

The Allegory of Love

"Adso thinks and writes like a monk who has remained impervious to the revolution of the vernacular, still bound to the pages housed in the library he tells about, educated on patristic-scholastic texts" (4). Thus the authorial voice that presents Adso's "manuscript" characterizes its narrator's idiom, point of view, and primary concerns. Eco has said that he used Adso's eighteen- (and eighty-) year-old monastic voice to deal with the problems posed by a narrative full of events not only obscure but irrelevant to most of the novel's readers. The youthful Adso's difficulty in recording experiences he does not fully understand, Eco speculates, probably enabled readers to identify with him (*PS* 32–40). Yet the preeminent feature of Adso's account is its representation of monastic thinking and writing. This chapter considers Adso's story as monastic narrative.

Adso's narrative displays on a grand scale what William illustrates on a smaller scale when, on approaching the abbey for the first time, he tells the monks searching for the abbot's runaway horse both what the animal looks like and its name. William is not clairvoyant; he simply understands "the way monks read the books of Scripture, and how they thought through them" (25). A similar sort of monastic determinism operates in all facets of Adso's narrative, which is structured on the plan of the canonical hours, divisions of the daily cycle of psalm singing that epitomized monastic attitudes toward the proper use of language.[1] Monastic modes of understanding, methods of interpretation, and appropriations of biblical language appear ubiquitously in Adso's narrative. His vision of the apocalyptic tympanum of the abbey church rich in quotations from the Book of Revelation, his meditation on the spiritual meaning of light inspired by the brightly illuminated scriptorium, his allegorical reading of Adelmo's "immodest" marginalia all illustrate how a monk "thinks and writes."

These monastic habits of thinking and writing achieve their most intense concentration in the chapter that concludes at the very center of the book with what is arguably the novel's most important moment, what one reviewer called the "sex scene, wonderfully bejewelled in quotations from the Song of Solomon."[2] Bringing into focus the central issues of Adso's narrative, the "sex scene" exemplifies how Adso's monastic voice contributes fundamentally to the central issues of the novel. More important, the scene represents the critical moment in Adso's semiotic *Bildungsroman*: here his inquiry into the meaning of signs becomes a matter of personal urgency rather than simply a facet of his developing intellectual curiosity.

I

Adso's encounter with the girl in the kitchen is the culminating moment in a tightly constructed sequence of episodes throughout which he faces the difficulty of interpreting his experience in light of the official teaching and language of monastic life and learning. The first episode is Adso's extended conversation with Ubertino di Casale, the saintly Franciscan who has taken refuge among the Benedictines. Seeking knowledge of Fra Dolcino's relation to the orthodox Minorites, Adso requests of Ubertino "enlightenment and counsel." The aged

1. See Paul Gehl, "Mystical Language Models in Monastic Educational Psychology," *Journal of Medieval and Renaissance Studies* 14 (1984): 219–43.
2. John Updike, "Baggy Monsters," *New Yorker*, 14 Nov. 1983, 195.

Franciscan, "almost with yearning himself," imagines Adso to be troubled by "yearnings of the flesh" rather than of the mind (221); he satisfies Adso's desire for enlightment with an account that emphasizes the Pseudo Apostles' carnality, a theme that gives him the opportunity to warn Adso of the dangers of the female.

It is ironic that Ubertino, not Adso, brings up the subject of fleshly yearnings.[3] At several important junctures Ubertino turns the novice's queries about heretical beliefs into occasions to remark on the connection between heresy and forbidden carnality. When Adso questions him about the relationship of Dolcino to the cellarer Remigio and to Salvatore, Ubertino protests Remigio's orthodoxy but laments, "'As for the rest, alas, the flesh is weak.'" When this remark naturally piques Adso's curiosity, Ubertino insists: "'These are not things you should know'" (230).[4] His reference to the cellarer's illicit activities anticipates Adso's encounter with the young woman who is the object of Remigio's lust as well. It also introduces the vital connection between transgressive acts of mind and body which Adso explores later in the chapter.[5]

According to Ubertino, the Pseudo Apostles' distortion of the teachings of Saint Francis was intensified by and imaged in their relations to women. They encouraged promiscuity, claimed for a woman the gift of prophecy, and permitted women to preach. Ubertino finds Dolcino particularly repugnant because he carried on the Pseudo Apostles' teachings after the death of Gherardo Segarelli and claimed "'that everything should be common in love, and that it was licit to lie indiscriminately with all women'" (225). Dolcino seduced, or was seduced by, the beautiful and "perfidious" Margaret, whom Ubertino cites as evidence that "'it is through woman that the Devil penetrates men's hearts'" (225–26). Ubertino sees in Margaret the Whore of

3. Cf. Ubertino's earlier conversation with William, p. 57.

4. The Italian text is slightly different here, emphasizing even more than the English version Ubertino's obsession with Remigio's illicit sexuality (*Il nome della rosa* [Milan: Bompiani, 1980], p. 233; hereafter cited as *Rosa*).

5. R. F. Yeager notes a similar connection between heresy, disordered sexuality, and writing in "Fear of Writing, or Adso and the Poisoned Text," *SubStance* 14 (1985): 50–51.

Babylon who may assume "the form of the most exquisite creature" (230). He holds her responsible for Dolcino's demise and, indirectly, for the flourishing of his heretical movement.

According to the fundamental strain in Christian theology that Ubertino's view represents, the antidote to the devilish carnality of woman is the sublimated femininity, the "immaculate love" of the Virgin Mary. In a passage that foreshadows Adso's efforts to find a language in which to render his carnal experience, Ubertino appeals to the exegetical tradition that read in the Song of Songs an allegory of femininity and saw in the Virgin Mary's body "a sign of the beauties of heaven." Having thus transmuted the attractions of the flesh, Ubertino points out a statue depicting "the Virgin's slender bust, held high and tight by a cross-laced bodice, which the Child's tiny hands fondled." He can now speak freely of the Virgin's "'breasts, which protrude slightly, only faintly tumescent, and do not swell licentiously,'" because he does so in the language of the doctors of the Church and through their authority supposedly transcends his own carnality (230).

It is both ironic and humorous that it is Ubertino's allegorized vision of the immaculate female, rather than any of his ravings against woman as the "vessel" of the devil, which causes Adso to be "stirred as if by an inner fire." For Adso, Ubertino's apparent exaltation of the spirit has only served to awaken the desires of the flesh. Whereas the saintly Franciscan has spoken of signs of heaven, Adso, responding as would most adolescents boys under similar circumstances, sees and hears of tumescent and swelling breasts. Yet Adso is aware that more is at stake here than the problem of sublimating the flesh. Just as, earlier, he had puzzled over similarities between the teachings of Ubertino and the Pseudo Apostles, and been confused by Ubertino's praise of the saintly Angela and Clare and his condemnation of the Pseudo Apostles' female prophets, so here he wonders how to distinguish the "fire of supernatural love" from the "raving of the senses." Ubertino proscribes love precisely because of the way it blurs distinctions:

"What is love? There is nothing in the world . . . that I hold as suspect as love. . . . Unless you have those weapons that subdue it, the soul plunges through love into an immense abyss. . . . Mind you, I do not say these things to you only about evil love . . . I say this also, and with great fear, of the good love between God and man, between man and his neighbor. . . . Because even the love felt by the soul, if it is not forearmed, if it is felt warmly, then falls, or proceeds in disorder." (230–31)

Given his fear of love's disorder, Ubertino's vilification of the female emerges as a means to "subdue" the soul and keep it from plunging "into an immense abyss." Like many such aggressive assertions of meaning in the novel, this is also an act of semiotic containment, directed to reinforcing boundaries and stabilizing polarities rather than tolerating ambiguities. Yet for all his polarization of opposites—woman is either a whore or a saint—Ubertino has the wisdom to know what he does not know: "'how difficult it is to distinguish [the good love] from the other'" (231).

Ubertino hardly furnishes Adso with the aid to his distressed soul that he had hoped to receive. Instead of providing the certain knowledge of heresy that the novice had sought, or the lesson on the unequivocal dangers of woman and the flesh that he himself had intended, Ubertino demonstrates—through his ranting against women, his allusions to Remigio's behavior, and his "rapturous" whisperings to Adso—the essential difficulty of distinguishing spiritual from physical love.[6] Thus Ubertino provocatively and graphically illustrates the ambiguity of love and its language which Adso experiences at this moment. In the "grip of contradictory thoughts" (228), Adso determines to go to

6. He thus anticipates Adso's far more dramatic and protracted experience of the same dilemma in the chapter's final episode, proleptically imaging its process and outcome. Ubertino's talk with Adso has overtones of a sexual experience: his mention of Remigio's fleshly weakness proceeds to a rapturous contemplation of the Virgin's statue in which the allegorization of her anatomy turns into the "sweetest of visions." He gives an increasingly impassioned speech about the perils of love, warning Adso that love plunges the soul into an "immense abyss" and likening the soul to a stone licked by flames. Adso's own encounter follows a similar course, including the apprehension of fire and the abyss (249). Ubertino's behavior here is the orgasmic fulfillment of a spiritual consummation; he is left with his face bathed "with tears but also by a faint perspiration," just as Adso after his physical consummation finds himself "damp with sweat" (249). The Italian text uses the word "sudore" in both instances (*Rosa* 234, 252).

the library on his own, mounting the stairs to the scriptorium "as Dolcino had climbed up Monte Rubello" (232). His analogy is a telling one, coming as it does immediately after Ubertino's warnings about love. Like his difficulty in drawing distinctions between Ubertino's holiness and Dolcino's heresy, feminine sanctity and seduction, spiritual and carnal passion, it hints at a connection in the novel between love and heresy which is deeper than the causal relationship Ubertino asserts in his commentary on the Pseudo Apostles.

Adso's analogy is also prophetic: as soon as he enters the scriptorium, his eye lights on a book about Dolcino's heresy. Books dominate in these next two scenes, as Adso confronts first this historical narrative about heresy and then the symbols of revealed authority as represented in the illuminations of the gospels and of the Apocalypse. Patterned in similar ways, the scenes in the scriptorium and the library call attention to the ambivalence that may issue from a reading of even the most authoritatively interpreted signs. In the abbey's semiotic storehouses Adso finds official texts whose verbal and pictorial signs both reinforce and increase the confusion Ubertino aroused in him.

What Adso reads about Dolcino is charged with contradiction, and, he tells us, "I took this circumstance as a supernatural sign, whether celestial or diabolical I still cannot say" (232). He recalls the trial and execution of the Fraticello Michael, an experience he now reflects upon in light of the interpretive dilemma posed by his conversation with Ubertino.[7] For Adso, Michael is a study in contradictions: the preacher and follower of Francis's rule of penance and poverty whom the church denounces as a heretic; the inquisitors' incarnation of evil whom the people compare to Christ before the Pharisees (235). Adso recalls won-

7. Adso's reminiscence seems to be based on the fourteenth-century anonymous eyewitness account of the history of Michael of Calci, who was burned at the stake in Florence in 1389; see John Fleming, *An Introduction to the Franciscan Literature of the Middle Ages* (Chicago: Franciscan Herald Press, 1977), pp. 105–7. See also Decima L. Douie, *The Nature and the Effect of the Heresy of the Fraticelli* (1932; New York: AMS Press, 1978), pp. 226–28. The fourteenth-century account appears in F. S. Zambrini, "Storia di Fra Michele minorita, come fu arso in Firenze nel 1389," in *Scelta di curiosita* (Bologna, 1864).

dering whether Michael was madman or seer, damned soul or holy martyr (238).

Adso registers his ambivalence in an image that reveals an allegorical habit of mind typical of his monastic language and education. Using a symbol that medieval commentators frequently glossed as the Virgin Mary, he makes the condemned heretic's funeral pyre a sign of God's presence on holy ground: "I would have said I was standing before the burning bush." He also recalls "some words . . . about ecstatic rapture" from Saint Hildegard: "'The flame consists of a splendid clarity, of an unusual vigor, and of an igneous ardor, but possesses the splendid clarity that it may illuminate and the igneous ardor that it may burn'" (239). Not surprisingly, this recollection brings to Adso's mind "some words of Ubertino about love." Ubertino, too, had spoken of fire and the soul that "'feels the true warmth of divine love and cries out and moans and becomes as stone flung in the forge'" (231). In that earlier conversation with Ubertino, Adso had faced an interpretive problem similar to that he confronts again in recalling Michael's death: the supposedly base sentiments of heresy and carnal passion find expression in the fervent and impassioned language of the raptures of holiness and spiritual love.

The very ambivalence that seems to inhere in the language of love compels Adso to mount the stairs to the library, where he encounters yet another hermeneutic problem. In the labyrinth he finds a richly illuminated gospel book decorated with the image of a lion, which "concentrates in itself all the characteristics of the things at once most horrible and most regal. So that image suggested to me both the image of the Enemy and that of Christ our Lord, nor did I know by what symbolic key I was to read it" (240).[8] In an illustrated Apocalypse, Adso sees the *mulier amicta sole* of Revelation 12, who reminds him of the statue of the Virgin Mary he had earlier contemplated with Ubertino, and who also resembles the whore of Babylon portrayed on a subse-

8. In medieval scriptural exegesis the lion was a *locus classicus* for contradictory readings in a good (*in bono*) and evil (*in malo*) sense; see Augustine, *On Christian Doctrine* 3.25.26, trans. D. W. Robertson (Indianapolis: Bobbs-Merrill, 1958), pp. 100–101.

quent page: "the forms were womanly in both cases, and at a certain point I could no longer understand what distinguished them" (241). Like his earlier encounters with contradictory signs, Adso's brief visit to the library emphasizes the difficulty of interpreting disparate things called by similar names and similar things called by disparate names. The particular collocation of ambivalent signs—in the scriptural text and woman—anticipates his experience in the monastery kitchen.

Adso's encounter with the peasant girl dramatically and literally enacts—and speaks—a semiotic ambivalence that is thoroughly consistent with his monastic narrative voice. His account of the lovemaking scene in the kitchen at some points resembles the raptures of a medieval mystic and at others the pious warnings of a guide book for the novitiate: "And while my rational instinct was to cry out 'Vade retro!' . . . something in my vis appetitiva urged me forward, as if I wanted to take part in some marvel" (242–43). The scene is most distinctively monastic in its resonant use of scriptural language. Eco readily admits that he constructed it "entirely on the basis of quotations from religious texts, from the Song of Songs to Saint Bernard and Jean de Fecamp, or Saint Hildegard of Bingen" (*PS* 45).[9] In so seamlessly incorporating biblical language and commentary into Adso's account, the novel captures an essential feature of monastic thinking and writing—its "deep impregnation with the words of Scripture." This characteristic of monastic study and writing made the person a sort of "living" biblical concordance. It accounts for the overlapping, associative quality of monastic works: words similar in sound to other words produce a "chain reaction" effect that brings together words with only chance

9. Eco amusingly claims to have constructed the scene from a random assemblage of notecards while "trying to follow with my fingers the rhythm of Adso's lovemaking": "Therefore I could not pause to select the most cogent quotation. What made the quotation cogent at that point was the pace at which I inserted it. I rejected with my eyes those quotations that would have arrested the rhythm of my fingers. I cannot say that the writing of the action lasted as long as the action (for there are times when lovemaking lasts fairly long), but I tried to shorten as much as possible the difference between the duration of the scene and the duration of the writing" (*PS* 45–46).

connections; words group themselves together like theme and variations.[10]

The biblical intertextuality of monastic writing is clearly illustrated in the *Rose*'s central scene, for not only Adso's account of his experience but the experience itself is shaped by his reading of Scripture and other holy texts. The extensive use of the Song of Solomon in this passage is a rhetorical and stylistic masterstroke, for no book of Scripture more deeply "impregnated" monastic thinking and writing than did the Song, the text most widely read and commented on in the medieval cloister. Monastic writers found in the Song of Solomon's portrayal of erotic longing a text about spiritual union, about the soul's love of God and God's relations with the soul. As the cardinal monastic text of contemplation, the Song of Solomon describes the search for God to which monastic love of learning, indeed all of monastic life, was directed.[11] It is supremely fitting that Scripture's most fervent and intensely allegorized portrait of passionate love should figure so largely in Adso's efforts to describe an experience in which carnal and divine love appear as one to him, an experience that leads him to question whether there is any difference between the two. The biblical text of erotic and spiritual love which was so important in the monastic cloister and in monastic spirituality is also extremely important to Adso's monastic narrative and to the novel's contemporary semiotic probing of medieval culture.

II

And she kissed me with the kisses of her mouth, and her loves were more delicious than wine and her ointments had a goodly fragrance . . . behold thou art fair, my beloved, behold thou art fair; thine eyes are as doves (I said), and let me see thy face, let my hear thy voice . . . thou

10. Jean Leclercq, *The Love of Learning and the Desire for God*, trans. Catharine Misrahi (1961; New York: Fordham University Press, 1974), p. 91; see also pp. 93–96.

11. Ibid., pp. 106–8.

hast ravished my heart, my sister . . . thy lips drop as the honeycomb, honey and milk are under thy tongue, the smell of thy breath is of apples, thy two breasts are clusters of grapes, thy palate a heady wine that goes straight to my love and flows over my lips and teeth. (246)

When Adso uses this pastiche of quotations from the Song of Solomon to record his passionate experience, he illustrates two principal features of high medieval monastic spirituality: its preoccupation with love—God's love for man and man's love for God—and its marked tendency to express that love in "human language borrowed from . . . human experience."[12] From the twelfth century on monastic spirituality exhibited a preoccupation with love, subsuming within a conception of *caritas* all forms of love between humans, taking a more positive attitude toward the feminine than had the older monasticism, and often preferentially imaging love for God in the love between man and woman.[13] This new monastic teaching on love was epitomized in the creation of a new genre of monastic writing, the treatise on love, which drew its primary inspiration from the Song of Solomon.

The preeminent poet and theologian of monastic love was Bernard of Clairvaux, whose commentary on the Song of Solomon even in his lifetime contributed enormously to increased interest in this book of the Bible and significantly influenced its interpretation.[14] Bernard found in the Song of Solomon's impassioned articulations what commentators long before him had recognized: an allegory of spiritual love. Ancient Jewish custom had read in the Song an expression of God's loving union with his people, and, building on this tradition, the fathers of the early Church appropriated the Song's imagery in ritual and litur-

12. Jean Leclercq, *Monks and Love in Twelfth-Century France* (Oxford: Clarendon Press, 1979), p. 9.

13. Ibid., pp. 12–16. Leclercq discusses the development of a monastic language of love in terms of the sociology of new monastic orders and the literature produced for them.

14. *PL* 183: 799–1198; for an English version see *On the Song of Songs*, trans. Irene M. Edmonds and Kilian Walsh, 4 vols. (Kalamazoo: Cistercian Publications, 1976–1980). On the influence of Bernard's commentary and the popularity of the Song in monastic spirituality, see Leclercq, *Monks and Love*, chap. 3, "A Biblical Master of Love: Solomon," pp. 27–61.

gical contexts that focused on the love of the soul for God.[15] Though different readings of the Song throughout the long history of its interpretation reflect general changes in attitude toward the literal sense of Scripture, the tradition of allegorical reading is remarkably consistent: the signal feature of the Song's hermeneutic tradition is the identification of its erotic sentiments with the experience of spiritual love.[16]

What is most notable about the consistent spiritual reading of the Song of Solomon is that the text allegorized as an expression of the soul's love for God speaks explicitly of erotic passion. It was the Song's language of physical love that monastic commentators necessarily labored to appropriate in terms of the models of behavior and belief that predominated in Christian religious culture. Thus Geoffrey of Auxerre, a disciple of Bernard whom LeClercq calls "an average witness . . . of monastic exegesis of the Song of Songs in the twelfth century," rigorously allegorizes everything potentially erotic in the Song: the breasts of the bride are understood as "teaching about faith and morals," her belly as "conscience."[17] Appropriations of the imagery and idiom of the Song of Solomon figure largely in monastic treatises on spiritual love, in which erotic diction and metaphors are used to describe the contemplative life and the soul's relation to God.[18]

In the Middle Ages, readings of the Song's eroticism as a fig-

15. Leclercq, *Monks and Love*, pp. 37–38. On the exegetical tradition of the Song, see Marvin H. Pope, *The Anchor Bible, Song of Songs: A New Translation with Introduction and Commentary* (Garden City, N.Y.: Doubleday, 1977), pp. 89–229; "Cantique des Cantiques," *Dictionnaire de Spiritualité* (Paris: Beauchesne, 1953), 2.1: 93–109; William E. Phipps, "The Plight of the Song of Songs," *Journal of the American Academy of Religion* 42 (1974): 82–100. Phipps describes the spiritualization of the Song on the part of Greek and early Christian exegetes (pp. 86–91).

16. On the continuity of the Song's interpretive tradition and the unanimity among its commentators, see Leclercq, *Monks and Love*, pp. 30–31; *Anchor Bible*, p. 90. Phyllis Trible offers a revisionary view; see *God and the Rhetoric of Sexuality* (Philadelphia: Fortress Press, 1978), pp. 144–65.

17. *Expositio in Cantica Canticorum*, quoted and summarized from the edition by F. Gastaldelli (Rome, 1974) in Leclercq, *Monks and Love*, pp. 54–56.

18. Leclercq discusses John of Fecamp's *Lament on Abandoned Quiet and Solitude*, which employs the ardent vocabulary of the Song to speak of the union with God, the desired end of a contemplative life (*Monks and Love*, pp. 44–45).

ure for the communities of Church and cloister or as the occasion for contemplation and spiritual union helped make this text a *locus classicus* of the progression from corporeal to spiritual meaning and love. Such interpretations reflect the widespread and fundamental acceptance within Christian culture of the scriptural text as symbolic language giving access to higher reality. Seen from the perspective of this interpretive tradition, monastic exegetes who wrote about love were simply following the transcendent movement of allegorical thinking, which assumes "an easy and quite natural shift from one level of the representation of love to the other." Accordingly, they could use even the most seductive biblical language, because they were confident that that "shift" from one level to the next would occur. They transformed figures in the human drama of love into "symbols of God and his beloved people, or of the human soul beloved by God" through the words of a biblical text that purified the emotions of carnal elements and "enabled them . . . to pass over, as it were, to a plane of faith reality."[19] This habit of allegorical reading, as summarized by Cistercian monk Jean Leclercq, maintains that the "symbolization of spiritual love in terms of carnal love is for monastic authors a matter of vocabulary: it in no way supposes personal experience of the realities dealt with. . . . It is simply a question of a healthy assimilation of Biblical imagery. . . . We find no innuendos, no double

---

See Leclercq's edition of the *Deploratio quietis et solitudinis derelictae* in *Un maître de la vie spirituelle au XI siècle* (Paris: J. Vrin, 1946), pp. 184–97. See also Leclercq's remarks on Adam of Perseigne's *On Mutual Love* and his letter to Agnes, a nun of Fontevrault, in both of which "the pastoral setting of the Song of Songs serves as the background to this 'heavenly marriage'" of the soul and God, its bridegroom ("An Interdisciplinary Perspective on Love and Marriage," in *Literary and Historical Perspectives of the Middle Ages*, ed. Patricia Cummins, Patrick W. Conner, and Charles W. Connell [Morgantown: West Virginia University Press, 1982], pp. 26–27). The treatise *On Mutual Love* is edited by Gaetano Raciti, "Un opuscule inédit d'Adam de Perseigne: Le livre de l'amour mutuel," *Citeaux. Commentarii Cistercienses* 30 (1980): 297–341; for the letter to Agnes see *PL* 211: 659–64. John Boswell comments on the use of passionate language in monastic writings and the valorization of love in spiritual contexts in the twelfth century; see *Christianity, Social Tolerance, and Homosexuality* (Chicago: University of Chicago Press, 1980), pp. 209, 220–22.

19. Leclercq, *Monks and Love*, pp. 31, 103.

meanings, nothing which can be considered as provocatively erotic."[20]

Adso's appeal to the Song of Solomon is surely intended to invoke that allegorical transition from the carnal to the spiritual plane which monasticism cultivated. Yet it also interrogates the hermeneutic assumptions of the exegetical tradition that took and (as Leclercq's remarks suggest) still takes such a transition for granted. The novel's probing of the Song in this way is reinforced by something both medieval and modern commentators have recognized: the scriptural text's inherent potential to signify simultaneously contrary or multiple meanings.[21] This feature of scriptural language doubtless helped make the Song of Solomon one of the most famous instances of an ancient poetic tradition that celebrated the accord of human and divine love.[22] Medieval writers frequently transferred its biblical erotic language to non-exegetical contexts, blurring the boundaries between the origin of such language and its use.[23] Despite the commentators who asserted the Song's unequivocally spiritual meaning, the tradition of commentary on the Song at times betrays a lingering discomfort with the very language it purports to contextualize so safely: both the hyper-allegorizing of the bride's physical body and the excessive eroticizing of the spiritual love the Song is supposed to signify complicate assertions about the simple and "healthy assimilation of Biblical imagery" by monastic writers who were not troubled by innuendo and double meanings.[24] Thus when a modern monastic commentator such as Leclercq criticizes the modern reader's mistaken inclination to see intentional "double meanings" where the medieval exegete and the scriptural text intended "hidden mean-

20. Leclercq, "Love and Marriage," pp. 26–27.

21. Augustine, *On Christian Doctrine* 3.25–27, pp. 99–102; Eco, *SP*, 147–53.

22. Peter Dronke, *Medieval Latin and the Rise of the European Love Lyric*, 2 vols. (Oxford: Clarendon Press, 1968), 1:6.

23. Ibid., 1:198–99; Boswell, *Christianity, Social Tolerance, Homosexuality*, pp. 190–91, n. 81.

24. For example, Phipps quotes Jerome's warning to virgins of how Jesus might titillate them: "Ever let the Bridegroom fondle you . . . He will put his hand through the opening and will touch your body. And you will arise trembling and cry, 'I am lovesick'" ("Plight of the Song of Songs," p. 89).

ings" according to a privileged hierarchy of truth, he effectively speaks from within the assumptions and authority of the very tradition he purports to explain.[25]

In the central chapter of *The Name of the Rose*, the language of the Song of Solomon evokes the connection—and the difference—between the possibility of double meanings and belief in the Song's hidden meanings. The Song appropriately provides the guiding text and language through which Adso experiences his encounter with the girl because it is a cardinal text for monastic education and spirituality, and because, as the most famous erotic text of the Judaeo-Christian tradition, it is invoked to describe carnal passion as a monk would be likely to describe it. The Song is also paradigmatic of the particular interpretive dilemma that Adso confronts in a passionate embrace on the kitchen floor: it brings to the fore the relation of erotic and spiritual love and language that is so central to its own interpretive tradition. So much so that to invoke the Song of Solomon is to invoke the subject of interpretation itself. In calling attention to its attendant exegetical tradition and to that tradition's simple but resonant starting point—the idea that one language of love may speak of distinctly different experiences of love—the Song of Solomon as a text invites the interrogation of the sign and its referent, the possibility of ambivalent readings and multiple meanings. These are the issues that underlie Adso's narrative reiteration of the Song.

In a sense, then, monastic commentary is correct; the "symbolization of spiritual love" *is* a matter of vocabulary. But as Adso confronts it in the central chapter of *The Name of the Rose*, a matter of vocabulary proves to be the only matter there

25. Leclercq, *Monks and Love*, pp. 35–36. See also Fleming's useful discussion of the confusion of the "real" and the "metaphorical" in religious experience (*Franciscan Literature*, pp. 251–55). Caroline Walker Bynum presents a different view in her comments on the spiritual use of what we might consider provocative imagery and in her plea for returning physical words and images to an original context in which they are not explicitly or even mainly sexual; see *Jesus as Mother: Studies in the Spirituality of the High Middle Ages* (Berkeley: University of California Press, 1982), pp. 110–69, and "The Body of Christ in the Later Middle Ages: A Reply to Leo Steinberg," *Renaissance Quarterly* 39 (1986): 406–7.

is. His impassioned meditation presents his experience of love as a linguistic problem that in effect undermines the confidence and precision with which monastic writers made distinctions between words and the realities they supposedly represent and with which they assert transference from one level of meaning to the next. His lovemaking in the kitchen replays the problem Ubertino had warned of when he spoke of the difficulty of distinguishing the "good love" from the other.

III

Adso develops his account of his seduction in the kitchen in terms of distinctions—between orders of experience, between sign and thing, between sign and sign. He describes his efforts to find the language that will best convey his experience and records his experience of difference itself in an account that is probably meant to acknowledge the predominate notion in recent language theory of the sign as a structure of difference. Though Adso eventually comes to understand the object of his affection in terms of the continuous deferral of presence that language theory attributes to the sign, initially he is caught up in the simple perception of difference. His confrontation with the girl signals first their language and their difference: he is the monk whose Latinity bespeaks learning and power, she the peasant whose Italian dialect identifies her as one of the *simplici*, the powerless. As monk and victim, Adso and the girl epitomize the dualities that dominate the conflict in the abbey to which Adso's narrative bears witness: the difference between the wealthy, traditional institutional Church and emergent spiritualist movements that draw upon the poor for their support; between entrenched ecclesiastical power and a changing secular world; and, on a more basic level, the difference between spiritual and earthly matters, between male and female. Adso and the girl are, in effect, a synecdoche not only for the novel's political narrative but for the dualistic framework through which it presents its central events and themes. (That they should, despite their duality and difference, unite in the novel's central chapter suggests modest yet not inconsequential semiotic possibilities.)

Adso's attention to signs and meaning is most obviously apparent in his recognition that he and the girl do not share a verbal language. Instead they communicate in the "language of gestures and of the face [which] is more universal than that of words" (244). The "speech" of the girl's fingertips draws Adso into "a kind of delirium":

> What did I feel? What did I see? I remember only that the emotions of the first moment were bereft of any expression, because my tongue and my mind had not been instructed in how to name sensations of that sort. Until I recalled other inner words, heard in another time and in other places, spoken certainly for other ends, but which seemed wondrously in keeping with my joy in that moment, as if they had been born consubstantially to express it. Words pressed into the caverns of my memory rose to the (dumb) surface of my lips, and I forgot that they had served in Scripture or in the pages of the saints to express quite different, more radiant realities. But was there truly a difference between the delights of which the saints had spoken and those that my agitated spirit was feeling at that moment? At that moment the watchful sense of difference was annihilated in me. And this, it seems to me, is precisely the sign of rapture in the abysses of identity. (244–45)

Faced with an experience for which he has no name, Adso relies on names and phrases he knows from other contexts to give us his impassioned, lyrical, intensely monastic account of his love. The words he chooses—from the Song of Solomon and its commentaries, from the Book of Revelation, from Ubertino's description of a statue of the Virgin Mary, from Saint Hildegard's mystic definition of ecstatic rapture—all come to him freighted with the meanings of their associations with more "radiant realities." Adso's ruminations on linguistic usage for the moment obscure the clarity and disturb the comfort of a monastic allegorical reading, offering in its place his pointed questions: how can he tell the difference between two orders of experience when he requires the same language to describe them? Can an identity of language reflect, or create, an identity of experience, in this case making his carnal passion a "radiant reality"? Adso's questions, implicit in the hermeneutic tradition of the Song of Solomon, offer more than a reflection on the allegorical possibilities of erotic scriptural language; they constitute an inquiry into the very nature and function of the linguistic sign: if the same words can communicate different experiences, to what do the words refer? are words a proper and fitting representation of experience and things, or is it possible that they help constitute whatever they purportedly communicate?

In the moments after his erotic encounter Adso attempts to deal with, or rather circumvent, these questions by appealing to the same monastic habits of mind that instinctively brought to his lips the words of the Song and its exegesis. He contains the semiotic resonances of his experience within institutionally sanctioned modes of speech and interpretation. First, he transmutes his "sinful encounter" into the verbal sacrament of penance, handing over with words "the burden itself of which they were the signifying voice" (277). The "consoling words" of absolution seem at first to settle his confusion about signification that began in a dark moment on the kitchen floor. Penance erases the discrepancy he had perceived between signifier and signified, identifying both sin and absolution with the words that speak them and resolving all difference in the "bosom of our lord."

But when this sacramental comfort wears off, Adso finds himself facing the particular ambivalence of the girl who appears to him as both "an occasion of sin" and "the vessel of every grace" (278). He resolves this ambivalence through the interpretive system privileged by monastic theology:

> It was . . . as if—just as the whole universe is surely like a book written by the finger of God, in which everything speaks to us of the immense goodness of its Creator, in which every creature is description and mirror of life and death, in which the humblest rose becomes a gloss of our terrestrial progress—everything, in other words spoke to me only of the face I had hardly glimpsed in the aromatic shadows of the kitchen. (279)

Adso invokes a famous medieval touchstone from Hugh of St. Victor ("the whole universe is a book written by the finger of

God") to order the troubling potential for discrepant meanings.[26] He redeems his experience and the girl by making her a part of God's text, "a chapter in the great book of creation, a verse of the great psalm chanted by the cosmos." Just as previously he had read her through the book of God's word, making her the beloved of the Song of Solomon, now he interprets her through the book of God's work. She and the rose (she is the rose) are signs that stand in for the "theophanic design that sustains the universe."[27] Thus he concludes that the girl he loves is a part of nature, chapter and verse of that book, and he is free to lose himself in love and contemplation. Like a good monk, he has translated his desire into prayer.

In reading the girl as a metaphor of divinity, Adso resorts to the solution that monastic hermeneutics offered to his quandary over reference, similarity, and difference. But the interpretive closure that this solution provides can by no means contain the interpretive turmoil, the fracture of familiar, prescriptive significations, which Adso had experienced on the kitchen floor.

I realize that to describe my wicked ecstacy . . . I have used the same words that I used . . . to describe the fire that burned the martyred body of the Fraticello Michael. Nor is it an accident that my hand . . . has penned the same expression of two experiences so disparate, because probably I experienced them in the same way both at the time. . . . There is a mysterious wisdom by which phenomena among themselves disparate can be called by analogous names, just as divine things can be designated by terrestrial terms, and through equivocal symbols God can be called lion or leopard. . . . Why did I, as a youth, depict the ecstacy of death that had impressed me in the martyr Michael in the words the

26. The quotation from Hugh of St. Victor's *Didascalicon* (*PL* 176:814) is reminiscent of the equally famous passage from Alan of Lille employing the metaphor of the world as book (*PL* 210:579) that appears earlier in the novel (23–24). See Eco's comments on the passage from Hugh in *SP,* 103–4. For a discussion of the cosmology Adso invokes here, see M.-D. Chenu, *Nature, Man, and Society in the Twelfth Century,* ed. and trans. Jerome Taylor and Lester K. Little (Chicago: University of Chicago Press, 1968), pp. 99–145.

27. With the exception of the final sentence of the *Rose,* the passage just quoted is the only one where the word—or the name—of the "rose" appears.

saint had used for the ecstacy of (divine) life, and yet I could not refrain from depicting in the same words the ecstacy (culpable and fleeting) of earthly pleasure? . . . What was similar in Michael's desire for death, in the transport I felt at the sight of the flame consuming him, in the desire for carnal union I felt with the girl, in the mystic shame with which I translated it allegorically, and in the desire for joyous annihilation that moved the saint to die in his own love in order to live longer and eternally? Is it possible that things so equivocal can be said in such a univocal way? And this, it seems, is the teaching left us by Saint Thomas, the greatest of all doctors: the more openly it remains a figure of speech, the more it is a dissimilar similitude and not literal, the more a metaphor reveals its truth. But if love of the flame and of the abyss are the metaphor for the love of God, can they be the metaphor for love of death and love of sin? Yes, as the lion and the serpent stand both for Christ and the Devil. The fact is that correct interpretation can be established only on the authority of the fathers, and in the case that torments me, I have no auctoritas to which my obedient mind can refer, and I burn in doubt. (247–48)

Identifying his experience of passion with the mystic and the heretic's transport of body and spirit, Adso wonders how such metaphoric transference occurs. The fluidity of language he observes here—the capacity of the same words to designate different experiences and of disparate words to designate the same thing—is thoroughly in keeping with the interpretive issues raised by his appeal to the Song of Solomon. Its exegetical tradition is largely the explanation of its evocative metaphors. Adso's meditation on the metaphoric propensities of language involves the recognition that the "hidden" meanings of a monastic, allegorical hermeneutics may in fact be "double" meanings. Posing in specific linguistic terms the confrontation with the equivocal he had experienced in the earlier scenes of the chapter, his discovery of the workings of metaphor sharpens his perception that the arbitrariness of the linguistic sign may enable it to mean several things of equal valence simultaneously. He longs for an authority to guide him out of his ambivalence but does not expect one to emerge from the "circle of hermeneutic legitimation" (*SP* 150) already broken by his perception of a play of equivocation.

IV

Though thoroughly embedded in the medieval hermeneutics of monastic culture, Adso's reading of the text and tradition of the Song of Solomon revises the monastic approach to language and interpretation in a direction that coincides with Eco's modern theoretical interests. In his essay on "Metaphor," Eco in fact takes up in more normative critical discourse the very same questions that arise for Adso out of his sexual encounter with the peasant girl.

Eco and Adso use the same examples to probe the workings of metaphor. Discussing the potential for ambiguity in the medieval cosmological code that made all creation a metaphor of divinity, Eco mentions contradictory meanings attributed to the lion as a figure of both Christ and the devil (*SP* 104). Adso employs these scriptural figures as evidence that the same verbal sign can represent vastly dissimilar things (248). Eco also poses Adso's question about the reading of such contradictory signs, acknowledging the role of an authority such as Adso had longed for to dispel his doubt: "How can an interpreter be sure that in a given context the lion stands for Christ and not for the Devil? . . . The medieval solution is that a preceding *auctoritas* should have already established the 'good' contextual selections" (*SP* 152). Eco's exploration of medieval *auctoritas* succinctly summarizes what Adso discovers with his probing of metaphor: that early Christian theology controlled the multiplicity of textual meaning with a hermeneutic circle—"the rules for good interpretation were provided by the gatekeepers of the orthodoxy, and the gatekeepers of the orthodoxy were the winners (in terms of political and cultural power) of the struggle to impose their own interpretation" (*SP* 151).

The coincidence of Eco's theory with Adso's love-inspired linguistics appears even more clearly when, to illustrate the difficulty of understanding metaphorical proportion in texts from a different culture, Eco singles out the following examples from the Song of Solomon:

"I have compared thee, O my love, to a company of horses . . ." (Song 1:9); "Thy teeth are as a flock of sheep which go up from the washing" (ibid., 4:2); "Her legs are as pillars of marble . . ." (ibid., 5:15); "Thy nose is as the tower of Lebanon . . ." (ibid., 7:4). . . . It cannot be denied that one is led to see sheep coming out of the water as *shaggy, dripping* creatures (bleating and smelly, as well): a terrible premise on which to build an analogy on the "black but comely" maiden whose "two breasts are like two young does that are twins." . . . Nevertheless, we can imagine how the biblical poet drops all those properties of sheep negatively identified above, so as to preserve only the characteristic of their *aequalitas numerosa,* their splendid unity in variety—as well as their whiteness. It is understood that the poet is able to do so because within his culture these most probably were the properties associated with sheep, *at least within the poetic tradition.* (*SP* 100–101)[28]

Eco's amusing account of the metaphors for the Song's bride calls attention to the "rich cultural framework" that produces such metaphors as well as to the codes that organize that multiplicity of reference into "networks of interpretants" that "decide (semiotically) the identities and differences of properties" (*SP* 127). Adso's use of the Song of Solomon "to express quite different . . . realities" enacts the richness of metaphor's cultural framework while challenging the codes by which he has learned to organize that framework.

The scriptural references that Eco shares with the narrator of his novel are but an aspect of a more important connection between their respective reflections on metaphor. Adso's internal debate on dissimilar similitudes dramatizes what Eco states more straightforwardly when he observes that every discussion of metaphor is founded on a view of language: either language is "by nature, and originally, metaphorical, and the mechanism of metaphor establishes linguistic activity" or it is "a predictive machine that says which phrases can be generated and which not, and which from those able to be generated are 'good' or 'correct,' or endowed with sense; a machine with regard to which the metaphor constitutes a breakdown, a malfunction, an unaccountable outcome" (*SP* 88). The opposition between these views, Eco observes, is an ancient one. In a sense, this formula-

28. Augustine cites "Thy teeth are as flocks of sheep" to comment on the pleasure and value of figurative language in Scripture; see *On Christian Doctrine* 2.6.7, pp. 37–38.

tion describes the interpretive debate played out in numerous arenas in his novel. Adso's erotically inspired meditation pits one view of language against the other, as his assumptions about statements that are "good or correct" give way to a view that recognizes the metaphoric founding of all language. His appeal to the allegorical cosmology of medieval Platonism, in which all creation reflects divinity, simply exemplifies institutionally sanctioned ways of validating the potential for linguistic and semantic flexibility inherent in metaphor.

Eco elaborates the connection between conceptions of metaphor and conceptions of language in a discussion of Aristotle on metaphor. Fortunately, he says (and probably with tongue in cheek), "of the thousands and thousands of pages written about the metaphor, few add anything of substance to the first two or three fundamental concepts stated by Aristotle" in his *Poetics* and *Rhetoric* (*SP* 88). Eco considers the philosopher's definition of metaphor—"the recourse to a name of another type or . . . the transferring to one object of a name belonging to another"—and his explanation of its four common types (*SP* 91).[29] Of greatest interest to Eco in Aristotle's analysis is the shift in focus he shows in his analysis of the fourth type: "In speaking of the first three types, he explains *how* a metaphor is produced and understood, whereas in speaking of the fourth type he explains *what* a metaphor enables us to know. In the first three cases, he says *how* the metaphorical production and interpretation *function*. . . . In the fourth case, Aristotle tells *what the metaphor says*, or in what way it increases our knowledge of the relations between things" (*SP* 99–100).[30]

29. *Poetics* 1457b–1459a, trans. M. E. Hubbard, in *Ancient Literary Criticism*, ed. D. A. Russell and M. Winterbottom (Oxford: Clarendon Press, 1972), pp. 119–22.

30. See *SP*, 89–100. Eco maintains that this "most ingenious and vigorous of Aristotle's conclusions" has frequently been ignored by metaphorological tradition (*SP* 100). Samuel R. Levin argues, with some qualification, that there is not much difference between Aristotle's first three types and his fourth; see "Aristotle's Theory of Metaphor," *Philosophy and Rhetoric* 15 (1982): 24–46, especially 27–28. Eco's claim that "Aristotle's limitation consists in his identifying the categories of language with the categories of being" (*SP* 103) coincides with Levin's observation that, for Aristotle, categorial relations are not defined by lan-

Eco's interest in Aristotle's conception of metaphor is hardly unexpected, given that William of Baskerville reconstructs (and Eco constructs) Aristotle's book on comedy, a book in which metaphor figures decisively, from the philosopher's *Poetics* and *Rhetoric*. Eco's view of the cognitive value of metaphor "as an additive, not substitutive, instrument of knowledge" (*SP* 89) states explicitly what Adso had implied in his erotically inspired meditation on language, in which he also explores metaphor as an index to the "relations between things." To the extent that his use of certain metaphors for carnal and spiritual love "puts before his eyes" relations that he had not seen or thought of before, these metaphors have cognitive value for him. Adso, seeing "'resemblances even in things that are far apart,'" as Aristotle says in the *Rhetoric*, also learns "that these likenesses were not only in things but also (perhaps above all) in the ways in which language defines things" (*SP* 103). In becoming conscious of metaphor Adso discovers relations of similarity between things that he has been led to believe are different.

Through metaphor he experiences meanings unaccounted for by any tradition of interpretation that he has at hand. For Adso, metaphor functions as an "additive instrument of knowledge," but what it adds are intimations of things he should not know, namely that there can be "additions" to knowledge. Adso's emergent perception that the meaning of words is not stable and unchanging, but shifting, multiple, and radically context-bound is hardly in keeping with the high medieval monastic perspective that shapes his interpretive frame of reference. According to that perspective, there are no new things, though "the same and everlasting truth" may be "rephrased in ever new ways: *non nova sed nove*" (*SP* 150).

Though the young Adso experiences his confrontation with forbidden knowledge—of metaphor and of the girl—mainly as a "total bewilderment of the senses," the older Adso understands

---

guage but exist a priori. See the discussion of metaphor along lines similar to the ones Eco pursues in Jacques Derrida, "White Mythology: Metaphor in the Text of Philosophy," *Margins of Philosophy*, trans. Alan Bass (Chicago: University of Chicago Press, 1982), pp. 231–45.

it as transgression. He retrospectively describes his youthful speculations about language as a manipulation of "the order of the stars and the sequence of their movements," an overstepping of boundaries by a "sinful and sick intelligence" (249). Adso's consciousness of transgression focuses on the linguistic terms through which he largely experiences it: he expresses greater remorse for the speculation about equivocal meanings he succumbed to after his sexual act than for the act itself.

V

Adso's nighttime reflections on linguistic order, his intimation of the arbitrary relation between sign and signified, and his struggle with equivocal meaning may rightly be seen in terms of Eco's own perspective on these prominent subjects of contemporary language theory. But they are just as much in keeping with, perhaps partly inspired by, a body of medieval themes and texts that link linguistic use and transgressive behavior. Classical and early medieval rhetoricians, for example, maintained that metaphor was a deviation from ordinary signification. The potential for transgression was in fact inherent in all tropes, since they "all involve some kind of *translatio* or transference of meaning."[31] To these early language theorists metaphor was an "alienation, denaturalization, translocation, or usurpation of linguistic property." Their distrust of metaphor as something "governed by . . . a law of juxtaposition, similarity and dissimilarity, and supplementarity" serves as a fitting gloss for Adso's nighttime ruminations.[32] His discovery of new relationships between words and things illustrates what Albert of Montecassino ob-

31. John Alford, "The Grammatical Metaphor: A Survey of Its Use in the Middle Ages," *Speculum* 57 (1982): 752.

32. R. Howard Bloch, *Etymologies and Genealogies: A Literary Anthropology of the French Middle Ages* (Chicago: University of Chicago Press, 1983), p. 116. Bloch cites Cicero, Quintilian, Augustine, and Isidore as proponents of this view, which coincides with Eco's description of a conception of language within which metaphor "constitutes a breakdown, a malfunction, an unaccountable outcome" (*SP* 88).

served about metaphor—that it "is a means of speech turned away from property in such a way as to innovate."[33]

Medieval commentators writing about language frequently realized the transgressive potential of tropes through sexual imagery, articulating linguistic and sexual deviance in terms of each other.[34] Thus in his *De planctu naturae* Alan of Lille mythologized illicit intercourse in terms of linguistic deviance. Alan contrasts the licit sexuality of Venus's marriage to Hymen, which is natural, correct, and proper, with Venus's seduction of Antigamus, which "transgresses the rule of natural genealogy and of grammatical rectitude." According to this schema, "adultery is both a sexual and a linguistic act," which is reflected in the ambiguity and mixing of meanings that characterize metaphor and other tropes.[35]

Within the general frame of reference provided by the medieval view of transgressive tropes, then, Adso's act of fornication appropriately coincides with his discovery of an adulterated language. But his transgressive acts of mind and body are even more fully realized through the novel's particular invocation of two medieval *topoi* that elaborate on the transgressive potential of linguistic behavior: the idea of an Adamic language and the connection between sexuality and reading.

Adso casts his experience in terms of the myth of Adam. The peasant girl removes her dress and stands naked before him "as

33. Quoted from his *Flores rhetorici* by Bloch, *Etymologies and Genealogies*, p. 119.

34. Alford notes that the sexual interpretation of grammatical terms goes back to ancient times ("Grammatical Metaphor," pp. 728–33).

35. Bloch, *Etymologies and Genealogies*, p. 134; see also Alford, "Grammatical Metaphor," pp. 751–54, and Boswell's analysis of Alan's endorsement of orthodox and proper modes of verbal and sexual intercourse (*Christianity, Social Tolerance, Homosexuality*, p. 310). For a detailed discussion of Alan's use of grammatical metaphors to express his ethical and theological views, see Jan Ziolkowski, *Alan of Lille's Grammar of Sex: The Meaning of Grammar to a Twelfth-Century Intellectual*, Speculum Anniversary Monographs 10 (Cambridge, Mass.: Medieval Academy of America, 1985). In the *De planctu* the issue of Venus's adulterous act is Jocus, or Mirth. The linking of the playful and the comic to transgressive behavior and linguistic ambiguity in the work's illegitimate genealogy corresponds to the *Rose*'s appeal to laughter and to its use of a treatise on comedy as both symbol and summation of its exploration of linguistic rectitude and transgression.

Eve must have appeared to Adam in the garden of Eden" (245). His encounter with her reenacts the Fall: he awakens from his postcoital sleep to find himself naked and, as he says, "aware that I had sinned" (250). It is hardly surprising that Adso identifies with Adam, with whom he shares a fall into knowledge. In fact, the cognitive dimension of his experience proves far more troublesome to Adso than the carnal, his intimations of linguistic multivalence appearing as profound a violation of order as Adam's transgression in Genesis. The Adamic resonances of this scene contribute to the monastic propriety of Adso's biblical idiom. Yet their importance to the novel's medievalism is more substantively related to the context in which the Middle Ages explored the Adamic myth.

For the Middle Ages the story of Adam was a story about language. Patristic and medieval writers looked to the Edenic myth for an account of the origins of speech and for an ideal of linguistic rectitude. They viewed Adam's Edenic speech as evidence of the harmony between God and creation. Adam realized this harmony in naming the animals, which showed "the natural affinity between rightly ordered speech and reality."[36] For many medieval writers the idea of an Adamic language meant a "primary instance of signification" that was identified with a "coincidence of words and things" against which the subsequent degeneration—or fall—of language could be measured.[37]

The concept of an Adamic language raises the fundamental and ancient question about the origin of human language in nature or convention. We have already seen how William invokes Adam's naming of the animals in his discussion of linguistic origin, concluding that although Adam may have designated the names of things according to their nature he was also given the freedom to exercise his judgment.[38] William's reference to the Adam who named and Adso's identification with the Adam who fell point up the fundamental connection between the medieval

36. Marcia Colish, *The Mirror of Language*, rev. ed. (1968; Lincoln: University of Nebraska Press, 1983), p. 176.

37. Bloch, *Etymologies and Genealogies*, p. 39.

38. The idea that "nomina sunt consequentia rerum" that William invokes was a commonplace of Roman law; see Colish, *The Mirror of Language*, p. 167.

preoccupation with an Adamic language and the idea of the sign that emerges from Adso's narrative.

This connection is illuminated by Eco's variations on the Edenic scenario in his essay "On the Possibility of Generating Aesthetic Messages in an Edenic Language."[39] Here Eco revises the medieval tradition that examined the foundations of meaning in an Adamic context in order to construct a model of signification in which the simple language of Adam and Eve, based on "their emotional responses to flora and fauna," is fundamentally and forever undermined by God's prohibition regarding the apple (*RR* 91). According to Eco's system, God's pronouncement designates as "bad and inedible" something that Adam and Eve's language designates as "good and edible." The resulting contradiction allows Adam to perceive that "language is responsible for ambiguities and deceptions" and that signs are arbitrary. These contradictions provoke Adam to manipulate the linguistic system, an act that leads him to comprehend that "system at the very moment he is calling the system into question and therefore destroying it. Just as he comes to understand the rigid generative law of the code which had governed him, so he realizes that there is technically nothing to stop him from proposing a new code" (101–2).

Eco's recasting of Adam's linguistic scenario offers a striking corollary to Adso's experience in *The Name of the Rose.* Like Adso, Eco's Adam learns that "the order of language is not absolute" and that the cultural universe of meanings he understands "may not be an unquestionable absolute after all." He reinvestigates the world and "discovers fresh cultural categories (. . . new perceptive realities), which oblige him to provide new names." His language grows, as does his world. "As a result of all this," Eco continues, "Adam discovers that Order, as such, is nonexistent; it is just one of the infinite possible states of repose which disorder occasionally arrives at" (102–3).

The particular genius of this essay lies in its appropriation of

39. The essay appears in *RR,* 90–104. Teresa De Lauretis discusses it in relation to the *Rose* and also draws a comparison between Adso and Adam; see "Gaudy Rose: Eco and Narcissism," *SubStance* 14 (1985): 13–14, 24.

the Adamic *topos* to make the point that Adam's initial transgression consisted in a necessary act of interpretation: "Adam was obliged to exit from the Garden of Eden after his first nervous manipulation of language. This was the mistake God made by disturbing the univocal harmony of the primitive language system by an ambiguously phrased prohibition. . . . From that moment onward (not from the time Adam really ate the apple), world history commenced" (103). Thus Eco's Adam glosses Eco's Adso, because they both apprehend the transgression entailed in the perception of ambiguity. For each the grasp of multivocal signification does not result from the Fall but rather helps to constitute it.

The conjunction of transgression and language, Adam's sin and his speech, which is manifested in Adso's experience, appears as well in canto 26 of Dante's *Paradiso*, one of several passages from the *Comedy* that echo in Adso's story. Sounding very much like Adso describing his erotic encounter, Dante tells Saint John of the most "sovereign" love: he has been "drawn from the sea of perverse love and placed . . . on the shore of right love" ("tratto . . . del mar de l'amor torto, / e del diritto . . . posto a la riva") (ll. 62–63).[40] The poet then meets Adam, from whom he seeks knowledge of "the true cause of the great wrath and the idiom" that he used ("la propria cagion del gran disdegno, / e l'idioma" (ll. 113–14). Adam remarks that his language is extinct, inevitably so because all creations of human reason are mutable; in language, nature's doing, man is left to his own pleasure (ll. 127–32). As for the true nature of his sin, Adam states that "the tasting of the tree was not in itself the cause of so long an exile, but solely the overpassing of the bound" of God's commandment—"solamente il trapassar del segno" (ll. 115–17). Though Adam clearly indicates that his sin was disobedience, the double entendre of his words suggests a dimension to that disobedience which both medieval writers and modern writers in a medieval tradition might have difficulty

40. Dante Alighieri, *The Divine Comedy: Paradiso*, trans. Charles S. Singleton (Princeton: Princeton University Press, 1970–1975), pt. 1, pp. 292–93; see the commentary on these lines, pt. 2, pp. 414–15. All citations in the text refer to this edition.

overlooking. For the "trapassar del segno" also suggests the "overpassing, or trespassing of the sign," a meaning that points precisely to that aspect of signification which medieval writers, however variously they construed it, deemed a consequence of Adam's fall. This resonant phrase from Dante and Adam's colloquy on language and the Fall thus coincides with Eco's rendering of the Edenic story in his essay on Adam's language. As a concrete instance of the linguistic multivalence that the "trapassar del segno" bespeaks, the phrase also epitomizes the overstepping of boundaries and the trespassing of signs that constitute the thematic focus of the central chapter of *The Name of the Rose.*

The medieval resonances of Adso's Adamic allusions are reinforced by the overtly sexual context in which they occur. Adso's experience fully realizes the link between sexuality, linguistic meaning, and interpretation frequently made in medieval texts. The final words of Adso's highly charged account describe how he awakens, only to find the girl gone and himself overcome by nausea (250): "I let out a cry and fell as a dead body falls" ("Lanciai un urlo e caddi come cade un corpo morto"). With the brilliant intertextuality of a near direct quotation, Adso echoes the final line of *Inferno* 5, in which Dante encounters Paolo and Francesca among the circle of the lustful. Francesca speaks to him of their mutual seduction, and the poet swoons: "io . . . caddi come corpo morto cade" ("I fell as a dead body falls") (l. 142).[41]

Clearly, Adso's narrative and the story of Paolo and Francesca both involve acts of sexual transgression. But the context in which Dante presents his lovers' transgression also has a bearing on Adso's situation: Francesca tells the poet how she and her lover were drawn to sin through an act of reading (*Inf.* 5. 127–38). Paolo and Francesca's seduction by means of a book furnishes a preeminent instance of the important medieval *topos* that connected sexuality and reading.[42] Through his impas-

41. *Divine Comedy: Inferno,* pt. 1, pp. 56–57.

42. On this aspect of *Inferno* 5 see Susan Noakes, "The Double Misreading of Paolo and Francesca," *Philological Quarterly* 62 (1983): 223. Some important medieval examples of the connection between sexuality and reading (see Noakes,

sioned swoon Adso joins the company of these medieval lovers and would-be lovers. The fateful act of reading that precipitated his amorous encounter involves the book about Dolcino (in Adso's mind inseparable from the temptress Margaret) which he finds in the abbey scriptorium after his unsettling talk with Ubertino: "I took this circumstance as a supernatural sign . . . and I bent eagerly to read the writing" (232). Adso's seduction is also the logical and inevitable outcome of the quandary over contradictory textual meanings that impels his nocturnal peregrination through scriptorium and library.

This interpretive struggle strengthens Adso's kinship with the lovers of *Inferno* 5 all the more, for it is something else he shares with Paolo and Francesca. Their fault is "the result of a misreading of a text which intends to edify"; their example poses "two warnings: against reading and against misinterpretation."[43] In Adso's case the form Francesca's misreading takes is also relevant: she is overcome by a carnal "amor," which she seems to construe in spiritual terms.[44] This is precisely the interpretive dilemma that Adso confronts as a result of his erotic experience: has he, in his use of biblical and theological language, misread texts meant to edify?

The allusion to *Inferno* 5 that concludes the central chapter

---

p. 238, n. 6) are Augustine, Abelard and Heloise, Chrétien's Cligés, Chaucer's Criseyde, and the Wife of Bath. See Eugene Vance's discussion of Augustine's analogizing of linguistic distractions and seduction of the flesh in "Augustine's *Confessions* and the Grammar of Selfhood," *Genre* 6 (1973): 19, "Augustine's *Confessions* and the Poetics of the Law," *MLN* 93 (1978): 619–20, and in general, "Désir, rhétorique et texte—Semences de la différence: Brunet Latin chez Dante," *Poétique* 42 (1980): 136–55. See also Jesse Gellrich, *The Idea of the Book in the Middle Ages* (Ithaca: Cornell University Press, 1985), pp. 117–18. On Chaucer, see Lee Patterson, who finds the *topos* in Chaucer's characterization of the Wife of Bath and his reading of the *Aeneid* in the *House of Fame* ("'For the Wyves love of Bathe': Feminine Rhetoric and Poetic Resolution in the *Roman de la Rose* and the *Canterbury Tales*," *Speculum* 58 [1983]: 660).

43. Noakes, "Double Misreading," pp. 226, 228.

44. Noakes (ibid., p. 236) notes this interpretation in relation to Dante's "lifelong poetic quest . . . for an understanding of the continuity" of carnal and spiritual love.

of *The Name of the Rose* illustrates with unusual clarity the complex tissue of medieval references through which the novel invokes the tradition that posited profound connections between language, sexuality, and interpretation. Adso's transgressive act is truly double: it involves monastic rules for the body and for language. Analogously, his experience of physical passion results in an effort to understand love which is inseparable from a desire to understand its language.

VI

In probing the language of love Adso confronts the fluidity of signification. He discovers that the workings of metaphor are metonymic of the workings of language itself. Metaphor's substitution of one sign for another, its making equivalent seemingly disparate signs, constitutes a paradigm of linguistic multivalence. In the novel's "sex scene" Adso indirectly poses the question that he fully articulates only much later in the novel, after William has cracked the symbolic code of the labyrinth and the contents of the unknown book have been revealed: do signs represent, or stand in for, an independent, transcendent, stable order of truth, or are they equivocal, temporal, determined by changing circumstances, referring only to other signs?

The rich texture of Adso's narrative derives from its grounding in a pattern of reference to medieval Latin and vernacular texts and its simultaneous reflection of the principal concerns of twentieth-century explorations of language. We have seen how the association of sexuality and textuality is integral to the interpretive tradition of the Song of Songs, as well as to medieval ways of talking about grammar, linguistic rectitude, and the perils of reading. The medieval conjunction of sexuality and interpretation also finds a perfect corollary in the eroticized reading through which Adso realizes one of the central tropes of contemporary theory.

Adso's carnal and hermeneutic experience may be read in light of an 'erotics' of the text in which meaning dissolves in "a ceaseless slipping and sliding of language."[45] Eco hints at such a connection in his *Postscript* when, in describing how he wrote the lovemaking scene, he claims to speak about "'writing' not in the Barthesian sense, but in the typewriter's sense" (46). Despite his disclaimers, the scene literalizes the link between writing, sexuality, and textual play. Adso in fact creates, or recreates, the girl as text. As the rose, the sign, and the referent, she is read—and misread—by Adso. Their sexual union emblemizes that identity between erotic and hermeneutic bliss conveyed in the notion of *jouissance*.[46]

If Adso's orgasmic semiotics discovers the *plaisir du texte* in the embrace of a peasant girl on a kitchen floor, his retrospective treatment of that experience also evaluates it in terms of the language and themes of contemporary literary theory, though in his reminiscences his youthful experience of *plaisir* seems to become a "prison house of language."[47] The connection between language and eros is accentuated by Adso's presentation of each as a problem of desire. The identity of the girl, the rose, and the sign is crucial here, for it makes Adso's remarks about his lost love of a piece with his understanding of the signs by which he knows her. In his meditations after their meeting he reflects more calmly on what she means to him:

> I desired, culpably, for her to appear at every moment. . . . The truth is that I "saw" the girl. . . . It was as if all creation spoke to me of her, and I desired to see her again, true, but I was also prepared to accept the idea of never seeing her again. . . . Everything . . . spoke to me only of the face I had hardly glimpsed in the aromatic shadows of the kitchen. . . . As if intoxicated, I then enjoyed her presence in the things I saw, and, desiring her in them, with the sight of them I was sated. And yet I felt a

45. Terry Eagleton, *Literary Theory: An Introduction* (Minneapolis: University of Minnesota Press, 1983), p. 82.

46. De Lauretis makes a similar point; see "Gaudy Rose," pp. 22–23.

47. It is also possible that Eco uses Adso to parody the tendency of modern critics to approach the erotic verbally and intertextually. Adso's whole account is not without its humor, if for no other reason than that he takes himself so seriously. Then too, Eco may be mirroring Adso in writing the novel, filtering passionate experience through literary models. I owe this good suggestion to Heather Dubrow.

kind of sorrow, because at the time I suffered from an absence, though I was happy with the many ghosts of a presence. (278–79)

Adso's reflections here appear in the passage in which he explains his "seeing" the girl in "all creation" in terms of the hierarchical "speaking" of a Platonically ordered cosmos. But counterposed to the signifying system by which he takes possession of her meaning is the dialectic of presence and absence, the "rhetoric of desire" that informs much contemporary thinking about the linguistic sign. Adso's momentary perception that meaning is produced by absence experienced as desire links his feelings for the girl to a poststructuralist conception of the sign as "the absence of everything from which it is differentiated." This sign "cannot literally represent that which it signifies, produce the signified as present, precisely because a sign for something must imply that thing's absence."[48] By this formulation, language is always empty, always a movement of desire.

Brilliantly literalizing the theoretical metaphor, Adso's desire is particularly acute because he has no name for speaking its absent object. When the girl is charged along with the other accused heretics, he laments her fate and his sorrow: "I burst shamefully into sobs and fled to my cell where all through the night I chewed my pallet and moaned helplessly, for I was not even allowed—as they did in the romances of chivalry I had read with my companions at Melk—to lament and call the beloved's name. This was the only earthly love of my life, and I could not, then or even after, call that love by name" (407). The Italian makes more explicit the connection between Adso's longing for the girl as presence and as sign and the novel's larger exploration of language and signification: "perche non mi era neppure concesso . . . di lamentarmi invocando il nome dell' amata" (*Rosa* 409). The name of the beloved ("il nome dell' amata") and the name of the rose ("il nome della rosa") are the same name.

48. Robert Young, "Post-Structuralism: An Introduction," in *Untying the Text: A Post-Structuralist Reader* (Boston: Routledge and Kegan Paul, 1981), p. 15.

Adso's erotic text based on other erotic texts calls attention to the eroticizing of all reading and interpretation that is inherent in a view of the sign founded in the experience of desire. Thus Adso achieves a nearly perfect harmonizing of his text's medieval and modern resonances. Not surprisingly, the theoretical dimension just described also finds its corollary in the ideals of the monastic milieu from which the narrative voice speaks. For the eroticized hermeneutics of Adso's narrative also illustrates monasticism's twin pursuits: the life of letters and the desire for God. When Adso unwittingly spiritualizes his erotic encounter, he does so with the monastic intentionality that experienced desire in terms of divinity. When he articulates that intention through the language of the Song of Songs, he appeals not only to the central monastic text on love but to a text that speaks of that love especially in terms of unfulfilled desire and of a dialectic of absence and presence.[49]

As the novel announces, then, Adso does think and write like a monk. While this thinking and writing thoroughly accord with the cultural setting of *The Name of the Rose*, they also contribute issues and vocabulary to the novel's larger meditation on contemporary literary and linguistic theory. In a single moment on the kitchen floor Adso tangibly and materially confronts what centuries of learned commentary—medieval and modern—have addressed in theological and theoretical discourse. His narrative's great achievement is that it manages to convey how very little difference exists between these two traditions of discourse.

49. Leclercq, *Love of Learning*, pp. 7–9; *Monks and Love*, p. 58, n. 13.

[3]

The Hermeneutics of Heresy

Eco remarks in his *Postscript to "The Name of the Rose"* that a novelist setting out to tell a story "must first of all construct a world, furnished as much as possible, down to the slightest details" (23). He describes how he went about constructing the "world" of his novel, how he paced his dialogue, studied architectural floor plans, and even counted the steps in a spiral staircase. One important constituent of his novel's world is "history." For while many aspects of a novel, "like the number of steps, can be determined by the author, . . . others . . . depend on the real world, which, in this kind of novel, happens to coincide with the possible world of the story" (27).

The fictional world that grew out of Eco's original inclination "to poison a monk" (*PS* 13) provides a minutely drawn portrait of fourteenth-century society, culture, and politics. Eco explains how this portrait followed from a certain historical and narrative logic: "I read and reread so many medieval chronicles; and as I read them, I realized that the novel had to include things that, in the beginning, had never crossed my mind" (*PS* 26). William of Baskerville, the fourteenth-century Fraticelli, and the debate about poverty are among the things Eco discovered his novel "had to include," as the necessity of having an investigator "with a great gift of observation and special sensitivity in interpreting evidence" led him first to the Franciscans after the time of Roger Bacon, then to the followers of Occam, and then to the politics of poverty in the fourteenth century.

Eco's account of the growth of his narrative from certain demands of the story itself is not entirely ingenuous: for instance, his assertion that he "could not move easily" (*PS* 26) in the fourteenth century is belied by his awesome dexterity in portraying the novel's historical setting. Nor are his observations simply another version of the familiar authorial assertion that the characters and situations "take on a life of their own." Rather, Eco's remark that his novel "had to include" certain things points toward the function of history in the novel and the role of fiction in fulfilling the historical purpose. His comments on the role of fictional characters in a historical novel illuminate this function and purpose:

> What the characters do serves to make history, what happened, more comprehensible. Events and characters are made up, yet they tell us things about . . . the period that history books have never told us so clearly. In this sense, certainly, I wanted to write a historical novel, and not because Ubertino or Michael had really existed and had said more or less what they say, but because everything the fictitious characters like William say *ought* to have been said in that period. . . . I ask myself if at times I did not endow my fictitious characters with a capacity for putting together, from the *disiecta membra* of totally medieval thoughts, some conceptual hircocervuses that, in this form, the Middle Ages would not have recognized as their own. But I believe a historical novel should do this, too: not only identify in the past the causes of what came later, but also trace the process through which those causes began slowly to produce their effects. (*PS* 75–76)

Here Eco describes both the practice and theory of history in *The Name of the Rose*: he intimates that the logic of events ("everything the fictitious characters . . . say *ought* to have been said") is not easily distinguished from the claims of the modern consciousness that employs "totally medieval thoughts" to create ideas that "the Middle Ages would not have recognized as their own." Thus the import of the novel's historical narrative resides not so much in the accumulation of significant detail, though the details are there in abundance, but rather in the probing of potential meanings and possible consequences of historical events and issues. History in *The Name of the Rose* is the present narrative of what was implicit in the past. It is a point where the medieval and the modern intersect.[1]

In *The Name of the Rose* history focuses on events that Eco claims did not initially "cross his mind," the controversy between Pope John XXII and the Franciscan Spiritualists on the question of poverty. This central episode in Franciscan history provides the ostensible raison d'être for the entire narrative, since William and Adso come to the monastery because the Franciscan is to serve as imperial emissary, mediator, and strategist in the dispute between John XXII and the Minorites over the interpretation of Christ's poverty. The chapter house meeting in which the two sides discuss the issue is the most overtly political event in a historical narrative otherwise committed to exploring the issue of poverty in social and philosophical terms. Eco's invention of this meeting is an imaginative and historical tour de force; it not only assembles the major and minor participants in the poverty controversy in the 1320s but also coincides with the actual timing of the historical debate. In December of 1327, Michael of Cesena, Minister General of the Franciscan order, was on his way to Avignon, having been summoned there by John XXII to account for and retract opinions he and the Franciscan chapter had endorsed.[2] The novel provides an interlude

1. The practice of history in *The Name of the Rose* corresponds to views about reading the past and writing history which have been set forth by recent theorists of history; among such views are the idea that history is a narrative constructed by historical agents, not a transparent record of documented knowledge; that these narratives "may be opened to some extent by the attempt to explore alternative possibilities in the past that are themselves suggested by the retrospective or deferred effects of later knowledge"; that, given the way that language "prefigures and informs the historical field," history is and can only be a conversation with the past. I adapt the characterization of these developments from Dominick LaCapra's *Rethinking Intellectual History: Texts, Contexts, Language* (Ithaca: Cornell University Press, 1983); material quoted here is from pp. 17–18, 75. LaCapra's remarks on the relationship of literature and history (pp. 57–58) further illuminate the role of history in Eco's novel. For a discussion of this view of history in the context of medieval studies, see Paul Zumthor, *Speaking of the Middle Ages*, trans. Sarah White (Lincoln: University of Nebraska Press, 1986), pp. 32–34, 87–89.

2. Decima L. Douie, *The Nature and the Effect of the Heresy of the Fraticelli* (1932; New York: AMS Press, 1978), pp. 153–201, especially pp. 154–55 and 165–66.

for Michael's journey, having him stop at the abbey "at the end of November."

In this chapter I address the uses of history in the novel, looking at the larger social and political context in which the chapter house meeting is situated. My concern here is with the conjunction of the novel's historical moment and its central themes and with the interpretive resonances of its historical events and persons. This chapter attends particularly to the novel's depiction and discussion of heresy, which figures in the political story in the same manner and to the same end as do the experience and language of love in Adso's monastic narrative. Both the discussion of heresy and the language of love provide opportunities for exploring how the linguistic sign signifies. Adso's meditation on the way language may or may not register distinctions between spiritual and carnal love is paralleled in the political story by an inquiry into the possibility of signifying through language the difference between heresy and holiness. In *The Name of the Rose* love and heresy bear a common tie to ambivalent linguistic signs. The novel probes the capacity of each to dissolve distinctions, to disturb order, and to render moral, emotional, and intellectual judgments uncertain.

While the personal and historical narratives of *The Name of the Rose* are thus linked by their respective inquiries into the nature and function of the linguistic sign, they are also connected more simply and fundamentally by the girl who plays such an important role in each. We have already seen how Adso's curiosity about the heretic Dolcino led him to knowledge of the touch of a simple peasant girl, who is the ambivalent object of his desire, both "an occasion of sin . . . [and] vessel of every grace" (278). From a historical and political perspective, she is a powerful instance both of the poverty on which heresy feeds and of the threatening female whom heretic hunters branded as a witch. The discrepancy between the girl's discrete meanings in the two narratives is striking: the token of allegorized passion that Adso's erotic experience appropriates in a biblical mode is also the simple girl who whores herself for a bundle of kitchen scraps. As an emblem of the way one sign stands in for another, the girl illustrates for both the novel's story and its theory how the metaphoric propensities of language make seemingly different things equivalent and equivalent things different.

I

Eco sets his novel in a historical moment marked by social transition.[3] The immediate past on which Adso and other characters reflect was an age that witnessed enormous changes in the social and economic aspect of Europe: the growth of towns, the expansion and diversification of population and professions, the emergence of new technologies, an increase in the amount and use of money. These developments all reflect the general turn toward the concrete, material world evident in Europe from the mid-eleventh century on.[4] They were accompanied by equally far-reaching changes in attitudes toward religious institutions and ideas of the spiritual life, as a Christian Europe increasingly faced the problem of reconciling the tenets of its faith with an expanding moneyed economy.

Historians of this period frequently depict the emergent characteristics of high medieval Europe in terms of the opposition between a new urban society and the feudally based monastic hegemony that it increasingly replaced. The administrative and economic organization of the monastery and the forms of cultural activity it fostered were singularly ill-suited to the modes of life that developed simultaneously with the rise of cities.[5]

3. Succinct summaries of historical events appear in the novel on pp. 12–13, 49–52, 145–48, 290–91, 338–40.

4. For an account of social and economic changes see John Baldwin, *The Scholastic Culture of the Middle Ages, 1000–1300* (Lexington, Mass.: D. C. Heath, 1971), pp. 15–34; Lester K. Little, *Religious Poverty and the Profit Economy in Medieval Europe* (Ithaca: Cornell University Press, 1978); M.-D. Chenu, *Nature, Man, and Society in the Twelfth Century*, ed. and trans. Jerome Taylor and Lester K. Little (Chicago: University of Chicago Press, 1968), pp. 37–39, and in general the two essays "Monks, Canons, and Laymen in Search of the Apostolic Life" and "The Evangelical Awakening." A general history of the period is John H. Mundy, *Europe in the High Middle Ages 1150–1309* (New York: Basic Books, 1973).

5. Chenu, *Nature, Man, and Society*, pp. 205–8, 230–31; Little, *Religious Poverty*, pp. 61–69.

Early in the *Rose* the Abbot invokes this conflict between monastic and urban life and values when he explains to William and Adso the threatened position of his order:

> "How many of our abbeys, which two hundred years ago were resplendent with grandeur and sanctity, are now the refuge of the slothful? The order is still powerful, but the stink of the cities is encroaching upon our holy places, the people of God are now inclined to commerce and wars of faction; down below in the great settlements, where the spirit of sanctity can find no lodging, not only do they speak (of laymen, nothing else could be expected) in the vulgar tongue, but they are already writing in it, though none of these volumes will ever come within our walls—fomenter of heresies as those volumes inevitably become!" (36)

The abbot's contempt for commerce and the vernacular is matched by Adso's nostalgic lament for the changing fortunes of Benedictine literary pursuits. Admiring the "scribe-monk imagined by our sainted founder, capable of copying without understanding, surrendered to the will of God, writing as if praying," he decries the degeneration of an order grown "too powerful," an order that now uses its accumulated knowledge as "barter goods" to try to recover the leadership in learning it has lost to "cathedral schools, urban corporations, universities" (184).

Significantly, both the abbot and Adso cast their remarks on the decline of their order in terms of shifting conceptions of its intellectual activity and its role in and attitude toward textual production.[6] They observe the appropriation of instruction and the pursuit of knowledge in secular institutions, the proliferation of books (and readers), and the growing influence of vernacular languages. The abbot's reference to the "stink of the cities" and Adso's concern for the competition the monastery faces from cathedral schools and universities reflect a real historical situation: one of the more severe blows to monastic power accompanying the urbanization of the West in the high Middle Ages was the break-up of the monastic monopoly on education. Shaped by the conditions of urban life, the cathedral schools and universities departed from monastic traditions of

6. Cf. the disgruntled monk Aymaro's more crabbed version of the same perception, p. 124.

study in their intellectual methods and goals and their position on spiritual matters.[7] These schools, like other new institutions in the towns in which they flourished, brought knowledge into the marketplace, where, their monastic rivals contended, it had no right to be.[8]

By reflecting on the decline of their order in specifically textual ways, Adso and the abbot provide a social and historical reference point for the novel's portrait of monastic letters and its larger interest in books, language, and signification. Their remarks bear witness to a moment in the history of the West which has been described as a "true historical mutation," a "profound shift in the status and uses of writing" which "affected virtually every area of social and cultural life." Whereas the so-called "Dark Ages" had restricted the locus of writing to the monasteries and the royal courts, the high Middle Ages witnessed "the irruption of a basically illiterate secular culture into writing, and the break, within writing, of a universal Latin culture into the disparate vernacular tongues. For the first time since the fall of the Roman Empire, the lay aristocracy of Western Europe possessed a cultural vehicle adequate to express its innermost tensions and ideals. And for the first time since the triumph of Christianity, the techniques of writing heretofore reserved for a caste (clerical and male) were massively disseminated among those exercising an ecclesiastical function as well as not."[9]

7. Little, *Religious Poverty*, pp. 174–75. A good account of the distinctions between monastic and scholastic aims and orientation can be found in Chenu, *Nature, Man, and Society*, pp. 270–330. I will consider the differences between monastic and scholastic attitudes toward language and knowledge in Chapter 5.

8. See Little, *Religious Poverty*, pp. 39, 177; G. Post, K. Giocarinis, and R. Kay, "The Medieval Heritage of a Humanistic Ideal: 'Scientia donum dei est, unde vendi non potest,'" *Traditio* 11 (1955): 195–234; Jacques Le Goff, "How Did the Medieval University Conceive of Itself?" in *Time, Work, and Culture in the Middle Ages*, trans. Arthur Goldhammer (Chicago: University of Chicago Press, 1980), pp. 123–27, and see pp. 58–70 and 107–21.

9. R. Howard Bloch, *Etymologies and Genealogies: A Literary Anthropology of the French Middle Ages* (Chicago: University of Chicago Press, 1983), p. 13; Brian Stock, *The Implications of Literacy: Written Language and Models of Interpretation in the Eleventh and Twelfth Centuries* (Princeton: Princeton University Press, 1983).

The Name of the Rose dramatizes the effects of this "historical mutation," its separate narrative strands delineating in personal, political, and intellectual terms the consequent shifts in relationships of power and authority brought about by the new "hegemony of writing" in the high Middle Ages. Yet the novel does not dwell in any historical detail upon the particular conflicts between representatives of the old and new learning nor upon the institutional factions and disputes that characterized much of the intellectual culture of the twelfth to fourteenth centuries.[10] Instead, it incarnates this important historical shift in the status of writing in its unremitting focus on and multilayered treatment of the relationship of language to what is and can be known, how and by whom. The novel emphasizes the cultural organization and production of knowledge by means of a narrative strategy that constitutes one of its most effective interminglings of medieval and modern.

Just as the basic dichotomy of monastery and city informs the *Rose*'s critique of the organization of learning in the fourteenth century, it also historically undergirds the discussion of evangelical and heretical movements that is so crucial to the novel's focus on the debate on poverty. In the history of high medieval Europe, the emergence of new religious movements and practices is an enormous and complex chapter. Historians customarily point out that the appearance of these movements coincides with the creation of a new urban class and the growth of a market economy, both of which clashed profoundly with the ethics and ideology of received Christian tradition.[11] The values of the *ordo monasticus*, whose exclusive claim to the attainment of perfection had up to that time furnished the model for the good Christian life, were no longer compatible with the religious aspirations of a mercantile society. Gradually, the authority of these values yielded to a new conception of the *vita apostolica* that spoke more effectively to the religious needs of lay society. This conception was realized in monastic reform, the rise of lay reli-

10. For a brief summary see Friedrich Heer, *The Medieval World: Europe 1100–1350*, trans. Janet Sondheimer (Cleveland and New York: World, 1962), chaps. 9 and 10.

11. Little, *Religious Poverty*, pp. 35–41.

gious movements, the appearance of vernacular scriptures and preaching, and the creation of new religious orders.[12]

The *Rose*'s portrait of fourteenth century Europe is populated with many representatives of the "evangelical awakening." The proliferation of lay religious movements provides the critical context for the historical narrative's exploration of poverty and heresy: Adso, for instance, is thrown into confusion by the anarchic proponents of the new evangelism. Yet the most crucial aspect of the novel's interest in the changing religious face of Europe is its emphasis on the Franciscan order. It is impossible to exaggerate the overall significance of the Franciscan element in *The Name of the Rose*. Eco has said that the kind of investigator he had in mind—a keen observer with a gift for interpreting evidence—had to be a Franciscan. His choice of a detective had far-reaching implications for his novel, which duly registers the many facets of Franciscan involvement in medieval society.

Significantly, the *Rose* is not preoccupied with the theology and spirituality of Franciscanism, nor is it principally concerned with portraying historical figures or events. With the exception of the meeting in the abbey between the supporters of John XXII and Michael of Cesena, in which Eco has apparently conflated several such encounters that occurred in the fourteenth century, all the major "events," turns of plot, and characters in *The Name of the Rose* are fictional. Yet they are fictional, as Eco has intimated, in a profoundly historical way, contributing to the historicity of the narrative through the plausibility and authenticity of incident, language, and behavior. William of Baskerville, for instance, is a near perfect exemplar of Franciscan

12. Chenu, *Nature, Man, and Society*, pp. 202–69; Little, *Religious Poverty*, pp. 113–45; Barbara H. Rosenwein and Lester K. Little, "Social Meaning in the Monastic and Mendicant Orders," *Past and Present* 63 (1974): 4–32; R. W. Southern, *Western Society and the Church in the Middle Ages* (Harmondsworth: Penguin, 1970), pp. 214–318; Jean Leclercq, François Vandenbroucke, and Louis Bouyer, *The Spirituality of the Middle Ages*, vol. 2 of *A History of Christian Spirituality* (New York: Seabury Press, 1968), pt. 2. On the rise of religious movements in times of radical social transition, see Victor Turner, *The Ritual Process: Structure and Anti-Structure* (1969; Ithaca: Cornell University Press, 1977), p. 133.

ideology thought through to its most probable and humane embodiment.

The historical period that brought about the changes in Western society represented in *The Name of the Rose* saw the emergence of what some historians identify as an "open" society that encouraged experimentation, growth in the intellectual and practical life, and tolerance. The appearance of such things as the mendicant orders, for example, is sometimes seen as an indicator of cultural pluralism and flexibility.[13] But the openness of that period was gradually replaced by a far less tolerant, uncompromising "closed" society, which seems "to have been bent on restraining, contracting, protecting, limiting, excluding."[14] The emergence of a "closed" Europe in the thirteenth and fourteenth centuries was accompanied by the development and consolidation of differentiated institutions (papacy and empire), the rise of nation states, and an increase in legislation; it was evidenced by the appearance during this period of pressure for conformity, antagonism toward all sorts of minorities, and the singling out of the poor as the source of social unrest.[15]

Eco's novel presents in detail the developments and consequences of a "closed" society in which the far more "open" voice of a William of Baskerville confronts the social and political repression and censorship engendered by institutions and persons bent on protecting established interests and power. The novel's portrayal of the conflict within the Franciscan order over the issue of poverty focuses on one important manifestation of this shift in high medieval Europe: how the "open" community founded by Francis developed into the complicated and influential institution that the Franciscan order became in the thir-

13. Eugene Vance considers Franciscan and Dominican preaching manuals in these terms; see "Mervelous Signals: Poetics, Sign Theory, and Politics in Chaucer's *Troilus*," *New Literary History* 10 (1979): 296.

14. John Boswell, *Christianity, Social Tolerance, and Homosexuality* (Chicago: University of Chicago Press, 1980), p. 270. Boswell adopts this characterization of the high Middle Ages from Heer, *The Medieval World*, who summarizes the ways in which high medieval Europe moved from an "open" to a "closed" society (pp. 1–13).

15. Boswell, *Christianity, Social Tolerance, and Homosexuality*, pp. 269–75; but see Heer's qualification of this model, p. 6.

teenth and fourteenth centuries. William comments on this profound and inevitable change in his order:

> "Francis wanted to call the outcast, ready to revolt, to be part of the people of God. . . . Francis didn't succeed, and I say it with great bitterness. To recover the outcasts he had to act within the church, to act within the church he had to obtain the recognition of his rule, from which an order would emerge, and this order, as it emerged, would recompose the image of the circle, at whose margin the outcasts remain." (202)

Yet, paradoxically, the very strategy that caused Francis's "failure" is from another perspective the very thing that enabled his order to succeed. As a consequence of institutional refinements and interventions, the order lost its original freshness and spontaneity; but "without this work of alteration and definition the Friars Minor might never have performed their great services to religion and learning."[16]

The history and ideology of the Franciscan order are ridden with such paradoxes. This characteristic of Franciscan life, thought, and letters accounts in part for the order's preeminence in the *The Name of the Rose*. It also contributes to the intermingling of medieval and modern in the novel, where the Franciscan order signifies much more than the group that nurtured a William of Occam and had as its founder an outrageous saint who talked to the birds.

II

The development of the Franciscan order was profoundly influenced by a feature of its original ideal: the "double movement" of its idea of the religious life, the yoking together of "the centrifugal spiritual aspirations of ascetic withdrawal and plenary, vigorous Christian service in the world."[17] To an extent, the Franciscans shared this aspect of their primitive ideal with

16. Douie, *Heresy of the Fraticelli*, p. 3. On the institutionalization of the Franciscan order, see also Turner, *Ritual Process*, p. 150.

17. John V. Fleming, *An Introduction to the Franciscan Literature of the Middle Ages* (Chicago: Franciscan Herald Press, 1977), p. 8.

other medieval orders and lay movements.[18] Yet the Franciscans are perhaps distinguished by the conspicuousness with which this "double movement" shaped their way of life, learning, and letters. Their double position is evident, for instance, in their perception of scriptural language as at once a concrete, material object and a divine articulation.[19] It is even more broadly attested by the whole problem that learning in general posed to the order, an issue related to the larger, more divisive debate on poverty. Saint Francis thought learning was incompatible with his ideal of poverty; he regarded knowledge as hoarding and so considered "learning as a possession, a form of property, a treasure."[20] Through the course of its history the order faced the problem of justifying the pursuit of knowledge. Though Francis had condemned learning, its pursuit was sanctioned by the heritage of his own radical engagement with the world and its creatures. Ironically, the order founded in the most humble, abject idea of divine service eventually produced both a practical theology and spirituality securely based in the world, as well as some of the most influential intellects of the high Middle Ages.

The Name of the Rose fully articulates the paradox of Franciscan learning. Reunited after a long separation, William and Ubertino discuss the value and danger of intellectual pursuits (53–64). Following the primitive dictates of Francis, Ubertino maintains that knowledge is pride, and he condemns William and his master Occam for idolizing reason. William counters that his pursuit of knowledge and study of nature can "better the human race." William and Ubertino illustrate the "double movement" of the Franciscan project nowhere more ironically than when, to Ubertino's admonition "'Mortify your intelligence, . . . throw away your books,'" William responds: "'I will devote myself only to yours'" (63).

Ubertino di Casale claims a rightful place in *The Name of the*

18. Chenu, *Nature, Man, and Society*, pp. 219–38; Fleming, *Franciscan Literature*, pp. 11–12.

19. Fleming, *Franciscan Literature*, pp. 22–24.

20. Le Goff, *Time, Work, and Culture*, p. 128; Fleming, *Franciscan Literature*, p. 5.

Rose because of the preeminent position he occupied among the Franciscan Spiritualists in the early fourteenth-century debate on poverty.[21] Yet rather than focus on his involvement in actual historical events, the novel creates a life for Ubertino after he "disappeared" from history, attending instead to the character of the man. Whereas his conversation with William reproduces the Spiritualist's celebrated anti-intellectualism, elsewhere in the novel Ubertino delivers "a learned disquisition" on the Spiritualist position on poverty (340). Trained in scholastic philosophy at Paris, Ubertino was a "brilliant speculative mind" who excelled "in academic debate, and in the conventional professional hairsplitting to which his opponents' charges of heresy drove him." His "attitude toward organized learning in the Franciscan life" was profoundly ambiguous.[22]

Ubertino is important in *The Name of the Rose* because he epitomizes the paradoxical conflict between asceticism and worldly commitment inherent in the primitive Franciscan ideal. The novel also develops him as a particular kind of personality—flamboyant, fervent, fanatical—whose ambivalence is most notably expressed in relation to the experience of human passion. Confident in the difference between the "high ecstasy of the heart loving Christ Crucified and the base, corrupt ecstasy of the Pseudo Apostles of Montefalco" (58), Ubertino ponders the transmutation of human desire into mystical experience. He is preoccupied with the erotic body, with female nature, and with love that "burns the viscera" (57).[23] We have seen in the previous chapter how Ubertino's provocative interpretations incite Adso to yearn for the very thing the aged Franciscan has

21. Douie, *Heresy of the Fraticelli*, pp. 120–52; Bernard McGinn, *Apocalyptic Spirituality* (New York: Paulist Press, 1979), pp. 155–56.

22. Fleming, *Franciscan Literature*, pp. 232–33; on the contradictions in Ubertino's literary production, see Douie, *Heresy of the Fraticelli*, p. 143. Fleming observes (pp. 101–2) a similar contradiction in the intellectual life of another Franciscan Spiritualist mentioned in the novel, Angelo Clareno; on Clareno see also Douie, pp. 49–80.

23. This aspect of the novel's portrait of Ubertino is supported by the historical literature; see Douie's comments on Ubertino's friendships with women, his life of Clare of Montefalco, and his attraction to the "charms of feminine beauty" in *Heresy of the Fraticelli*, pp. 122–25, 127, 148.

warned against. As Adso puts it: "I confess that the way Ubertino stigmatized the vice of others did not inspire virtuous thoughts in me" (57). By the tensions within his character Ubertino effectively links the issues of the historical narrative—the Franciscan story—with those of Adso's personal story. His impassioned warnings and ecstatic spiritual love are an exaggerated, intensely personal version of the essential doubleness that the Franciscan order manifested in its search for the transcendent in the everyday, material world. The Franciscan ideal, as represented by Ubertino, and the amorous Adso both exemplify interpretive ideologies that focus on the relation between the realms of flesh and spirit. Ubertino's efforts to polarize the two are only the other side of Adso's desire to unite them.

The embodiment of this paradox of the Franciscan ideal in *The Name of the Rose* is one important dimension of the order's ideological presence in the historical narrative. But in the novel's richly detailed portrait of Franciscan ideas, figures, and beliefs it is overshadowed in significance by an aspect of Franciscan history to which it is also closely related: the consistent linking of developments in the order with particular written texts and the Franciscans' critical involvement with problems of textual interpretation and authority. The very being of the Franciscan order is informed by a marked self-consciousness about the meaning, idiom, and authority of the written and spoken word. This fundamental feature is manifested in the order's primary belief in the radiant continuity of the Word and the word; in the radical biblicism of its history, hagiography, and homiletic writings; in its penchant for vulgarization; and in its genius for adapting styles of speaking and writing, which helped make it the vernacular order par excellence.[24]

The Franciscan involvement with language and textual interpretation makes the order a likely preoccupation of a novel with patent textual and semiotic concerns. *The Name of the Rose* acknowledges these prominent features of Franciscan language and hermeneutics. When Jorge excoriates Saint Francis as the clown

24. Fleming, *Franciscan Literature*, pp. 27–31, 250–57; see also Fleming's *From Bonaventure to Bellini: An Essay in Franciscan Exegesis* (Princeton: Princeton University Press, 1982), pp. 25–29.

who "'preached sermons giving a performance like a mountebank's, . . . spoke with animals and plants, transformed the very mystery of the Nativity into a village spectacle, [and] called the lamb of Bethlehem by imitating the bleat of a sheep'" (478), he in effect summarizes episodes from Franciscan hagiography that illustrate the saint's particular talent for exploiting language and interpretive traditions in his mission. In fact, in the Middle Ages, the matter of Francis's biography was a central and controversial issue in the order's larger involvement with hermeneutics and textual production. The search for "a definitive and 'authentic' Francis, and for a single 'true' account of his vision of fraternal life" was inseparable from the order's image of itself, its authority, and its social presence.[25] That search was intimately connected to the two overlapping issues of Franciscan hermeneutics which *The Name of the Rose* examines in detail: the order's alliance with Joachite apocalypticism and the question of poverty. The novel makes both these issues paradigmatic of the inevitable variability of interpretation in the face of competing claims for an authorized and absolute truth.

In the thirteenth and fourteenth century the Franciscan debate on poverty was profoundly affected by the teachings of Joachite apocalypticism. Nearly from the time of Francis's death in 1226, the Franciscan order was divided between those who wished to follow the strict observance of the founder and those who wished for moderation in the practice of poverty, an approach more consistent with that of the older, traditional orders. This conflict in the order was played out in its literature, its organization, and its politics. In the mid-thirteenth century it gathered momentum and polemical force as the supporters of the strict observance, or Spirituals as they came to be called, appropriated the views of the twelfth-century Cistercian Joachim of Fiore, whose revolutionary Trinitarian reading of Scripture and secular history had prophesied the approach of a Third Age that would

25. Fleming, *Franciscan Literature*, p. 32, and, for a general history of the controversy, pp. 32–72. On Bonaventure's effort to still the controversy and fulfill the quest, see Ewart Cousins, "Introduction," in *Bonaventure: The Soul's Journey to God, The Tree of Life, The Life of St. Francis* (New York: Paulist Press, 1978), pp. 37–46.

supersede the age of Christ and the New Testament, just as these had superseded Judaism and the Old Testament. The new Age of the Spirit, as Joachim called it, was to be distinguished by a superior religion and culture and by a democratized communal monasticism in society. Joachite apocalypticism offered a new reading of history particularly well-suited to the Franciscan Spirituals, who, in seeking validation for the observance of absolute poverty, saw themselves as the harbingers of the spiritual men of Joachim's Third Age.[26]

In appropriating Joachite prophecy the Franciscan Spirituals were simply exhibiting a biblical mode of thought common to the historically minded of their day, a mode "in which human time and divine time could be reconciled and in which current events could be seen as the reflex and afterlife of biblical events."[27] This biblicized historicism endowed apocalyptic exegesis with polemical force, as scriptural authority could be made to align variously with historical event.[28] The interpretive ges-

26. For brief summaries of Joachite apocalypticism and the cause of the Franciscan Spirituals, see Steven Ozment, *The Age of Reform 1250–1550: An Intellectual and Religious History of Late Medieval and Reformation Europe* (New Haven: Yale University Press, 1980), pp. 98–115; Richard K. Emmerson, *Antichrist in the Middle Ages: A Study of Medieval Apocalypticism, Art, and Literature* (Seattle: University of Washington Press, 1981), pp. 59–61, 68–69. For more detailed commentary on Joachism, see Marjorie Reeves, *The Influence of Prophecy in the Later Middle Ages: A Study of Joachism* (Oxford: Clarendon Press, 1969); Bernard McGinn, *The Calabrian Abbot: Joachim of Fiore in the History of Western Thought* (London: Macmillan, 1985); and the essays collected in Delno C. West, *Joachim of Fiore in Christian Thought: Essays on the Influence of the Calabrian Prophet*, 2 vols. (New York: Burt Franklin, 1975). For further commentary on Joachism and the Franciscan Spirituals, see Gordon Leff, *Heresy in the Later Middle Ages: The Relation of Heterodoxy to Dissent, c.1250–1450*, 2 vols. (New York: Barnes and Noble, 1967), 1:51–255. See also the texts collected in McGinn, *Apocalyptic Spirituality*, and in that work his introduction to the section "Franciscan Spirituals," pp. 149–58.

27. John Fleming, *From Bonaventure to Bellini*, p. 25, and, for a brief overview of medieval attitudes to history and prophecy, pp. 20–23.

28. See Emmerson, *Antichrist in the Middle Ages*, pp. 62–72. The very elements of Joachite prophecy that Franciscan Spirituals used in their favor were just as easily turned against them in the thirteenth century by William of St. Amour's *De periculis novissimorum temporum*, which identified the fraternal orders with Antichrist and the Pseudo Apostles. For an overview of this important and influential conflict between St. Amour and the friars, see Penn R. Szittya, "The Antifraternal Tradition in Middle English Literature," *Speculum* 52

ture by which the Franciscan Spirituals allied themselves with Joachite exegesis and history had far-reaching implications: Joachite apocalypticism posed a radical vision of the future that severely challenged the hierarchy of church authority. It was doubtless these affiliations with Joachism that provoked the institutional church to suppress the Spirituals' promotion of absolute poverty. But it was also the ideological commitment to the ideals of Francis that motivated the Spirituals to appeal to Joachite interpretations to authorize their strict observance of the founder's vow of poverty.

The apocalyptic context of the poverty debate in the Middle Ages also colors its portrayal in *The Name of the Rose*. Apocalypticism's sense of the imminence of the end lends urgency to the poverty debate in the novel and furnishes its rhetoric. The interpretation of the Friars Minor as both the "spiritual men" of Joachim's Third Age and as Pseudo Apostles, messengers of the Antichrist (61–63), illustrates how competing readings of Joachite prophecy fueled the poverty debate.

The conflict over competing interpretations of the scriptural text and secular history which characterizes the Joachite dimension of the Franciscan poverty debate is most clearly illustrated by the particular textual problem at its very heart and hence at the heart of the Franciscan story of *The Name of the Rose*: the meaning of the Franciscan *Rule*.[29] At issue in the conflict over

---

(1977): 287–313, and his new book, *The Antifraternal Tradition in English Literature* (Princeton: Princeton University Press, 1986).

29. On the poverty debate in general, see Douie, *Heresy of the Fraticelli*, pp. 153–201; and John Moorman, *A History of the Franciscan Order from Its Origins to the Year 1517* (Oxford: Clarendon Press, 1968), pp. 307–19. For a recent theory of the origins of the controversy within the Franciscan order, see David Burr, "The *Correctorium* Controversy and the Origins of the *Usus Pauper* Controversy," *Speculum* 60 (1985): 331–42. For an account of the literary work inspired by the debate, see Fleming, *Franciscan Literature*, pp. 73–109. The medieval *Rule* existed in two versions, an early one of 1221, the *Regula non bullata*, which is thought to have been built upon the primitive rule that Francis presented to Innocent III, and a later version, the *Regula bullata*, which was accepted as definitive by Honorius in 1223. Shortly before his death, Francis also wrote a *Testament*, intended to counteract efforts by the institutional church to "domesticate" the primitive Franciscan ideal's strict observance of poverty; see Ozment, *Age of Reform*, p. 100. Texts of the earlier and later *Rules* and the *Tes-*

the *Rule* was the exact meaning of poverty. Poverty was at the center of the Franciscan ideal, but Francis had never "defined in unambiguous jural terms what he meant by poverty and what this entailed with regard to property."[30] The problem of interpreting the *Rule,* then, was in part a function of Francis's own spiritual style: his thinking was not systematic or formulaic; his writings, such as they are, are simple, laconic. As the legends about him suggest, he preferred to speak with his whole body rather than with his pen. For Francis the *Rule* was realized only in the living of it.

The conflicts about the meaning of the *Rule* were embedded in the Franciscan approach to its very language. Thirteenth-century Franciscans saw "their founder's rule as having something of the authority and inviolability of Scripture"—a status that necessarily heightened the importance of its valid interpretation. Francis had "considered both the language and the intent of the *Rule* plain and simple, and . . . commanded his followers to abstain from exegesis." But their interest in recovering that intent, as it became wedded to other exigencies, turned that "plain and simple" document into "the object of thousands of pages of *explication de texte.*"[31]

The debate on poverty coincided with the development of the order from the small fraternity that had followed the saint from Assisi to an international movement with thousands of members.[32] *The Name of the Rose* appropriately contextualizes the debate on poverty in the grand historical sweep of thirteenth-

---

tament can be found in *Francis and Clare: The Complete Works,* trans. Regis J. Armstrong, O.F.M. and Ignatius C. Brady, O.F.M. (New York: Paulist Press, 1982), pp. 107–45 and 153–56. Fleming describes the Franciscan conception of the *regula*; (*Franciscan Literature,* pp. 25–26).

30. Turner, *Ritual Process,* pp. 145 and 146–47. See the critique of Turner's reading of the Franciscans by Caroline Walker Bynum, "Women's Stories, Women's Symbols: A Critique of Victor Turner's Theory of Liminality," in *Anthropology and the Study of Religion,* ed. Robert L. Moore and Frank E. Reynolds (Chicago: Center for the Scientific Study of Religion, 1984), pp. 105–25.

31. Fleming, *Franciscan Literature,* p. 95.

32. Armstrong and Brady, *Francis and Clare,* pp. 107–8; Douie comments on early interventions by papal decretals that affected the meaning of the *Rule*; see *Heresy of the Fraticelli,* pp. 2–3.

and fourteenth-century Europe, showing how the matter of interpreting the *Rule* had enormous social and political consequences. For the Franciscans, the debate on poverty reflected the order's effort to define itself in relation to the intentions of its founder—in effect, to reconcile Francis's ascetism with his charge for a worldly mission. The "very essence" of Franciscan history, that effort repeatedly confronted the paradox of the double movement at the center of the Franciscan ideal.[33] In *The Name of the Rose* the conflict over interpretations of the *Rule* reflects the competing exegetical efforts to construe it as an authoritative document bespeaking a singular truth. The novel tells the story of that battle for univocal significance—its opposing parties, their interests, motivations, and political agendas. As in its manipulation of the competing apocalyptic signs só intimately connected to the poverty debate, the novel appropriates the central interpretive issue of medieval Franciscanism in its larger inquiry into linguistic signification and the search for authoritative and original meaning.

III

Adso's musings on the meaning of poverty give a human immediacy to the issue epitomized in the problem of interpreting the Franciscan *Rule*. Describing the death of the Fraticello Michael, who was burned as a heretic in Florence, Adso recalls that, as he witnessed the event, he wondered "why the men of the church and of the secular arm were so violent against people who wanted to live in poverty and held that Christ had not owned worldly goods" when, rather, "they should fear men who wish to live in wealth and take money away from others, and lead the church into sin and introduce simoniacal practices into it." Adso innocently, and mistakenly, assumes that the preaching of poverty involves primarily doctrine and ethics; he cannot understand what could possibly be heretical in wanting to follow the poverty of Christ. But he also recalls another spectator's explanation for Michael's death: preaching poverty creates con-

33. Fleming, *Franciscan Literature*, p. 75.

flict because people who follow poverty make things difficult for clerics who don't; it "put you on the side of the Emperor, and this did not please the Pope" (237).

Adso's reminiscence identifies two features of the preaching of poverty which are closely related to the interpretive dilemma it presents to him and to its significance in the novel. Like its handmaiden heresy, the preaching of poverty is primarily a social problem; further, its social force is seen as a challenge to established power.

In casting the problem of poverty in this light, *The Name of the Rose* simply reiterates a commonplace of medieval history: that the heretical movements of the Middle Ages had a strong social basis and origin.[34] The Europe Adso reflects upon when he recalls the "mire that flowed over the paths of our world, [and] with them mingled preachers in good faith, heretics in search of new victims, agitators of discord" (190), marked the late phase of a movement that had begun in the eleventh century with the "shaping of an evangelical truth to a determined socio-economic form."[35] Almost from their very inception the apostolic and evangelical movements of the high Middle Ages posed numerous threats to institutional authority. These threats had less to do with doctrine than with the social and economic organization, and hence the established powers, of the Christian community.[36] Tacitly questioning clerical roles and functions, the orders and movements founded in the call to poverty understood that condition not only as a form of "moral asceticism among members of a fraternity that held their goods in common, but as the proper institutional condition of the kingdom of God in this world."[37]

Just as the call to poverty distinguished itself from the mode

34. Douie, *Heresy of the Fraticelli*, p. 209; Le Goff, *Time, Work, and Culture*, p. 109. For a critique of this view see Stock, *Implications of Literacy*, pp. 92–101.

35. Chenu, *Nature, Man, and Society*, p. 235. Chenu discusses the role of poverty in the apostolic movements emerging after the first millennium (pp. 204–19) and the social context in which the call to poverty gained authority and momentum (pp. 240–46).

36. See, for example, Little's remarks on the Waldensians in *Religious Poverty*, pp. 127–28; and, in general, pp. 99–145.

37. Chenu, *Nature, Man, and Society*, p. 242.

of life of traditional institutions, so too did it find its audience among those outside traditional social groupings. The new fraternal orders, for example, drew their recruits from ministerials, knights, patricians, and burghers, groups who "commanded vast material resources but lacked commensurate social prestige and political power."[38] Saint Francis, after all, was the son of a cloth maker from Assisi. The order that he founded owed its success in part to his particular genius for understanding and anticipating the challenges to the reigning institutions that the call to poverty presented; Innocent III's approval of his order was his first tactical victory.

The social context in which the apostolic movements pledged to voluntary poverty emerged adds another dimension to the representation of the Franciscan poverty debate in *The Name of the Rose*. For the paradoxical relation of Franciscan ideals to the actual destiny of the order coincides with the manner in which a new moneyed economy accommodated itself to the call to poverty. The novel's focus on the poverty debate, then, follows a double course: the poverty question not only illuminates the nature, history, and ideology of the Franciscan order but also illustrates the disruptive social force inherent in apostolic movements. Like love, its hermeneutic counterpart in Adso's personal narrative, the poverty question is allied to a potential for transgressive behavior.

William's approach to the poverty question clarifies Adso's muddle by establishing the link between poverty as a sign and as a social phenomenon. His analysis of recent Italian politics describes poverty's linguistic multivalence and its transgressive power: "'In the Italian city . . . goods serve to procure money. And even priests, bishops, even religious orders have to take money into account. This is why, naturally, rebellion against power takes the form of a call to poverty. The rebels against power are those denied any connection with money, and so every call to poverty provokes great tension and argument'" (126–27). William's discursive account of the relation between signification, society, and evangelism is for Adso poignantly re-

38. Little, *Religious Poverty*, p. 161; see also Chenu, *Nature, Man, and Society*, p. 243.

alized in the fractured life of Salvatore, who represents for him the many men he has encountered along the road and even "the splendid epitome" of Italy itself. A refugee from his native village, always poor and always hungry, Salvatore brings together in a single unwitting interpretive act the voluntary poverty of the apostolic movements and the abject poverty of his social marginality. Listening to the Franciscan preachers, Salvatore "understood that the poor and vagabond life he led should be taken, not as a grim necessity, but as a joyous act of dedication, and he joined penitential sects and groups whose names he could not pronounce properly and whose doctrine he defined in highly unlikely terms. . . . He had passed from one group to another, gradually assuming as a mission his vagrant state, and doing for the Lord what he had done till then for his belly" (191).

William's analysis and Salvatore's example define the high stakes in the battle for interpretive control of the meaning of poverty. Each in his distinctive way illustrates how the desire to elicit from the Franciscan *Rule* and its companion scriptural texts an original, authoritative meaning is guided by a social agenda. William and Salvatore indicate how the competing readings of poverty within the Franciscan order and the serial pronouncement of papal bulls intended to establish the "true" interpretation of both Scripture and the *Rule* are analogously motivated political acts. The interpretation of poverty is no simple matter because every interpretive gesture implies a stance toward the church's material goods and its involvement in the material world. As William explains: "'the question is not whether Christ was poor: it is whether the church must be poor. And "poor" does not so much mean owning a palace or not; it means, rather, keeping or renouncing the right to legislate on earthly matters'" (345).

The political magnitude of the problem of interpreting poverty is illustrated in the meeting between the papal envoys and the Franciscan officials gathered at the abbey. The exchange between John XXII's representatives and the Spiritualist sympathizers shows how Scripture can be manipulated in the service of conflicting readings of the Franciscan *Rule* (338–48). As the meeting dissolves into a cacophony of competing voices, Adso asks William if there is no argument that will "'prove or refute the poverty of Christ.'" William's response implies that the entire meeting is gratuitous: "'Why, you can affirm both positions . . . and you will never be able to establish on the basis of the Gospels whether, and to what extent, Christ considered as his property the tunic he wore'" (345).

William's observation on the variability of scriptural interpretation is strengthened by his own address to the meeting, in which, as noted earlier (p. 18f.), he interprets Genesis to argue for the conventionality of the verbal sign. But William is neither a linguistic nor a political relativist. Rather, his very consciousness of the flexibility of interpretation, of the power and danger that follow from the sign's conventionality, undergirds his own political position and his rhetorical style, which is a tour de force of irony, understatement, and feigned humility. William argues for a rationally ordered, democratic society in which the "legislation over the things of this earth, and therefore over the things of the cities and kingdoms, has nothing to do with the custody and administration of the divine word, an unalienable privilege of the ecclesiastical hierarchy" (353). He wishes to get the Church out of the business of controlling meanings and, consequently, controlling secular society. He is supremely aware that the institutional components of the poverty debate, papal and Franciscan, purvey "truths" that are founded on vastly different authorities. There is no purely hermeneutic solution to the problem of poverty.

The novel elaborates on William's position by showing how the problem of conflicting interpretations besets every aspect of the poverty debate, particularly the heretical movements it was credited with fostering. Adso ponders the spiritual and moral distinctions between heresy and holiness, recalling the bands of flagellants he has encountered, at one time deemed "saints" by the local populace, at another heretics. "And yet," he muses, "they were the same people" (122). His questions link the social and interpretive dimensions of the poverty debate: "Was the simoniacal and corrupt Pope right in considering the mendicant monks preaching poverty the equivalent of bands of outcasts and robbers?" (190). Adso's quandary is epitomized in his obsession with Dolcino, who serves in the novel as a resonant sign upon which the major issues of the historical narrative converge.

For both William and Adso, Dolcino effectively incarnates the problem of distinguishing between similar phenomena with different names and different phenomena with similar names. According to William, Dolcino was "'a man who did insane things because he put into practice what many saints had preached. At a certain point I could no longer understand whose fault it was, I was as if . . . dazed by an air of kinship that wafted over the two opposing camps, of saints who preached penitence and sinners who put it into practice'" (119). William's trouble with Dolcino resides not so much in what the Pseudo Apostle has done as in what he represents: the fading of the apparent dichotomy between sinner and saint into the gray area in which the heretic's faith looks remarkably like the most elevated forms of orthodox holiness. Dolcino emblemizes the difficulty of differentiating between the Pseudo Apostles and the Franciscan Spiritualists; Adso brazenly asserts to Ubertino that he and the "heretic" actually preached the same thing (227).[39] In one breath William speaks confidently of the difference between Minorites and Pseudo Apostles, whom the abbot lumps together as heretical followers of Joachim of Fiora. Yet in the next breath he acknowledges that the Pseudo Apostles can be reproached only for "'putting into practice without much consideration things that the Spirituals preached with greater temperance, animated by true love of God, and here . . . the borderline between one group and the other is very fine'" (150).

Dolcino's semiotic variability in the novel's historical narrative corresponds to two related interpretive issues that Eco has discussed elsewhere, in a more openly theoretical context. Within a "network of cultural information" a sign is susceptible to many different readings. Medieval approaches to such a network customarily restrict these readings to allow only a few, generally contradictory properties. Eco provides the telling ex-

39. Cf. Ubertino, who "could have become one of the heretics he helped burn, or a cardinal of the holy Roman church" (65).

ample of the lion seen as "a *figura Christi* or as a figure of the Antichrist." In order to determine meaning "a *co-text* is necessary. The tradition provides a typology of possible co-texts, so that the best interpretation is always the one recorded by some . . . *auctoritas*" (*SP* 104). The hermeneutic fortunes of Dolcino and of heresy in *The Name of the Rose* illustrate the problem of choosing the "co-text" that will establish the proper meaning of the sign. Dolcino can be named both a saint (*figura Christi*) and a heretic (figure of the Antichrist) because the Pseudo Apostle and the institutional church each invoke competing co-texts.

For William neither of these readings is satisfactory; neither is simply "true." William is aware that the co-texts of the poverty debate validate what Eco calls "cultural properties," not "ontological realities." He explains to Adso how Dolcino's story, like the entire poverty debate, is a story about the cultural production of meaning. When Adso finally passes over the opportunity to discuss with his master the "differences among heretical groups" in order to talk about "the problem of difference itself" (196), he learns that reform movements are a function, not of systems of belief, but of the condition of the people—the simple—who flock to such movements: "'I think the mistake is to believe that the heresy comes first, and then the simple folk who join it (and damn themselves for it). Actually, first comes the condition of being simple, then the heresy'" (200). Because of poverty, hunger, and ignorance the simple are attracted to movements of renewal because such movements offer the "possibility of a different life" (152). They do not "choose" heresy; it chooses them. The simple distinguish neither fine points of doctrine nor the urge for renewal from other impulses. Rather, they lump all doctrines and urges together in one undifferentiated swell of revolt, which conveniently serves the enemies who wish to show them as "'one jumble of diabolical contradictions which offend common sense.'" Thus, William asserts, "'what makes them live is also what makes them die'" (200).[40]

Adso also learns that the cultural construction of heresy is

40. William's analysis of the social formation of heresy is incarnated in Remigio's account of the life he and Salvatore led with Dolcino, pp. 271–73.

part of a larger process. Reform movements do not simply owe their nature and their unfortunate fate to the social conditions from which they emerge; their existence and continuation are also guaranteed by the very social and institutional structures that presumably would suppress them. As William explains it, this is the function of social marginality. The Christian community is composed of insiders—those who govern and who interpret the word of God—and outsiders—the peasants, the unconnected city dwellers, the fringe elements whose exclusion from the social order is signified by the archtypal sign of exclusion, the leper. While the insiders fight with each other over their respective rights, the outsiders fulfill their role by eliciting the opprobrium of the powers that be and, above all, by staying outside. They latch on to movements of renewal that offer the possibility of making them insiders, of reordering the distinctions between margin and center. This was the perception that motivated Saint Francis, who wanted to recover the outcasts but failed (202). Such gestures are always doomed to failure, William maintains, because true recovery of the outcasts would demand "'reduction of the privileges of the powerful,'" who brand the excluded as heretics so that they will remain excluded. As William puts it: "'Every battle against heresy wants only this: to keep the leper as he is'" (203). Every battle against heresy is an act of semiotic containment of the margin by the center.

Heresy, then, is not the result of demonic challenges to orthodoxy; heretics are created.[41] They are a function and a sign of social organization and social relations, their existence signifying the insiders' desire for self-protection, revenge, and power. Adso had intimated as much when he observed that the difference between heretics and true penitents "did not lie in the ac-

41. The novel's social and anthropological analysis of heresy coincides with the conclusions of recent historians. See Stock, *Implications of Literacy*, pp. 145–51. Carlo Ginzberg argues that Counter-Reformation heresy was shaped not by a specific belief, but by acts of interpreting printed texts in light of the traditions of oral culture; see *The Cheese and the Worms: The Cosmos of a Sixteenth-Century Miller*, trans. John and Anne Tedeschi (Harmondsworth: Penguin, 1982), pp. 6–7, 51. Victor Turner's analysis of millenarian religious movements is also relevant here; see *Ritual Process*, pp. 111–12, 129–30.

tions of the one or the other, but in the church's attitude when she judged this act or that" (123).

The novel shows how those judgments vary according to the particular interests of the judge. When the doctors of the Sorbonne found that the friars were becoming too influential, they declared their Joachite teachings heretical (50). The wealthy Benedictines, hardly interested in apostolic poverty, nevertheless supported the Franciscan Spiritualists, called heretics by some, because they were united in a common opposition to the pope, whose increasing power threatened a declining monastic hegemony's control of the social order (145–46). The abbot of the novel's monastery sees all movements for renewal as the same, all heresies that "'endanger the order that sustains the people of God.'" He supports the empire, he says, "'because it guarantees this order for me'" (153).

IV

The unexpected events occurring at the abbey while the papal envoys and Franciscans are gathered there give full play to this analysis of heresy. Bernard Gui's seizure and questioning of Salvatore and Remigio exemplify the issues of the poverty debate, showing in particular how meanings are constructed to mark the excluded as heretics. What begins as a formal, institutional confrontation between papal and imperial forces on the question of poverty and the Franciscan *Rule* ends with the rooting out of individual heretics. International politics give way to very local problems, as Bernard Gui finds himself caught up in the abbey's peculiar transgressions. But the shift in focus here is a shift of scale not of substance, for the impulse to establish authoritative meaning in the documentary context of the debate over the *Rule* coincides with Gui's efforts to detect and name heresy in action.

The novel presents Gui as the "scourge of heretics" who will manipulate meanings and appearances to serve the powerful interests of the pope whom he represents.[42] The abbot rightly anticipates that Gui "'will try to insist that the theses of Perugia are the same as those of the Fraticelli, or the Pseudo Apostles'" (211). Gui also brings to life William's more graphic assertion that the "'simple are meat for slaughter, to be used when they are useful in causing trouble for the opposing power, and to be sacrificed when they are no longer of use'" (152).

The novel shows Gui at work in his arrest of Salvatore and Adso's beloved young girl and in his inquisition of Remigio. Each episode is a tour de force of medieval significations. When Salvatore is caught with the paraphernalia of his attempted sorcery and the girl is apprehended with the rooster she has accepted as payment for her favors, Gui quickly seizes the opportunity to interpret these pathetic tokens as evidence of witchcraft. Ironically, Gui's accusation accords with Salvatore's own foolish belief in sorcery, as Salvatore had earlier explained it to a disgusted Adso (308–9). But Salvatore's spells were intended only to "make every woman succumb to love," not to call up Satan himself, and the girl's "little dead rooster" is the mark of a desperate hunger. In Gui's world these signs of an ignorant man's lust and a peasant girl's poverty become clear tokens of devil worship, a point that Gui makes easily by calling on a host of authoritative witnesses (328). Once he establishes the meaning of these signs in the institutional context of theological heterodoxy, little effort is required for him to link Salvatore's putative sorcery with "'necromancies . . . prepared to make attempts on the life of our lord Pope himself'" (329).

William calls attention to the rhetorical move that enables Gui to link the abbey's so-called heretics with papal politics and

42. The novel's portrait of Bernard Gui is perfectly consistent with his historical role in the repression of medieval heresies. As the novel mentions (210), Gui was the author of a manual for inquisitors. John Mundy notes that Gui recorded "with gruesome joy the slaughter of Dolcino of Novara and Margaret," the Pseudo Apostles who figure so prominently in the *Rose* (*Europe in the High Middle Ages*, pp. 16, 553–55; on inquisitorial excesses, see pp. 549–61). Portions of Gui's *Practica inquisitionis heretice pravitatis* are edited and translated by Walter L. Wakefield and Austin P. Evans, *Heresies of the High Middle Ages*, Records of Civilization: Sources and Studies 81 (New York: Columbia University Press, 1969), pp. 373–445.

thus to establish the basis for discrediting and threatening the abbey and the Franciscans it harbors. Gui's method is consistent with the idiom of his speech. His icy control of the languages of patristic authority, scholastic reasoning, and papal fiat suffices as the burden of proof for Salvatore's and Remigio's guilt. When he asserts, "'Now the case seems clear to me. A monk seduced, a witch, and some ritual,'" he shows confidence in the names and systems he has used to condemn the simple victims. The power of his language is underscored by the futile shouts of Adso's apprehended lover, who "was as if mute." Her vulgar peasant tongue goes unheeded, not because it is foreign but because the simple are "not granted the boon of self-expression in the universal tongue of knowledge and power" (329–30).

Gui's inquisition of Remigio is an example of that "universal tongue" speaking to overtly political ends (370–90). Whereas Salvatore's arrest affords Gui the opportunity to imply that persons in the abbey threaten the pope, his examination of Remigio enables him to bring to light the cellarer's former affiliation with Dolcinian heresy. Once Gui's language of "knowledge and power" forces Remigio to "confess" not only to heresy but to crimes he did not commit, the inquisitor concludes that the heresy of those who preach poverty inevitably leads to other crimes and that those who harbor heretics are no better than heretics themselves. Gui thus brings down Remigio in order to imply that the abbey is a haven for heresy, particularly of a Franciscan tinge. Acting, he says, only as the "'humble instrument of the truth,'" he thus accomplishes through inquisitorial strategies what he was originally to effect through formal debate.

Gui's "truth" declares rather than discovers heresy. Like the "justice" that he also purports to represent, it authorizes a meaning for the ambivalent fervor that may be either holiness or rebellion against poverty. Gui's approach to interpretation is directly opposite to that of William, who readily admits the difficulty he has in making the distinctions that Gui so easily propounds. The difference between William and Gui is also manifested in the sharp irony William displays in their exchanges (301–2; 328; 378–79). The double meanings on which William's irony depends have no place in Gui's universe.

Their respective approaches to language and interpretation may be illuminated in terms of the distinction that Eco draws elsewhere between the dictionary and the encyclopedia as semiotic and philosophical concepts. Gui prescribes meaning with reference to a "dictionary," understood as "a stable and univocal image of a semantic universe" (*SP* 86). William, in contrast, recognizes that the semantic universe is in fact an "encyclopedia," which is "virtually *infinite* because it takes into account multiple interpretations realized by different cultures . . . [and] because every discourse about the encyclopedia casts in doubts the previous structure of the encyclopedia itself." Whereas Gui's semantic universe is organized as a global system, an encyclopedia permits "only 'local' and transitory systems of knowledge, which can be contradicted by alternative and equally 'local' cultural organizations" (*SP* 83–84). According to Eco's categories, the inquisitor's semiotic manipulations—of heresy, poverty, sorcery—might be seen as an attempt to recognize as unique and "global" the local organizations of the encyclopedia.

The truth that Adso seeks at first resembles Gui's rather than William's. Discussing heresy with his mentor, Adso asks, "'Why don't you take a position, why won't you tell me where the truth is?'" (205). William directs his reply not to the political intent of Adso's question but to the basis on which such an inquiry can be made. He considers the "simple" people of heresy in relation to conditions of knowledge rather than social structure:

"The simple have something more than do learned doctors. . . . The simple have a sense of the individual, but this sense, by itself, is not enough. The simple grasp a truth of their own . . . but then they destroy it in unthinking actions. . . . How are we to remain close to the experience of the simple, maintaining, so to speak, their operative virtue, the capacity of working toward the transformation and betterment of the world? . . . If the sense of the individual is the only good, how will science succeed in recomposing the universal laws through which, and interpreting which, the good magic will become functional? . . . How can I discover the universal bond that orders all things if I cannot lift a finger without creating an infinity of new entities? For with such a movement all the relations of position between my finger and all other objects change. The relations are the ways in which my mind perceives the connections between single entities, but what is the guarantee that this is universal and stable?" (205–7)

William's reflections move the implicit concerns of the political narrative into the explicitly philosophical realm: the empirical knowledge of singular things which satisfies the simple (they are nominalists of sorts) may be knowledge in its most authentic form. But in that form it is of little value, and indeed is capable of doing great harm. Hence, William says, we need "universal laws," even though we know they are constructions, ways of talking about an experience that is always individual. The only thing about which we may be certain is the impossibility of certainty; even so, we must act at times as if it were possible. As Adso sums up William's position: "'You act, and you know why you act, but you don't know why you know that you know what you do?'" (207).

As he acknowledges, William's view here owes much to the philosophy of his "friend" William of Occam.[43] William embodies the sobriquet frequently applied to the nominalists in their own day. Yet he is of the *moderni* in a double sense, both through the role he plays in the medieval story and through the strategy that links his "nominalist" point of view with contemporary thinking about language and epistemology. With William as its interpreter, the entire political story is gradually subsumed in the novel's articulation of contemporary language philosophy. As the burden of historical and cultural paradox, the dilemmas of Franciscan textuality and hermeneutics, come to focus on the distinction between heresy and holiness as a philosophical problem, we see how the narrative's interest in the construction of social and political meanings provides a paradigm for the prob-

43. For brief summaries that point up the similarity of Occam's life and thought to William's, see Ozment, *Age of Reform*, pp. 55–63; Gordon Leff, *The Dissolution of the Medieval Outlook* (New York: Harper and Row, 1976), pp. 55–92; Heiko Oberman, "The Shape of Late Medieval Thought: The Birthpangs of the Modern Era," and Charles T. Davis, "Ockham and the Zeitgeist," both in *The Pursuit of Holiness in Late Medieval and Renaissance Religion*, ed. Charles Trinkhaus and Heiko Oberman (Leiden: Brill, 1974), pp. 9–10 and 59–65, respectively.

lem of naming, of representing anything to consciousness. When William turns Adso's query about the "truth" of particular heresies into a consideration of scientific laws, he suggests that Adso's concerns finally come to rest in the confidence with which we may know any experience of the individual that is of necessity knowable—and communicable—only through what it is not.

These are heady issues. William suggests as much to Adso as the two try to figure out the plan of the library. Still preoccupied with their analysis of heresy, Adso draws William into a discussion of mathematics with this provocation: "'Then you do admit universal notions.'" William takes the bait at first, only to retort, "'Stop dragging me into discussions of metaphysics.'" He then quickly diverts Adso's attention to something more practical, ordering him to take up "'a parchment, a tablet, something you can make signs on, and a stylus'" (215). William's rejoinder offers some momentary relief from a narrative that quite regularly does drag the reader into metaphysics. Ironically, most often it is the nominalist William who does the dragging, and then only to reject the possibility of metaphysics. William's exchange with Adso here anticipates his more explicit and protracted philosophical debate with Jorge, which provides the novel's ideological finale.

It is also significant that William here turns Adso away from philosophy and toward a specific and directed act of writing. The shift in focus from the "universal notion" to the "making of signs" is a synecdoche for the novel's primary philosophical concerns. It is also a gesture that aptly coincides with Eco's assertion that "those things which we cannot theorize about, we must narrate."

V

The Name of the Rose does not simply offer medieval history as an object of representation whose faithful reproduction enhances the work as historical novel. Rather, it selectively represents medieval "events" that make possible a critique of historical representation itself. The fundamental issues of the historical narrative are hermeneutic. It looks at the Franciscan story and the problems of heresy and poverty in order to show how the terms, concepts, and structures of history involve much larger issues: the cultural production of meaning and the conditions under which knowledge is constituted. Yet the concerns of the historical narrative are also profoundly social. William's hermeneutic positions are consistent with his analysis of social relations. He understands that strategies of exclusion and social marginality intersect with "the conquest of power"; he knows that social structure and conflict reflect the ground of knowledge (203–4).

Though deeply rooted in details of the medieval period, the concerns of the novel's historical narrative coincide with recent critiques of traditional history that have drawn attention to processes of cultural exclusion and prohibition and to the social discontinuities that produce outsiders. Michel Foucault's well-known examination of madness, criminality, and other forms of social deviancy analyzes how such exclusions occur and are held in place by a "positive unconscious of knowledge."[44] In *The Archaeology of Knowledge* Foucault describes how the so-called "objects" of knowledge are constituted by discourse according to certain "rules of formation." A "discursive formation" is not an entity but a practice, a complex group of "relations . . . established between institutions, economic and social processes, behavioural patterns, systems of norms, techniques, types of classification, modes of characterization." These relations "are not present in the object . . . when the object is being analysed." Rather, they are "what enables it to appear."[45] An object emerges in discourse through certain "authorities of delimitation" that name and establish it. Such authorizing occurs according to the function of the discourse "in a field of non-discursive practices" and the "rules and processes of appropriation

44. Michel Foucault, *The Order of Things: An Archaeology of the Human Sciences* (New York: Pantheon, 1970), p. xi.

45. Foucault, *The Archaeology of Knowledge and the Discourse on Language*, trans. A. M. Sheridan Smith (New York: Pantheon, 1972), pp. 38, 45.

of discourse": it determines, as in the case of a language, who speaks, who understands, who uses the discourse.[46]

In Foucault's analysis, the object of knowledge thus constituted is vested with power, understood particularly on the level of social practice.[47] This theme, prominent in all his work, is articulated with unusual economy in his *Discourse on Language*, which asserts that "in every society the production of discourse is at once controlled, selected, organised and redistributed according to a certain number of procedures."[48] These procedures are as various as the purposes for which discourse may be controlled. Foucault singles out three "great systems of exclusion governing discourse—prohibited words, the division of madness and the will to truth." A historical phenomenon (the division between true and false emerged between the time of Hesiod and Plato), the will to truth "relies on institutional support. . . . But it is probably even more profoundly accompanied by the manner in which knowledge is employed in a society, the way in which it is exploited, divided and, in some ways, attributed."[49] The will to truth is evidenced in the way a society's discursive formations define themselves as true, at the same time consigning to the realm of exclusion, even silence, whatever is unauthorized by the system. Thus Foucault offers the notion of speaking *dans le vrai* (within the true) to indicate the condition of speaking within the rules of some "discursive policy."[50]

In *The Name of the Rose* the discussion of the relation of heresy to power and truth offers an exemplary instance of this "ar-

46. *Archaeology of Knowledge*, pp. 41–42, 67–68.

47. Edward W. Said, "The World, the Text, and the Critic," in *The World, the Text, and the Critic* (Cambridge: Harvard University Press, 1983), pp. 186–88, 216.

48. *The Discourse on Language* is appended to the *Archaeology of Knowledge*, pp. 215–37; the quotation here is from p. 216.

49. Foucault, *Discourse on Language*, p. 219. For a discussion of the concept of truth in relation to history, see Foucault's "Nietzsche, Genealogy, History," in *Language, Counter-Memory, Practice*, ed. Donald F. Bouchard and trans. Donald F. Bouchard and Sherry Simon (Ithaca: Cornell University Press, 1977), pp. 142–44.

50. *Discourse on Language*, p. 224.

chaeological" historicism. In fact, the novel's historical narrative might be seen as an extended elaboration of Foucault's observation that "questions of heresy and unorthodoxy in no way arise out of fanatical exaggeration of doctrinal mechanisms; they are a fundamental part of them."[51] The novel appropriates the revisionist historical view that sees heresy in terms of a discursive system of social and linguistic relations. For example, when William explains the difference between the heretic and the saint by describing the interaction of social groupings, sacred and secular authorities, and the languages of city and Church, he in effect describes the discursive formation that in his view enabled the so-called heresies of the high Middle Ages to appear. Similarly, the inability of Adso's beloved to speak "the universal tongue of knowledge and power" may be seen as her exclusion from the discursive rules that lie *dans le vrai*. Gui's examination of Remigio and Salvatore's heresy exemplifies the exclusionary practices of the will to truth in a most destructive form.

The historical narrative of *The Name of the Rose* acknowledges the conditions that make possible its approach to "history." Adso responds to William's analysis of the complex circumstances that create heresy with this demand: "'Why won't you tell me where the truth is?'" (205). His remark betrays his belief that, once all the social constituents of heresy are sorted out, there still exists some final basis on which the truth may be determined. Adso's position is that which the contemporary critique of traditional historicism attempts to undo: he desires to make discourse "the sign of something else, and to pierce through its density in order to reach what remains silently anterior to it"; to define its object in "reference to the *ground*, the *foundation of things* . . . the depth of a primal soil." Adso would believe in "a sort of ideal discourse that is both ultimate and timeless, and which choices, extrinsic in origin, have perverted, disturbed, suppressed, or thrust towards a possibly distant future."[52]

Implicit in Adso's desire is a concept of linguistic function

51. Ibid., p. 226.
52. Foucault, *Archaeology of Knowledge*, pp. 47–48, 70.

that informs the entire novel: the idea that language serves as a "reservoir of value-free vehicles of representation," that, in this case, beyond the welter of meanings arising from his probe of heresy, there is an end point to signification.[53] William counters the novice's longing for absolutes with his scientific example emphasizing the priority of the individual over the universal, indeed calling into question the very existence of universals. He stresses the perception of particular things—what signs may help us do rather than any a priori ground of knowledge that they represent. It is a position to which Adso reluctantly gives accord: "'Then I can always and only speak of something that speaks to me of something else, and so on. But the final something, the true one—does that never exist?'" (317).

Through their discussion of heresy William and Adso accomplish a kind of "archaeology of knowledge" that incorporates a critique of traditional historicism into this most densely historical novel. Their analysis of social ills and meanings points toward what Foucault terms an "effective" history, which recognizes that "the world we know is not this ultimately simple configuration where events are reduced to accentuate their essential traits, their final meaning, or their initial or final value. On the contrary, it is a profusion of entangled events . . . without a landmark or a point of reference."[54] Yet although the novel illustrates how the problems in history and the problem of history are founded in language and interpretation, it by no means implies a simple reduction of its history to matters of linguistic signification. William does not undo the traditional "unities of discourse" simply to replace them with a nominalist proliferation of individual signs. Both he and Adso are all too painfully aware of the conditions in which historical meanings are lived. William's coolly philosophical observations about "things in their individual truth" are frighteningly realized in the novel's profoundly particularized examples of heresy: the dismembered Dolcino; Adso's memory of Fraticello Michael at

53. Robert Weimann, *Structure and Society in Literary History* (Baltimore: Johns Hopkins University Press, 1984), p. 294.

54. Foucault, "Nietzsche, Genealogy, History," p. 155.

the stake; the peasant girl "kicking and screaming like an animal being led to the shambles" (330); a desperate and battered Remigio confessing to crimes he did not commit. These individual examples represent, perhaps, the most meaningful form of history; they instance "effective" history's inversion of the "relationship that traditional history . . . establishes between proximity and distance," its shortening of "its vision to those things nearest to it—the body, the nervous system, nutrition, digestion, and energies."[55]

The Name of the Rose suggests, then, that there are meanings in history; they result from studying "what is closest" and from affirming "knowledge as perspective."[56] Long before he wrote his novel Eco had made this very point, but in a semiotic rather than an overtly historical context. Practitioners of semiotics, when considering the origin or ground of discourse (or its absence), will be preoccupied with the question, "who speaks?" That is an ideological question, Eco observes, sustained by a social system that enables "a certain category of human beings" to contemplate being and to feel the urgency of that question. But for those without the power "to contemplate," the "slaves" whose work supports the order of contemplation, another question will be preeminent. In place of "who speaks?" these people ask "who dies?" The slave—one could think of William's "simple" peasants—is not primarily concerned with the "proximity of being." Rather, he is concerned with "the proximity of his own body and those of the others." The slave has his own philosophy, authorized, like any other philosophy, by his own more immediate priorities.[57]

Eco posits two equally valid rationales for knowing, one based on questions of reference and control of the universe of discourse, the other founded in the material body, with its capacity

55. Ibid.

56. Ibid., p. 156.

57. Umberto Eco, *La structure absente: Introduction à la recherche sémiotique*, translated from the Italian *La strutture assente* by Uccio Esposito-Torrigiani (Paris: Mercure de France, 1972), pp. 384–86; hereafter cited as *SA*. Translations are my own. Teresa De Lauretis discusses this passage in light of Eco's novel; see "Gaudy Rose: Eco and Narcissism," *SubStance* 14 (1985): 25–26.

for pleasure and pain, its potential for exclusion and transgression. Just as they figure prominently in Adso's story of monastic love, these two rationales frame the novel's historical narrative. The pressure Adso feels to interpret his love in terms of the relation between the material and spiritual realms has its counterpart in his effort to understand how the fervor of the heretic confuses the spiritual ends of the saint with the material transgressions of the body. According to the authority to which Adso regularly appeals, heresy and romantic love are corporeal perversions of impulses that should refer to a higher realm, a source of being. But paradoxically, these impulses may find their fullest expression only in the very materiality that appears to compromise them. Adso's obsession with forbidden acts of body and speech corresponds with the more openly social ways in which heresy challenges social and sexual arrangements. Dolcino's heresy is always equated with his sexuality. Whereas love's transgression is a sin, heresy's is a crime.[58]

The features that link the monastic and historical narratives also figure prominently in the novel's mystery story. Transgressive behaviors and words, the relation between problems of reference and the material body—these are the prominent issues in the murder plot, the search for the book, and the discussion of laughter. The abbot intimates a connection between heresy and the mystery when, as William puts it, he implies that the murders have their source "'in some obscure story dating back to the heretical past of one of the monks'" (154). Gui insists "'that the heresy of those who . . . preach poverty . . . can only lead to criminal acts'" (381). Each defines a causal relationship between the politics of heresy and the murders, when the link between the two rests rather in the features heretical movements have in common with the subject of the unknown book, comedy. Her-

58. John Boswell notes the regular identification of heresy with transgressive sexual behaviors; see *Christianity, Social Tolerance and Homosexuality*, pp. 283–84, 290, 330. On the relation between charges of heresy and sexual promiscuity in the thirteenth and fourteenth centuries, see Robert Lerner, *The Heresy of the Free Spirit in the Later Middle Ages* (Berkeley: University of California Press, 1972), pp. 10–34. The *Rose* bears out Jacques Le Goff's comment that "the history of heresies is, in many respects, a history of woman in society and religion" (*Time, Work, and Culture*, p. 230).

esy and comedy both embrace marginal things, focus on the simple, and transgress traditional order. At one point William even mistakenly guesses that the mysterious book is "a dangerous heretical text" (285). Remigio describes the heretical rebellion inspired by Dolcino as "a feast of fools, a magnificent carnival" (272). William most provocatively suggests a connection between heresy and comedy when, after Gui's political victory, he reminds Adso: "'I must concern myself with something else. I had two missions: one has failed, at least the other must succeed. I want to get my hands on a book, and on a man'" (393). He implies that his search for the book concerns things more important then the battle between pope and emperor. He is quite right.

[4]

A World Upside Down

The problems of textual interpretation that ground the stories of love and heresy in *The Name of the Rose* are writ large in the novel's mystery plot. Like these other stories, the mystery depends upon a central text. More obviously than the Song of Solomon in Adso's narrative and the Franciscan *Rule* in the political story, Aristotle's lost book on comedy presides over the mystery plot. The search for the lethal book lends an overriding narrative purpose to the novel's preoccupation with textual hermeneutics: in the mystery story everything and everyone in the abbey are parts of the text that William and Adso strive to interpret. Their assumption that identifying the book will also identify the murderers endows the unknown text with extraordinary power. For some, reading the book is quite simply a matter of life and death. For William and Adso, identifying the book—their arrival at the right answer for all the wrong reasons—is a figure for the hermeneutic process itself.

The novel intimates the subject of the mystery's unknown book in its attention to laughter. The secrecy and prohibition attending the slightest mention of laughter may provide William with clues for decoding the mystery, but they also hint at the central role laughter plays in the novel. The discussion of the forms of laughter constitutes a précis of comic theory that coincides with the novel's deeper probing of contemporary theories of language.[1]

This modernizing of laughter in *The Name of the Rose* by no means occurs at the expense of the novel's medieval elements. Rather, the debate on laughter and the uses of the comic reproduces a venerable tradition whose medieval manifestations had an ancient heritage. Classical writers had considered the relationship of the comic and the serious not merely in rhetorical terms but as "an ideal of life," showing little discomfort with the mixture of styles and values. In contrast, early Christian writers as far back as Saint Paul took a dim view of laughter. The novel poses the questions of a vigorous intellectual debate that attracted the interest of eminent medieval thinkers—did Christ ever laugh? is laughter proper to human nature? can holiness and laughter mix? (130–33).[2] Jorge is quick to remind William that the Benedictine *Rule* took an extremely cautious position on laughter (78, 131). But William's recollection of Prudentius's account of Saint Lawrence on the gridiron—"Manduca, iam coctum est" ("Eat, for it is well done") (95)—points up how the medieval Church itself contributed to the comic spirit in literature and culture, through official writings such as Latin hagiography, unofficial rites and texts, and sacred parodies.[3] One of these, the *Coena Cypriani*, provides the structure and imagery of Adso's climactic dream, which precipitates William's solution of the mystery.

1. Of the many ways in which the *Rose* may be understood, one is as a document in the field of "gelotology," a term coined for the study of laughter; see G. B. Milner, "Homo Ridens: Towards a Semiotic Theory of Humour and Laughter," *Semiotica* 5 (1972): 3.

2. Ernst Curtius, *European Literature and the Latin Middle Ages*, trans. Willard Trask (1953; New York: Harper and Row, 1963), pp. 417–22. The similarities between the novel and Curtius on this subject are striking enough to provoke us to wonder if Eco, like an entire generation of medievalists, has used Curtius as his crib. Who else could have drawn his attention to the line of Carolingian poetry with which Jorge reprimands William (133): "Tum podex carmen extulit horridulum" ("Then the rear brings forth a rough song")? See Curtius, p. 435.

3. Ibid., pp. 425–28 and 435, n. 40. For an overview of medieval comic and parodic rites, see Mikhail Bakhtin, *Rabelais and His World*, trans. Helene Iswolsky (Cambridge, Mass.: MIT Press, 1968), pp. 13–15.

Medieval writers, for the sake of convention and their own rhetorical purposes, customarily offered jesting compositions for their "earnest" and edifying ends. The prominence of this medieval *topos* is sufficient evidence "that the Middle Ages loved all kinds of crossings and mixtures of stylistic genres . . . which, to our modern taste, schooled by classicistic aesthetics, absolutely exclude any such mixtures."[4] This medieval penchant for mixing verbal styles gives us a key to the larger import of laughter in the Middle Ages and in *The Name of the Rose*. The polarizing and integration of competing styles and rhetorics implied in the collocation of "jest and earnest" reflects attitudes not only to the cultural artifact but to the organization of culture itself. Laughter is closely connected to modes of learning and discourse, to forms of representation, to hierarchies of society and speech, to philosophies of experience and interpretation. It carries all these associations in the novel, where it figures as a code word for a model of culture based on oppositions—between serious and comic, official and unofficial, spirit and flesh, high and low. This chapter decodes the meaning of laughter in the novel.

I

In *The Name of the Rose* the discussion of laughter always occurs in relation to books. Laughter is not only identified with the mysterious book linked to the deaths in the abbey, it is also intimately connected to the many bookish issues the novel explores: the nature and justification of literature, indeed of all imaginative art; the uses of authority; even the actual making of books. Adelmo, the mystery's first victim, is an illuminator of manuscripts who specializes in marginalia. His book-making craft inspires the novel's first mention of laughter. The psalter Adelmo had been working on at the time of his death

> delineated a world reversed with respect to the one to which our senses have accustomed us. As if at the border of a discourse that is by definition the discourse of truth, there proceeded, closely linked to it,

4. Curtius, *European Literature*, p. 424.

through wondrous allusions in aenigmate, a discourse of falsehood on a topsy-turvy universe, in which dogs flee before the hare, and deer hunt the lion. . . . Sequences of anthropomorphic animals and zoomorphic dwarfs joined, sometimes on the same page, with scenes of rustic life in which you saw . . . all the life of the fields, plowmen, fruit gatherers, harvesters, spinning-women. . . . Next to the psalter there was . . . an exquisite book of hours. . . . The entire margins of the book were invaded by miniscule forms that generated one another. . . . At one point, as if to continue the triple "Sanctus, Sanctus, Sanctus" repeated on three different lines, you saw three ferocious figures with human heads, two of which were bent, one downward and one upward, to join in a kiss you would not have hesitated to call immodest if you were not persuaded that a profound, even if not evident, spiritual meaning must surely have justified that illustration at that point. (76–78)

Adelmo's marginalia are far from unique; they recall the countless images that decorate Gothic manuscripts as well as the sculpted grotesqueries of the great European cathedrals. Just as typical is Adso's monastic impulse toward allegorical interpretation. The inclination to save even the immodest appearance through an appeal to a higher reality comes to Adso's aid in his bewilderment before "illustrations [that] naturally inspired merriment, though they were commenting on holy pages" (78).

Adso's response highlights the teasing double nature of Adelmo's marginalia, which introduce the major issues of the debate on laughter and the comic. The young monk's drawings depict reversals and inversions of traditional form and order, illustrating the familiar classical and medieval *topos* of the "topsy-turvy" universe or world upside down.[5] Adelmo's marginalia realize in a very literal way the novel's preoccupation with reversal itself, not only as a comic *topos* but as a figure for the ordering—and disordering—of culture.[6] Reveling in the variety and abundance of creation, Adelmo's marginalia also embody

5. Ibid., pp. 94–98. See also Barbara A. Babcock, "Introduction" to *The Reversible World: Symbolic Inversion in Art and Society*, ed. Babcock (Ithaca: Cornell University Press, 1978), pp. 13–36.

6. For more sinister examples of reversal, see pp. 15, 403–4. Verlyn Flieger observes that a major theme of the novel is "reversal, the voluntary or involuntary overturning of norms" ("The Name, the Thing, the Mystery," *Georgia Review* 38 [1984]: 179).

materiality itself. They depict a profusion of body parts and physical activities and evoke the fecundity of the material earth. Adso's appeal to their "spiritual meaning" is an attempt to contain this corporeal abundance. Finally, the very marginality of Adelmo's drawings is significant. Their position on the borders of the manuscript page not only marks their "marginal" relationship to the monastic "discourse of truth" but also sums up laughter's relation to such discourse. Through their reversals and their marginality, Adelmo's drawings figure as a synecdoche for laughter's inversion of discursive and representational cultural norms, its alliance with material creation, and its relation to authoritative discourse. Adelmo's drawings are to the manuscript page's "discourse of truth" what Adso's erotic encounter is to an allegorized Song of Solomon and what heresy is to orthodox social hierarchy.

The discussion that follows Adso's discovery of Adelmo's drawings explains their import. This discussion takes place during William's first meeting with his ideological nemesis, Jorge of Burgos, who counters Adso's pleasure at the images with Benedict's proscription against laughter: "Verba vana aut risui apta non loqui" (78). Appropriately, their conversation occurs in the scriptorium, for it is over the import and the impact of the scriptorium's products that William and Jorge differ so profoundly.

William defends humorous and fantastic illustrations on the basis of their "edifying ends." He appeals to Pseudo-Dionysius and Hugh of St. Victor to argue that "'God can be named only through the most distorted things. . . . The more the simile becomes dissimilar, the more the truth is revealed to us under the guise of horrible and indecorous figures, the less the imagination is sated in carnal enjoyment, and is thus obliged to perceive the mysteries hidden under the turpitude of images'" (80). William's response challenges Jorge on several levels. Deriving from fundamental principles of Neoplatonic cosmology and epistemology, his justification instances a mainstream Christian exemplarism, which maintained that the corporeal world is the reflection and expression of divine being and that intelligible reality is accessible through the sense-perceptible world. The authorities to whom he refers were touchstones of the medieval exemplarist tradition, which, though mediated by diverse philosophies, was nonetheless united in a common conviction that "all natural or historical reality possessed a *signification* which transcended its crude reality and which a certain symbolic dimension of that reality would reveal to man's mind."[7] This "symbolist mentality" also lent philosophical import to literary and artistic forms; William makes just such an application here.

William's defense of Adelmo's marginalia is thoroughly appropriate to his role as a Franciscan. The exemplarist tradition's emphasis on the uses of the material world provided a foundation for the techniques of the Franciscan spiritual mission, which was distinguished by a consistent appeal to carnal sensation and physical participation. The Franciscans regularly conjoined imaginative fictions and images "operating within the world of sensible objects with a profound inner spirituality which sought to transcend the corporeal world."[8] The exemplarist recovery of the material world was also a critical element in the philosophical disposition that eventually resulted in the Franciscans' major contributions to medieval nominalism. William's expressed tolerance for carnal sensation here anticipates the more pointed statements he makes elsewhere about the uses of knowledge of the material world.[9]

Jorge's response to William's defense of imaginative art criticizes precisely the characteristics that form the backbone of the Franciscan's justification. Jorge condemns images of distortion and reversal because "'they lie about the form of creation and show the world as the opposite of what it should be, has always been, and always will be throughout the centuries . . . under the pretext of teaching divine precepts!'" (79–80). He invokes Bernard of Clairvaux's famous rejection of architectural orna-

7. M.-D. Chenu, *Nature, Man, and Society in the Twelfth Century*, ed. and trans. Jerome Taylor and Lester K. Little (Chicago: University of Chicago Press, 1968), p. 102; see also, in general, pp. 49–145.

8. John Fleming, *An Introduction to the Franciscan Literature of the Middle Ages* (Chicago: Franciscan Herald Press, 1977), p. 248 and pp. 254–55.

9. To be sure, William is no simple endorser of Christian exemplarism. As he shows elsewhere, his acknowledgment of an exemplarist view of creation and of the human mind's ability to create symbols is an acknowledgment of an ordered epistemological structure, not necessarily of the truth.

ment and, in the shadow of the venerable Cistercian, asserts that the "'man who depicts monsters and portents of nature to reveal the things of God per speculum et in aenigmate, comes to enjoy the very nature of the monstrosities he creates'" (80).[10] According to Jorge's reading, the images that exemplarism deems signs of divine things lead their makers and viewers to a delight in the "works of man" in and of themselves, to an attachment to the world and its pleasures. His stance makes clear that arguments for the legitimacy of an enigmatic and fanciful art relate the uses of the comic to larger questions of hierarchy and order. For Jorge, the users of such images are abusers of order who invert a divinely ordained hierarchy by privileging the creations of man over the creations of God, the humorous falsehood of impossibilities over the certainty of revealed truth.

Following the typical medieval habit of identifying "strategies of the verbal and the visual," the novel illustrates how the lines of argument advanced by William and Jorge regarding Adelmo's imagery also apply to the humorous collocations of verbal signs.[11] Venantius observes that the "'truth can be revealed through surprising expressions, both shrewd and enigmatic.'" Citing Aristotle, he queries "'whether metaphors and puns and riddles, which also seem conceived by poets for sheer pleasure, do not lead us to speculate on things in a new and surprising way'" (82). Venantius refers here to the philosopher's comments in the *Poetics* and *Rhetoric*, where he considers the function of metaphor and other devices as vehicles of knowledge and relates these workings to the strategies of the verbal joke.[12] His remarks bring an abrupt end to the debate at this point, but later discussions between William and the monks point up how the appeal to Aristotle's analysis of poetic diction to validate laughter applies to all imaginative uses of language. William and

10. See Fleming, *Franciscan Literature*, p. 243; John Phillips, *The Reformation of Images: Destruction of Art in England, 1535–1660* (Berkeley: University of California Press, 1973), pp. 19–20.

11. Fleming, *Franciscan Literature*, p. 243.

12. The relevant passages in Aristotle are *Poetics* 1457b–1459a and *Rhetoric* 3.10–11. For a discussion of the workings of pun which is reminiscent of Adso's consideration of metaphor and William's defense of Adelmo's marginalia, see Milner, "Homo Ridens," p. 18.

Jorge's debate in fact reiterates an age-old controversy in Western culture about the truth and falsehood of imaginative literature. Whereas Jorge distinguishes between the pagan poets' use of metaphor to convey falsehood and the truthful use of linguistic figures in the poetry of the divinely inspired psalms (111–12), William defends fables and fictions because they share with the comic the same possibilities for revealing the truth in unexpected and surprising ways (130).

The novel's easy passage from a furtive reference to Aristotle on poetic figures to the invocation of some classic positions of Western literary criticism is based on their common ties to questions regarding the signifying capacities of language. Metaphors, puns, and riddles depend upon flexibility of reference and multiple or equivocal meanings.[13] They call attention to the way words resist easy codifications of meaning by signifying many different things at once, expressing the excesses and possibilities of language. Fictions raise questions about the status of imaginative discourse in relation to a ground of truth and to other ostensibly nonfictive modes of discourse. Poetic figures and fictions all challenge univocal conceptions of linguistic reference by showing how their meanings depend on meanings outside themselves, the human interventions that perceive the metaphor's dissimilar similitude or the fiction's creation, not falsification, of a world.

Metaphors, puns, riddles, and fictions imply a view of language that Jorge finds particularly dangerous. He maintains "'that Jesus had urged our speech to be yes or no, for anything further came from the Evil One; and that to mention fish it was enough to say 'fish,' without concealing the notion under lying sounds'" (112–13). Jorge is a spokesman for univocality. Perhaps because the meaning of the linguistic sign is not naturally founded, he would have that meaning tinkered with as little as possible. Jorge objects to laughter for the same reasons he objects to literary uses of language and to representational art—

13. See Eco's comments on the flexibility of "good" metaphor in *SP*, 120. For an assessment of the workings of pun and metaphor in a medieval context, see Paul Zumthor, "From Hi(story) to Poem, or the Paths of Pun: The Grand Rhetoriqueurs of Fifteenth-Century France," *New Literary History* 10 (1979): 261–62.

laughter is not the "real thing"; it suggests that truth may be something other than fixed, single, and immutable, approached only through a "strait and narrow path" (81). He tells William the real danger of laughter: "'He who laughs does not believe in what he laughs at, but neither does he hate it'" (131). Like the good use of metaphor, which, according to Aristotle, "perceives resemblances," laughter obscures distinctions and encourages ambiguity and contradiction.[14] "Laughter foments doubt," which must be resolved by recourse to an authority (132). The problem of laughter is a problem of interpretation.

Thus Adso's simple observations about the comic strategies of Adelmo's art lead him once more to hermeneutic questions. In the mystery story, as in the novel's other narrative strands, the theme (in this case, laughter) reveals itself as a debate on how and why meanings are made. William hints at these narrative connections when, to defend the comic reversals of Adelmo's marginalia, he uses the same words that Adso employs in his erotically inspired meditations on the workings of language. Both Adelmo's "indecorous figures" and Adso's equivocal metaphors express truth through a "dissimilar similitude" (248), a phrase that medieval thinkers employed to describe efforts to understand the transcendent by bridging "the apparently nontraversible gap that the mind perceived between two realities otherwise akin."[15] William and Adso's statements about the strategies of laughter and language are further linked by the common emphases of their "dissimilar similitudes": William appeals to the mysteries hidden within figures of "carnal enjoyment," while Adso calls upon the "great theophanic design that sustains the universe" (279) to redeem his sexual encounter with the peasant girl. The relationship of matter and spirit was fundamental to the formulations of exemplarist epistemology and theology. But the novel appropriates these familiar topics of

14. *Poetics* 1459a, trans. M. E. Hubbard, in *Ancient Literary Criticism*, ed. D. A. Russell and M. Winterbottom (Oxford: Clarendon Press, 1972), p. 122.

15. Chenu, *Nature, Man, and Society*, p. 131. The phrase "dissimilar similitude" originates with William's authority Pseudo-Dionysius. On the transmission of this concept in the Middle Ages and on the relation of metaphor and the symbolist mentality, see Chenu, pp. 131–44.

medieval thinkers to destabilize the traditional hierarchy of these relationships, to look at the potential for and significance of their reversal.

Laughter is also pointedly connected to the narratives of love and heresy by their shared relation to Jorge's nemesis—doubt. Adso's erotic encounter prompts him to appeal to an *auctoritas* that will free him from tormenting doubt (248). Bernard Gui exemplifies the authority that dispels the ambiguities of heresy in the clear light of inquistorial definition. The impulse shown by Jorge, Adso, and Gui to mark off an unequivocal authority in the face of doubt, whether inspired by laughter, love, or heresy, resembles the compositional format of Adelmo's manuscript page, where the reversals of the margins stand outside of but are "closely linked" to the central discourse of truth. Besides being a source of laughter, then, Adelmo's marginalia are also a figure for a structure of communication and an organization of society and culture.

II

After the fourth death in the novel, Jorge delivers a sermon on the coming of the Antichrist which adumbrates the relationship between the novel's discussion of literary values and larger social and cultural issues. Although the sermon trails off into the "usual mystical prophecies" that everyone has come to expect from Jorge, it also fulfills William's prediction that the blind monk will speak out of a very precise purpose:

"The work of our order . . . is study, and the preservation of knowledge. Preservation of, I say, not search for, because the property of knowledge, as a divine thing, is that it is complete and has been defined since the beginning. . . . It is a property of knowledge, as a human thing, that it has been defined and completed over the course of the centuries, from the preaching of the prophets to the interpretation of the fathers of the church. There is no progress, no revolution of ages, in the history of knowledge, but at most a continuous and sublime recapitulation. . . . I am He who is, said the God of the Jews. I am the way, the truth, and the life, said our Lord. There you have it: knowledge is nothing but the awed comment on these two truths. . . . Beyond that there is nothing further to say. . . . Now, my brothers, what is the sin of pride that can tempt a scholar-monk? That of considering as his task not preserving but seeking some information not yet vouchsafed mankind, as if the last word had not already resounded in the words of the last angel who speaks in the last book of Scripture: 'For I testify unto every man that heareth the words of the prophecy of this book. If any man add unto these things, God shall add unto him the plagues that are written in this book: and if any man shall take away from the words of the book of this prophecy, God shall take away his part out of the book of life, and out of the holy city, and from the things which are written in this book.' . . . These words only adumbrate what has recently happened within these walls, whereas what has happened within these walls adumbrates only the same vicissitude as that afflicting the century in which we live, determined in word and deed, in cities as in castles, in proud universities and cathedral churches, to seek anxiously to discover new codicils to the words of truth." (399–400)

Jorge's sermon illustrates a near perfect coincidence of the novel's theoretical concerns and its portrait of medieval culture. The repressive control of information that Jorge espouses is perfectly compatible with monastic values. Ironically, Jorge's aggressive censorship is based on the Benedictine order's most revered ideals of language and learning: knowledge is circumscribed and the business of language is to repeat and to praise what is already known. Jorge's view epitomizes monasticism's moral and religious conception of all language education, which was founded on the belief that "language is a sacred medium of human participation in the divine plan" whose proper use is in "expressing the ultimate reality." As that goal was impossible to achieve, monasticism cultivated and praised silence. Thus religious tradition dignifies Jorge's proscriptions and his distrust of language, sanctioning restraint, formalized speech, and silence as the only appropriate human responses to the inexpressible.[16]

16. Paul Gehl, "Mystical Language Models in Monastic Educational Psychology," *Journal of Medieval and Renaissance Studies* 14 (1984): 225, 226. Jorge's thoroughly monastic conception of language complements the structuring of the novel's narrative according to the canonical hours of the monastic office.

This effort to control what is known and what is spoken resonates throughout the novel. Jorge's telling quotation of the warning in Revelation 22 against "adding to" or "taking away from" the "book" is strongly reminiscent of Adso's fear of overstepping the boundaries of the universe through equivocal signs that would enable him to think of new relations and thus add to the order of knowledge. Jorge's comparison between "what is happening within these walls" and the "vicissitude . . . afflicting the century in which we live" connects his reproof of the monks' textual activities to new spiritual models and new forms of learning outside the cloister. His allusion to Revelation has a social import as well, evoking the visionary prophecy that attended the medieval debate about the role of the Franciscans in history. Jorge's efforts to contain language and learning within the abbey are thus of a piece with the cultural context and the social and political controversies that are at the center of the novel's historical narrative.

But most pointedly, Jorge's stance in this speech fulfills the prohibitions adumbrated in the discussions of laughter. His objections to the equivocation of comedy, metaphor, and marginalia, his insistence that speech "be yes or no," are justified by his observations here on the appropriate role of language and learning in the cloister; the sermon provides the interpretive context for his desire to suppress laughter. His sermon and his prohibitions provide a model of distinctions—between eternity and the temporal order, truth and falsehood, the revealed Word and the individual voice—a model that embraces systems of communication, definitions of authority, and the cultivation of power. Jorge's pronouncements move the issues of explicit textual interpretation central to all the novel's stories into the larger arena of textual production and social practice. Jorge's suppression of laughter expresses an ideology of culture.

The model of distinctions emerging from the discussion of laughter in *The Name of the Rose* corresponds to a typology of medieval culture favored by contemporary semiotic and structuralist analysis. This typology comprises two central terms: a divinely ordained, hierarchical model identified with the dominant religious and juridical culture, and an "antimodel," an "other," a "different" culture that absorbs what is extraneous to the hegemonic, official culture, transgressing its order and its norms. Believing in its divine sanction, the dominant culture determines an order of semiotic value for what is within it and what is outside it. Things within the dominant culture are positive, eternal; things outside it are negative, historical. These pairs of values generate a series of homologous oppositions: high/low, closed/open, ordered/disordered, wise/foolish, official/unofficial, spirit/flesh, serious/comic.[17] The dominant culture prescribes a society that is "static, fixed, immutable, without . . . any possibility of movement from class to class, or any . . . proliferation of classes"; it also stipulates that man "must set his sights on *rendering stable the volume of information which is proper to him*; . . . this entails a rejection of knowledge for knowledge's sake."[18]

All cultures might be characterized in the general terms of this model, particularly if we understand culture as modern theorists do, that is, as a "system of discriminations and evaluations . . . for a particular class in the State able to identify with it; . . . culture is a system of exclusions legislated from above but enacted throughout its polity, by which such things as anarchy, disorder, irrationality, inferiority, bad taste, and immorality are identified."[19] This model has recently gained wide currency among social historians, anthropologists, and literary theorists and critics interested in medieval and early modern European culture. Versions of this cultural typology inform discussions of medieval folk humor, folk custom, and heresy, relating these manifestations of cultural difference to the efforts of ecclesiastical culture to block or efface them. Studies of the interaction of ritual behaviors and social structure address the strategies by which unofficial culture challenged established medieval hier-

17. Maria Corti, "Models and Antimodels in Medieval Culture," *New Literary History* 10 (1979): 341, 344–45, 350. Corti notes (p. 345) that over the medieval centuries this model adapted its structure to accommodate social change.

18. Ibid., p. 341.

19. Edward W. Said, "Secular Criticism," in *The World, the Text, and the Critic* (Cambridge: Harvard University Press, 1983), p. 11. See also Corti, "Models and Antimodels," pp. 339–41, 344–46.

archies. Anthropological analyses of social organization have been used to locate medieval religious communities in the binary system of cultural modalities which characterized hegemonic culture and its difference.[20]

These readings of medieval and early modern European culture show an interest in metaphor and symbol, in strategies of reversal and transgression, in principles of exclusion, in the ambiguity and ambivalence of social phenomena, in the social ordering of discourse. That is, they convey a conception of culture that is thoroughly consistent with the portrait of the Middle Ages in *The Name of the Rose*, so much so that we might see the novel as a deliberate attempt to realize modern theories of cultural organization. The central oppositions developed in the novel—spiritual love versus erotic passion; holiness versus heresy; the serious versus the comic—are appropriately viewed as variations in the "other" culture's challenge to the dominant culture. The interpretive difficulties attendant upon the novel's individual readings of love, heresy, and laughter mark them off, according to the binary typology, as elements "open towards the different, the discordant, the opposite with respect to official codification."[21] As Adso struggles to balance the personal truth of his experience and the truth of an authority that privileges the spiritual over the physical, he confronts monasticism's full participation in the ideology of the hegemonic culture. William's defense of the intellectual pursuits of Bacon and Occam against the admonitions of Ubertino and the abbot recalls Jorge's prohibitions against "adding to the book" and more generally attests to the dominant culture's interest in "rendering stable" the volume of information deemed suitable for humankind. The

20. The studies I have in mind here are those of Natalie Zemon Davis, *Society and Culture in Early Modern France* (Stanford: Stanford University Press, 1975); Bakhtin, *Rabelais*; Jacques Le Goff, *Time, Work, and Culture in the Middle Ages*, trans. Arthur Goldhammer (Chicago: University of Chicago Press, 1980), especially the essays collected in pt. 3, "High Culture and Popular Culture"; Carlo Ginzberg, *The Cheese and the Worms: The Cosmos of a Sixteenth-Century Miller*, trans. John and Anne Tedeschi (Harmondsworth: Penguin, 1982); Victor Turner, *The Ritual Process: Structure and Anti-Structure* (1969; Ithaca: Cornell University Press, 1977), chaps. 3–5.

21. Corti, "Models and Antimodels," p. 350.

novel's portrait of monastic opposition to the "stink of the cities" (36), with their new commerce and social groupings, is an instance of the structuring model's response to phenomena outside official codification. Similarly, the novel identifies the world of heresy with the people who fall between the cracks of social structure and have no voice because "what does not fit into the model does not exist at the level of signs."[22] This world is the context for Salvatore's macaronic babble and the "mute" shouting of Adso's apprehended love, whose silence speaks volumes, attesting as it does to the exclusionary mechanisms by which the dominant culture suppresses its difference.[23] The opposing hermeneutic options explored in each of the narrative lines participate in this typology, which furnishes the ideological structure of the entire novel, enabling its discourse on the problem of meaning in terms that weigh the legitimizing authority of the cultural model against the fragmented, pluralizing character of the individual experiences that contradict the model's stereotypes.

The Name of the Rose also appropriates the particular emphases of the cultural model. According to Maria Corti, the "most striking aspect" of the different culture in all its manifestations is a stress "on the bodily nature of things." It values the material over the spiritual and consequently reverses all the model's oppositions: "the *high/low* opposition, homologous to that of *spirit/flesh*, is turned upside down not merely on the individual plane but at the level of the collectivity as well, since it is the people who are the chief carriers of these material, bodily values."[24] This positive valuing of the material on the individual and collective planes is central to the novel's characterization of the "other." Adso essentially inverts the monastic reading of the Song of Solomon to articulate his physical passion. His carnal interpretation challenges the dominant cultural codes, which speak of the body only as a "function of something

22. Ibid., p. 341.
23. Ibid., p. 350.
24. Ibid., p. 351.

else which is not corporeal."[25] Ubertino and Gui condemn heresy in part because its overturning of orthodox rules and values is inseparable from its carnal, populist character. Heresy is linked to the sheer human materiality of the different culture, the catalogue of maimed, wounded, and bleeding vagrants and the champions of corporeal transgression who roamed over Europe (189–90). The materialist inversions of heresy are particularly associated with the sum and image of corporeality—woman.

The novel illustrates the stress the different culture places on "material, bodily values," most emphatically in its ludic forms, language, and imagery. Mikhail Bakhtin's work on medieval carnival is useful in this context, for it details the relation of laughter to the corporeal preoccupations of the "other" culture. Carnival is a social celebration of materiality, with its own time, place, and mode of thinking and living. Carnival forms and images participate in a universal, populist, ambivalent "festive laughter," which "is gay, triumphant, and at the same time mocking, deriding."[26] Carnival laughter expresses itself in spectacle, parodic verbal compositions, and abusive language. Its imagery is the grotesque realism of the "material bodily principle," which degrades "all that is high, spiritual, ideal, abstract . . . to the material level, to the sphere of earth and body."[27] The imagery of the grotesque body is that of food, drink, defecation, and sexual life; it involves banqueting—even chewing and swallowing—and the kitchen, the place where food is prepared. Grotesque realism is extremely graphic in its treatment of body parts; it is a realism of the belly, mouth, phallus. It is intensely scatological as well as explicitly sexual.

25. Ibid., p. 353; cf. Corti's comments on Gilbert of Tournai's reading of the Song of Solomon and Ubertino's interpretation of the statue of the Virgin Mary (230).

26. Bakhtin, *Rabelais*, pp. 11–12. For a useful summary of Bakhtin's version of carnival, see Dominick LaCapra, "Bakhtin, Marxism, and the Carnivalesque," in *Rethinking Intellectual History: Texts, Contexts, Language* (Ithaca: Cornell University Press, 1983), pp. 294–306; see also Robert Anchor, "Bakhtin's Truths of Laughter," *Clio* 14 (1985): 237–57.

27. Bakhtin, *Rabelais*, p. 19.

The novel explicitly invokes medieval carnival in Remigio's description of Dolcinian heresy: "'It was—I don't know how to say it—a feast of fools, a magnificent carnival. . . . there was an atmosphere . . . can I say of freedom? . . . it was . . . a new experience. . . . There were no more masters. . . . In carnival time everything is done backward'" (272–73). And its interest in the ludic corporeality of carnival is manifested in three prominent loci of grotesque imagery: the monastery kitchen, the character Salvatore, and Adso's dream of the *Coena Cypriani*. These are focal points for the imagery, language, and ideology of the "other" culture; each is central to the cultural typology encoded in the novel's debate on laughter.

III

The monastery kitchen occupies the ground floor of the Aedificium—the novel's presiding structure and the locus of its most important events. The Aedificium represents culture interpreted as a typology of opposites. It is an emblem of the dominant culture itself, symbolically structured, hierarchically ordered, and institutionally sanctioned. Adso's first glimpse of it elicits a description in terms of the interpretive systems of an official culture that finds order and meaning in number:

> This was an octagonal construction that from a distance seemed a tetragon (a perfect form, which expresses the sturdiness and impregnability of the City of God). . . . Three rows of windows proclaimed the triune rhythm of its elevation. . . . As we came closer, we realized that the quadrangular form included, at each of its corners, a heptagonal tower, five sides of which were visible on the outside. . . . And thus anyone can see the admirable concord of so many holy numbers, each revealing a subtle spiritual significance. Eight, the number of perfection for every tetragon; four, the number of the Gospels; five, the number of the zones of the world; seven, the number of the gifts of the Holy Ghost. (21–22)

With the library at the top, the scriptorium in the middle, and the kitchen and refectory at the bottom, the Aedificium represents the hierarchy implicit in the dominant culture. And if in the Aedificium's hierarchy the library is identified with order, tradition, and the codification of official truth, the kitchen and refectory represent the force of competing values. In semiotic terms the scriptorium is a place of mediation where the transmission of official culture occurs. Thus the scriptorium is open to challenges to the dominant culture—Adelmo's marginalia and the intellectual curiosity of Venantius and William, who see things in books other than what monastic hegemony prescribes. The Aedificium emphasizes the opposition between the cultures of library and kitchen by cordoning off the library as forbidden territory to which access is either denied or kept secret.[28]

The opposition of the dominant and dissident cultures of library and kitchen is sustained until the end of the novel, when ordered typology gives way to chaos, and the blazing library floor comes crashing down to the scriptorium. The novel's final pages present an aged Adso, who, having returned to the Aedificium after many years, finds culture overgrown by nature: "across vast stretches of the kitchen the eye ran to the open heavens through the breach of the upper floors and the roof. . . . Everything that was not green with moss was still black from the smoke of so many decades ago" (499–500). The conflagration of the Aedificium effaces the typology's oppositions, reducing its order to random fragments of parchment.[29]

Through their familiar substances—food and drink—and their basic functions—cooking and eating—the kitchen and refectory ally themselves with the material nature of things. In making the kitchen a prominent locus of ludic materiality in the novel, Eco acknowledges an ancient tradition that associated various comic *topoi* with kitchens and imagery of food and drink.[30] Medieval Latin recreational literature of the twelfth and thirteenth centuries provides one pointed example; its "banquet images . . . are usually centered around the figure of a monk, portrayed as a drunkard, glutton, and lecher." This is the

28. Cf. Walter E. Stephens, "Ec[h]o in Fabula," *Diacritics* 13 (1983): 57–58.

29. See Eco's humorous gloss on this scene in *PS*, 28–29.

30. Curtius provides classical, Carolingian, and later medieval examples of "kitchen humor"; see *European Literature*, pp. 431–33.

tradition Rabelais drew upon for his chapter in *Gargantua,* "Why Monks Love Kitchens."[31]

The mythic gluttony of monks, as well as the dark underbelly of monasticism's association with the material body, inform the *Rose*'s portrait of monastic banqueting. William and Adso are welcomed to the monastery with a prodigious meal preceded by the intonation "Edent pauperes." Here compunction impels Adso to justify such indulgence (93–94), but, later, when he describes the banquet offered to the legation visiting the abbey, he abandons all reservation:

> We had a ragout of pigeon, marinaded in the wine of those lands, and roast rabbit, Saint Clare's pasties, rice with the almonds of those hills —the blancmange of fast days, that is—and borage tarts, stuffed olives, fried cheese, mutton with a sauce of raw peppers, white broad beans, and exquisite sweets, Saint Bernard's cake, Saint Nicholas's pies, Saint Lucy's dumplings, and wines, and herb liquers that put everyone in good humor . . . an elixir of lemon verbena, walnut wine, wine against the gout, and gentian wine. It seemed an assembly of gluttons, except that every sip of every morsel was accompanied by devotional readings. (307)

Adso's ironic observation relates this transgressive consumption to the prescriptions of the monastic rule and thus effectively contains it within the dominant culture.

Kitchens and banquet imagery are ludic because eating and drinking signify the ambivalence of the grotesque body; both positive and negative activities, they reveal how "the body transgresses . . . its own limits" and takes in the world.[32] The activity in and imagery of kitchen and refectory in *The Name of the Rose* carry this transgressive force. Whereas the library is the locus of the official culture's ideal of semiotic containment and protectionism, the kitchen and refectory are open to discord. It is thus perfectly appropriate that free passage in and out of the library is denied to Aristotle's work on comedy, and that Adso learns of the delights of the flesh from the peasant girl in the

31. Bakhtin, *Rabelais,* pp. 294, 300.

32. Ibid., p. 281; see also the entire chapter on "Banquet Imagery," pp. 278–302.

kitchen. Seen from the perspective of a culture structured by oppositions, Adso's roamings up and down the Aedificium's stairs on that eventful night constitute a peregrination between the competing cultural values epitomized in the structure of the Aedificium.

It is even more significant that Adso first sees the unrecognizable form of the girl as he stands on the *threshold* between refectory and kitchen: "sul limine tra refettorio e cucina" (242; *Rosa* 245). The Italian "limine" at once identifies the locus of Adso's experience and characterizes it with a term that figures prominently in discussions of the kind of cultural modeling I argue for here. Adso's pause on the "threshold" indicates his entry into liminality, a phase that anthropological analyses of social structure employ to single out a distinguishing characteristic of the "other" culture. Liminal phenomena fall "between the cracks" or to the bottom of social structure, or they lie outside it altogether. They are often regarded as "dangerous, inauspicious, and polluting," because they transgress the norms that govern structure and ambiguously suspend order and hierarchy.[33] The term "liminal" aptly describes the experience that ensues from Adso's perception on the threshold; indeed, his experience even follows the three-stage pattern that anthropologists distinguish for liminal rites of passage. In his movement through separation, margin (*limen*), and aggregation, he "passes through a cultural realm that has few or none of the attributes of the past or coming state."[34] For Adso, the kitchen is a new "cultural realm" of sexual arousal and multiple meanings, providing a fitting locus for his transgressive experience of the material body and language. His heightened consciousness of the ambiguities of this experience underscores the fundamental pattern of cultural oppositions that structures the novel.[35]

33. Turner, *Ritual Process*, pp. 108, 125, 128. Turner contrasts liminality with the characteristics of official culture (his term is "status system"); see pp. 106–8.

34. Ibid., p. 94.

35. The Italian edition of the novel makes explicit the analogy between the Aedificium and the cultural model that I argue for here. See Walter Stephens's discussion of the original dust jacket for *Il nome della rosa*, where Eco's gloss on

The cultural otherness and liminality with which the novel endows the monastery kitchen also characterize my second example of transgressive corporeality, the former Dolcinian and would-be Benedictine, Salvatore. He is the very incarnation of the marginal type that Victor Turner identifies as the liminal persona who eludes or slips through the "network of classifications that normally locate states and positions in cultural space. Liminal entities are . . . betwixt and between the positions assigned and arrayed by law, custom, convention, and ceremonial."[36] Adso is fascinated by Salvatore largely because of the many ways Salvatore stands outside the cultural structures with which Adso is familiar.

Like the Aedificium in which the kitchen is contained, Salvatore embraces opposing cultural values. This opposition is most evident in his hybrid language: his speech is a mixture of the Latin of the dominant culture and the vernaculars spoken by the vagabonds and *simplici* of the different culture. It is at best a "Babelish language . . . of primeval confusion," or as Adso suggests, no language at all, since it exhibits no rules and observes neither a necessary nor conventional relationship between sign and thing. Salvatore is an "anti-logos . . . an organic representation of confusion and discord."[37] Yet ironically, Adso and others understand this fragmented speech comprised of "disiecta membra of other sentences," an indication perhaps that Salvatore's semiotic confusion is but the underside of a living intertextuality.

Salvatore is a figure of ambivalence, a crude tapestry of contrary meanings. His gaze, Adso observes, "was innocent or malign . . . perhaps it was both" (46). His appearance commingles high and low, official and unofficial culture:

---

the pictured floor plan of a labyrinth plays up the opposition between official proscription and unofficial transgression which is encoded in the Aedificium as a whole ("Ec[h]o in Fabula," p. 54).

36. Turner, *Ritual Process*, p. 95. For an interesting reading of Salvatore, indeed of the entire novel, in light of a thermodynamic modeling of change, see Robert Artigiani, "The 'Model Reader' and the Thermodynamic Model," *SubStance* 14 (1985): 68–69.

37. Stephens assesses Salvatore in terms of Eco's semiotic concepts; see "Ec[h]o in Fabula," p. 56.

> His speech was somehow like his face, put together with pieces from other people's faces, or like some precious reliquaries I have seen (si licet magnis componere parvis, if I may link diabolical things with the divine), fabricated from the shards of other holy objects. At the moment, when I met him for the first time, Salvatore seemed to me, because of both his face and his way of speaking, a creature not unlike the hairy and hoofed hybrids I had just seen under the portal. (47)

Resembling Adelmo's marginalia, Salvatore's holy grotesquerie conjoins sacred and profane. His mingling of the official and the different cultures is further figured in a physical presence that cloaks the sympathies of a Dolcinian "heretic" in the robes of a hegemonic Benedictine. He epitomizes in a specific human form the abstract or philosophical point that the novel continually asserts: the difficulty of making distinctions. It is, after all, the account of Salvatore's life that provokes Adso to claim "everything looked the same as everything else" (191).

Still, the novel allies Salvatore most strongly with the lower, marginal term of the oppositions commingled in him, with the Dolcinian over the Benedictine, the flesh over the spirit, the profane over the sacred, the comic over the serious. Early in the novel Salvatore interrupts Adso's visionary reverie as a voice that "came from behind me . . . a different voice, because it came from the earth" (45). Salvatore's association with the material earth is of a piece with his identity among the "people," the simple and unlearned whose interests and actions stand outside the force of institutions (188–89). In William's terms, Salvatore is a perfect example of social marginality understood as heresy: the story of his life illustrates William's position that the truth of heresy can only be known as the truth of the individual. For Adso, Salvatore represents the hordes of human beings wandering over the face of Europe; indeed, to Adso, Salvatore *is* the face of Europe, "the splendid epitome of so many events and movements that made the Italy of that time fascinating and incomprehensible" (194).

Salvatore's identification with the "bodily nature of things" is realized in his job in the monastic community as assistant to the cellarer, the procurer of provisions. The kitchen is his domain; food is his business and his love. The story of his life begins as a story about food, or the lack of it, a story of the extreme hunger and abject poverty that afflict the socially outcast and dislocated. This is the historical reference point for the portrait of Salvatore's nearly mythic gluttony. His ideal world, Adso reports, would be the glutton's utopia, a "land of Cockaigne, where wheels of cheese and aromatic sausages grow on the trees that ooze honey" (189).[38] The political and the mythic dimensions of Salvatore's hunger mingle in his description of his early days. While he "merrily" devours a mutton pie "as if he had never eaten before in this life" (187), Salvatore tells with Rabelaisian gusto a tale of grave-robbing, of the murder and dismembering of bodies, of cooked human flesh, and of cannibalism (190–91). Salvatore's prandial confession is ambivalent: his grotesque consumption suggests, on the one hand, a carnivalesque version of eating as a "triumph of life over death" and a festive "expression of social justice."[39] On the other hand, as his delight in mutton pie merges with the "grimace of the desperate man eating the corpse" (188), it also furnishes a bold reminder of other connections between life, death, and food, of the perils of starvation and the politics of hunger.

Salvatore's fixation on the belly makes him a quintessential example of grotesque realism. Since he epitomizes the other culture's emphasis on the bodily nature of things, it is fitting that he is responsible for bringing the peasant girl into the kitchen and that he acts as procurer for Remigio's lust. His suppression by Gui's men, arch-enforcers of the hegemonic terms of the cultural model, asserts the dominance of the official culture over his own difference.

The grotesque imagery of banqueting and the body and the cultural oppositions signified by the monastic kitchen and Salvatore are gathered together in the novel's most impressive instance of transgressive corporeality—Adso's dream of the *Coena Cypriani*, which enacts the reversals of difference on a large his-

38. See Bakhtin, *Rabelais*, p. 297.

39. Ibid., pp. 283, 302. Significantly, Salvatore tells his life story while eating, thus illustrating what Bakhtin describes (*Rabelais*, p. 296) as the "power of food and drink to liberate human speech."

torical and narrative scale. The *Coena Cypriani*, or Cyprian's Supper, numbers among the many medieval comic literary compositions—sacred and learned Latin parodies of ecclesiastical forms, rites, and teachings—that, drawing upon the varieties of folk humor and carnival laughter, emerged from within the Church.[40] Probably composed in the fifth or sixth century, the *Coena Cypriani* parodically transforms sacred history from Adam to Christ into a "fantastic clownish banquet using in grotesque fashion its most important events and symbols."[41] Enjoying great popularity from the ninth to sixteenth centuries, the *Coena* survives in many manuscripts.

Works such as the *Coena* were produced within the heart of medieval monasticism as a complement to the Church's legalized round of feast days that called for suspension of the usual rules and hierarchies. These works had the recreative aim of transposing sacred texts and received wisdom to the level of the material body, which is the sphere of low, folk culture.[42] Whatever functions such appropriations of low culture by the high served, official justification for them could be found. For example, Rabanus Maurus, Abbot of Fulda, defended the "gay and degrading" tone of the *Coena*, dedicating his abridged version to King Lothar II *ad jocunditatem*, for his amusement.[43] Adso describes a typical rationale of hegemonic culture when, with William's prompting, he recalls that, "though [the *Coena*] is banned or execrated by the more austere among novice masters, there is still not a convent in which the monks have not whispered it to one another . . . declaring that behind a veil of mirth it concealed secret moral lessons, and others encouraged its circulation because, they said, through its jesting, the young could

40. My discussion of the *Coena* and sacred parody is indebted to Bakhtin, *Rabelais*, pp. 76–86. For an illuminating discussion of the *Coena*'s literary history, its intertextual strategies, its use of reversal, and its role in the novel, see Douglass Parker, "The Curious Case of Pharaoh's Polyp, and Related Matters," *SubStance* 14 (1985): 74–85.

41. Bakhtin, *Rabelais*, p. 84.

42. On the authorization of such parodies and the appropriation of low or folkloric culture by hegemonic culture, see Corti, "Models and Antimodels," pp. 352–55 and 357–64; Le Goff, *Time, Work, and Culture*, pp. 156–57.

43. Bakhtin, *Rabelais*, p. 76.

more easily commit to memory certain episodes of sacred history" (437).

According to Adso's official interpretation, the *Coena* has allegorical and mnemonic value. But as the shaping force of his dream, it bespeaks the values and imagery of difference. William's explanation of the dream draws together the *topoi* and key words that punctuate the novel's preoccupation with laughter: he speaks of a world upside down, of a "kind of comedy," of carnival, of Adelmo's marginalia, and finally of a dream that does not distinguish between true and false, life and death (437–38). Adso's dream reproduces the *Coena*'s ludic reversal of Scripture; it offers "a vast selection . . . of all festive images of the Bible and the Gospels," combined "into the grandiose picture of a banquet, full of life and movement, presented with extraordinary carnivalesque . . . freedom."[44] The imagery of the *Coena* is that of grotesque realism, debasing the contents of Scripture to the level of earth and the body.

Adso's dream of the *Coena Cypriani* defies all of Jorge's admonitions against laughter, impossibilia, and reversals of order (427–35). Like another moment of Adso's heightened experience, this is set in the kitchen and refectory; here too he finds himself on the threshold. Here too he confronts the ambivalence of his surroundings, unable to decide if the clamorous, food-laden kitchen is hell or a Salvatorian paradise. The dream enacts the principal transgressive strategies of carnival laughter: it reduces all the reverent persons and signs of Scripture and all the serious characters and incidents of the novel to the "material bodily principle," reversing their customary significations in a room that is itself adorned with images of reversal. The *Coena*'s necessary connection with the forms of feasting is realized here in the abbot who rules with a fork in place of a scepter and in Jorge, who drinks wine and swears "by God's belly." The scriptural characters take on the cellarer's role, becoming procurers

44. Ibid., p. 287. A critical edition of the *Coena Cypriani* appears in *Monumenta germaniae historica: Poetae latini aevi carolini* 4.2 (1923): 857–900. On the link between the *Coena* and the novel's invocation of Rabelais through the reference to "Magister Alcofriba," see Stephens, "Ec[h]o in Fabula," pp. 59–60.

of food and drink. Remigio is given the "higher" status of providing the "devotional" reading for the grotesque banquet; his stories of Christ joking with the apostles accompany "eating at full tilt."

Images of the grotesque body, its distortions, reversals, and transformations punctuate Adso's dream. He is welcomed to the feast by "dwarfs with huge pot-shaped heads." The banquet's drunks fall into jars "with only their legs sticking out," a position like that of the dead Venantius, earlier in the novel. Wine flows from Adam's rib, and Berengar, in a parody of the gesture Bernard Gui had ascribed to devotees of Satan, pulls up "everyone's habit, man and woman, kissing them all on the anus" (431).

Prominent in the dream's devouring and consuming, its energetic and graphic rendering of the physical body, is the evocation of the female—as a scriptural figure, cultural symbol, and character in the novel. The girl of Adso's erotic encounter appears both as the "maiden terrible as an army with banners" and as the girl herself, seized with her black rooster and labeled a witch. Here the novel's specific identification of woman with threats to monastic vows of chastity and to orthodox Christianity yields to another vision of the female as a repository of all transgressive meanings and functions, as the epitome of materiality. The *Coena*'s festive banquet gives way to a dismembering of the girl that recalls the fate of the heretical Dolcino's Margaret and recapitulates the martyrdom of the saints: "Peter crucified her head down, Stephen stoned her, Lawrence burned her on a grate, Bartholomew skinned her" (432). Her fragmented body is simultaneously defiled in the most grotesque aspects and revered "among the glass cases and gold-and-crystal reliquaries of the crypt."

In its essential ambivalence—sacred and profane, a "single immense body . . . the masterpiece of creation . . . shattered into plural and separate accidental forms"—the girl's fragmented body reveals its connection with the novel's other fragmented totalities (432–33). It recalls the "disiecta membra" of Salvatore's speech and of his body, "composed of scraps of humanity," and anticipates the scattered pieces of text with which Adso concludes his story.[45] And it images those disparate individualities in which, William asserts, our only knowledge inheres. After all its ludic merriments and violations, Adso's dream synthesizes the specific ambivalences of the individual narratives in the image of

> a single dead body, lacerated and tormented like Dolcino's body after his torture, transformed into a loathsome and resplendent treasure. . . . It was the same body that at the supper had eaten and tumbled obscenely but here, instead, appeared to me fixed in the intangibility of its deaf and blind ruin. . . . But, wondrous mystery, that scene no longer instilled fear in me, . . . because now I knew all about the mortal human body, its sufferings and its corruption, and I feared nothing any more. (433–34)

Adso's vision of the *Coena Cypriani* confirms what Jorge had said about laughter: that it is "something very close to death and to the corruption of the body" (96). But it also accepts the body as a "loathsome and resplendent treasure," as fundamentally mixed in its very nature as the commingling of spirit and flesh in humankind itself.

The novel's use of the *Coena Cypriani* as the model for Adso's dream is a narrative masterstroke. It validates a point made consistently in monastic literary theory and in the novel's monastic narrative: the reading and writing of texts ("A dream is a scripture," William says [438]), are shaped by prior knowledge of other texts. More important, the dream's ludic inverted Scripture recapitulates the narrative itself. The grotesque gathering of biblical saints and prophets merges with the characters and events of the novel: Michael of Cesena is anointed by the Marys and tempted by Adam; Christ's fingers betray the black stains that identify the readers of the forbidden book; Adso's love is persecuted by Abel, Adam, Nebuchadnezzar, Elijah, and Noah. Thus, in appropriating an important medieval comic form, Adso's dream submits the entire narrative to grotesque reversal, ef-

45. Stephens, "Ec[h]o in Fabula," pp. 62–63.

fecting within the time required for the singing of the Office of the Dead, the "carnivalization of the novel."[46] Adso's dream of the *Coena* concentrates the interpretive issues of the stories of love, heresy, and laughter in an energetic endorsement of an ambivalence that mediates between high and low, serious and comic, spirit and flesh, life and death. It is the culminating sign of the reading of medieval culture that structures the novel.

IV

In *The Name of the Rose* the ludic imagery of kitchen, heresy, and dream richly typifies the transgressive corporeality of medieval carnival. But as evocative tokens of an idea of culture, such imagery directs attention to the overall purpose of this representation and to the meaning of these specific transgressions, in both cultural and narrative terms. To some, the carnivalesque challenge to the dominant culture's codes may seem to have not merely a symbolic but an actual subversive function as an agent of social change, a function obviously complicated by the dominant culture's tendency to appropriate carnivalesque transgressions.[47]

Eco himself has assessed the theory of carnival as revolution, acknowledging the "profound drive towards liberation and subversion in Medieval carnival."[48] But he severely critiques the "hyper-Bachtinian ideology of carnival as *actual* liberation":

> Carnival, in order to be enjoyed, requires that rules and rituals be parodied, and that these rules and rituals already be recognized and re-

46. Barbara Babcock-Abrahams borrows the phrase from Julia Kristeva; see Babcock-Abrahams's "Novel and the Carnival World," *MLN* 89 (1974): 913, 923–24.

47. On this point see Turner, *Ritual Process*, p. vii; Ginzberg, *Cheese and the Worms*, pp. xvi–xvii, 164, note to p. 86; Davis, *Society and Culture*, pp. 102–3; Corti, "Models and Antimodels," p. 353. On the relation of Bakhtin's ideal type of carnival to social practice, see LaCapra, "Bakhtin, Marxism, and the Carnivalesque," pp. 295–96.

48. "The Frames of Comic Freedom," *Carnival!* ed. Thomas Sebeok, Approaches to Semiotics 64 (Berlin, Amsterdam, and New York: Mouton, 1984), p. 3; hereafter cited as FF.

> spected. One must know to what degree certain behaviors are forbidden, and must feel the majesty of the forbidding norm, to appreciate their transgression. Without a valid law to break, carnival is impossible. . . . Carnival can only exist as an *authorized* transgression. (FF 6)

Eco maintains that this containment or regulation of transgression applies not just to carnival but to comedy as a whole: both "represent paramount examples of law enforcement. They remind us of the existence of the rule" (FF 6).

Eco singles out the *Coena Cypriani* as one important medieval example of such "authorized transgression," for its biblical burlesque is not only limited but made possible by the more frequent and normative serious reading of Scripture (FF 6). Not surprisingly, he invests his novel's appropriation of the *Coena* with the same containment he distinguishes as a feature of authorized transgression. Adso's dream of the *Coena* is doubly contained: by his own monastic narrative voice, a product of official culture, and by the novel itself, produced from within the learned culture of university professors and literary theorists.

The "authorized transgression" that the *Coena* illustrates holds true for the other paramount acts and figures of transgression in the novel. Adso's encounters with interpretive ambivalence and the delight of the flesh are ultimately contained by the comfort of cosmic allegory; Salvatore's heresy is openly and dramatically suppressed. Even the substance of comedy is regulated by official philosophy, Aristotle's theory, his book of comedy.

But the novel by no means suggests that its acts of transgression are simply gratuitous. Laughter and comedy mean something besides the rules that bring them into being. Eco provides an escape hatch from the notion that "the comic is only an instrument of social control and can never be a form of social criticism." For besides the carnival forms of laughter—the reversals of folk societies, marginal people, and lower classes—he mentions other types of the comic: "Aristotle, for instance, speaks in the *Rhetoric* of a verbal comic, of wits, of sophisticated plays with words that seem to have a more critical power" (FF 7). This other form of the comic—Eco calls it "humor"—differs from the carnivalesque in the way the relationship between rule and violation is balanced. Like simple comedy, humor encourages us to see the contradiction between the transgression and the rule; but it also scrutinizes the rule itself. Humor is "always . . . metasemiotic: through verbal language or some other sign system it casts in doubt other cultural codes. If there is a possibility of transgression," Eco states, "it lies in humor rather than in comic" (FF 8).

It is, I think, an appreciation of humor rather than an endorsement of the comic that *The Name of the Rose* finally achieves. Unlike the comic, which "takes place at the level of . . . narrative structures," humor "works in the interstices between narrative and discursive structures." It

> does not pretend, like carnival, to lead us beyond our own limits. It gives us the feeling, or better, the picture of the structure of our own limits. It is never off limits, it undermines limits from inside. It does not fish for an impossible freedom, yet it is a true movement of freedom. Humor does not promise us liberation: on the contrary, it warns us about the impossibility of global liberation, reminding us of the presence of a law that we no longer have reason to obey. In doing so it undermines the law. It makes us feel the uneasiness of living under a law—any law. (FF 8)

William, the perennial doubter, the prober of signs and cultural codes, is the locus of humor in the novel. Ironically, he gains access to the mystery's codes by virtue of the "authorized transgression" of Adso's dream of the *Coena*: "'I believe that your sleeping soul understood more things than I have in six days'" (438). The dream acts as a "liminal" phenomenon for William, ushering him to the threshold of the narrative moment when he is able to identify the contents of the lost book. The discovery of Aristotle's book on comedy enables him to draw together the interpretive issues of all the narratives, displacing the comic's laughter with a humor that both pictures "the structure of our own limits" and "undermines limits from inside."

[5]

Medievalizing Theory

Logic, chance, and knowledge of other books at last enable William to identify the deadly text—the second book of Aristotle's *Poetics,* the book on comedy. The identification of the book simply makes explicit what has been implicit in the narrative all along. Aristotle's book on comedy is allied with the view of society and culture emerging from the discussion of laughter, and is itself a precise illustration of the novel's binary model of culture. For its account of comic phenomena, the marginal, and the different in words and in things, is made available only through the hegemonic, official voice of the philosopher.

The novel's reconstruction of *Poetics* II is itself a tour de force. Eco has said elsewhere that the loss, even the nonexistence, of the second book of the *Poetics* is only a "minor inconvenience," because what Aristotle "could have said about comedy can be extrapolated from two sources: the observations on comedy and witty manipulation of language" in *Poetics* I and the *Rhetoric,* and anonymous treatises on comedy, such as *Tractatus Coislinianus* from the post-Aristotelian Greek and Latin tradition (FF 1).[1] The reconstruction Eco envisions has in

1. In the novel Benno makes a similar recommendation for reconstructing Aristotle's views on comedy (111–12).

fact recently been made, a happy coincidence that reinforces the integrity of the fictional book on comedy.[2]

The novel's reconstructed *Poetics* II effectively captures the Aristotelian idiom and incorporates what "Aristotle could have said about comedy":

> As we promised, we will now deal with comedy . . . and see how, in inspiring the pleasure of the ridiculous, it arrives at the purification of that passion. . . . We will then define the type of actions of which comedy is the mimesis, then we will examine the means by which comedy excites laughter, and these means are actions and speech. We will show how the ridiculousness of actions is born from the likening of the best to the worst and vice versa, from arousing surprise through deceit, from the impossible, from violation of the laws of nature, from the irrelevant and the inconsequent, from the debasing of the characters, from the use of comical and vulgar pantomime, from disharmony, from the choice of the least worthy things. We will then show how the ridiculousness of speech is born from the misunderstandings of similar words for different things and different words for similar things, from garrulity and repetition, from play on words, from diminutives, from errors of pronunciation, and from barbarisms. (468)

Here we find a reprise of the issues that knit together the novel's several narratives: the reversal of traditional order, debasement of high to low, the focus on the vulgar and unworthy, and the ambivalence generated by the conventional nature of language. The fake *Poetics* II owes a large debt to Aristotle's *Rhetoric*, particularly in its view of the origins of laughter and its attention to the verbal bases of humor.[3]

The interest in manipulations of language in the lost Aristotle clarifies the relation of the mysterious poisoned text to the narrative as a whole: laughter, like allegory and like political dis-

2. Richard Janko, *Aristotle on Comedy: Towards a Reconstruction of Poetics II* (London: Duckworth, 1984). Janko's reconstruction is based on the *Tractatus* Eco mentions. For a discussion of the existence of a second book of the *Poetics*, see pp. 63–66, 88–90; the reconstruction is on pp. 91–99. The versions of *Poetics* II by Eco and Janko share the same general strategy and intention and the same appreciation for the Aristotelian voice; see Janko's explanation of his procedure, p. 91.

3. Aristotle, *The Art of Rhetoric* 3.3, 10, 11, trans. John Henry Freese, Loeb Classical Library (Cambridge: Harvard University Press, 1926).

course, centers on problems of equivalence and difference. As we have seen, Aristotle addressed these issues in his discussion of metaphor in *Poetics* I; it is hardly surprising that William's exegesis of *Poetics* II recalls the philosopher's view of the cognitive value of metaphor: "'Here Aristotle sees the tendency to laughter as a force for good, which can also have an instructive value: through witty riddles and unexpected metaphors, though it tells us things differently from the way they are, as if it were lying, it actually obliges us to examine them more closely, and it makes us say: Ah, this is just how things are, and I didn't know it'" (472).[4] William asserts a value for comedy specifically in terms of those aspects of the verbal sign that he elsewhere identifies with other uses of language: comedy enlarges knowledge and shows that the categories of truth are fluid rather than fixed.

William's reading of Aristotle on comedy at the climactic moment of the novel initiates the final phase of his debate with Jorge. His exegesis emphasizes precisely what Jorge finds objectionable in laughter and the forbidden book. It also illuminates their conflict over laughter as a philosophical quarrel, which can be construed in light of the novel's binary model of culture. This chapter examines the philosophical implications of their positions on laughter and their place in the cultural model. Because their competing views of laughter reflect attitudes toward language and interpretation, William and Jorge's debate takes its place in the novel's representation of theory. At the same time, their conflict is also firmly anchored in the medieval social and cultural environment with which each is associated. The opposition between William and Jorge, then, gives us access to the shape of the novel's overarching medievalizing of theory.

I

William asks Jorge: "'Why did this one [book] fill you with such fear?'" The blind monk's response addresses the Francis-

4. See *Rhetoric* 3.11.1412a; p. 409, and cf. Eco's discussion of Aristotle on metaphor in *SP*, 101–3.

can's generously optimistic sense of the relation of knowledge and the verbal sign. Jorge also explains his censoring of Aristotle as an effort to contain the dangerous qualities of the cultural other. His objection to the book on comedy is an objection to Aristotle's entire philosophical project, which "'destroyed a part of the learning that Christianity had accumulated over the centuries.'" The medieval glossing of Aristotle had overthrown the sufficient knowledge of the "power" and "divine mystery of the Word" achieved by the fathers, replacing it with "a human parody of categories and syllogism": "'We knew everything about the divine names,'" until Aquinas, the Dominican "seduced" by Aristotle, "'renamed them, following the proud paths of natural reason.'" This proliferation of words displaced reverence for the Word, fundamentally transgressing an order of language and truth complete from its beginning. Aristotle's cosmology overturned the view of Jorge's hero Pseudo-Dionysius, who had maintained that the cosmos "'revealed itself to those who knew how to look up at the luminous cascade of the exemplary first cause.'" Aristotle's philosophy reconceived the universe as "dull and slimy matter" and, mediated by the work of Aquinas, turned the "luminous cascade" into a "preserve of terrestrial evidence" from which the heavens can be known (473).[5]

Jorge is a Platonic extremist; his aversion to Aristotle's philosophy is an aversion to the material nature imaged in laughter, which is "weakness, corruption, the foolishness of our flesh" (474). Laughter summons the "'dark powers of corporal matter . . . that are affirmed in the fart and the belch'" (477). Jorge's lengthy diatribe against laughter reiterates the identification of laughter with the cultural "other": it is a "defense for the simple," a tool for plebians, rebels, and kings of fools. Jorge knows that he cannot do away with laughter's reversals, nor does he

5. Jorge hates the abbot because of his association with Aquinas, the Dominican "seduced by" Aristotle. The abbot rose to power on the prestige of Aquinas, becoming famous "because at Fossanova he managed to get a body down some circular stairs" (464). Jorge's repugnance for Aquinas's reputed obesity might be seen in light of his philosophical objection to such emphatic corporeality. Eco has elsewhere shown amused interest in Aquinas's obesity; see his preface to his book on the Beatus Apocalypse manuscripts, quoted in Teresa De Lauretis, *Umberto Eco* (Florence: La nuova Italia, 1981), p. 6.

wish to. He acknowledges that "'even the church in her wisdom has granted the moment of feast, carnival, fair, this diurnal pollution that releases humors and distracts from other desires and other ambitions.'" Eventually, "'carnival is consumed, and it does not matter whether during the feast the epiphany of the world upside down will be produced on earth for a brief time'" (474). Like Eco himself, Jorge acknowledges here that carnival cannot help but validate the very law it transgresses (FF 6). His effort to censor the book on comedy stems from other motives—he wishes to keep the reversals of laughter from being legitimized by the name of Aristotle. Laughter and its material forms can be tolerated as long as they maintain their otherness and marginality, as long as they are not dignified with the official labels of "art," "philosophy," and "theology" (474). Aristotle's *Poetics* on comedy threatens to provide such a legitimation.

According to Jorge, the legitimation of laughter would "'strike the Luciferine spark that would set a new fire to the whole world, and laughter would be defined as the new art, unknown even to Prometheus, for canceling fear.'" His imagined world reverses the effort of traditional medieval Christianity "'to redeem, through the thought of that which is lofty, the wretchedness and temptation of that which is base,'" making way for "'false scholars [who] . . . try to redeem the lofty with a diabolical reversal: through the acceptance of the base'" (475). In such a world laughter redeems fear; distinctions between margin and center dissolve; the customary rhetoric and topics of philosophy are dismantled—at least according to Jorge's predictions of the probable consequences of laughter's unleashing of signification.[6]

Jorge suitably authorizes his own plea for authority. He sees his suppression of Aristotle as the main action in a providential narrative in which he plays a central role: "'I know, I know as if I saw it written in adamantine letters, with my eyes, which see

6. Walter E. Stephens speaks in this context of the "threat which unlimited semiosis poses to the closure" of liturgy and cosmos; see "Ec[h]o in Fabula," *Diacritics* 13 (1983): 57.

things you do not see. I know that this was the will of the Lord, and I acted, interpreting it'" (479). But from William's perspective Jorge's well-ordered narrative is only a gathering of discrete events; his adamantine will of God only a devilish "'arrogance of spirit, faith without smile, truth that is never seized by doubt.'" To Jorge's authorized certainty, William opposes "'the infinite whirl of possible things [in which] God allows you also to imagine a world where the presumed interpreter of the truth is nothing but a clumsy raven'" (477). Believing himself to be "the hand of God," Jorge epitomizes the hierarchical officialdom to which William's "otherness" is opposed.

The blind monk tellingly identifies William's "otherness" with his Franciscanism: "'You are worse than the Devil, Minorite. . . . You are a clown, like the saint who gave birth to you all'" (477–78). William's identity as a Franciscan is important to the novel's medievalism and to its reflections on the organization of culture; it is as central to the role he plays as the Franciscan debate on poverty is to the novel's larger treatment of the problem of interpretation. We have already considered the hermeneutic implications of the historical role of Franciscanism in the novel. William further focuses the semiotic significance of the Franciscan presence. When Jorge condemns William as a follower of the saint who "'de toto corpore fecerat linguam'" (478) ("who made his whole body a tongue"), he makes explicit his earlier reproval of the Franciscan attraction to "merriment" and "nonsense" (79, 133). But his aversion to Franciscan frivolity, like his aversion to laughter, is merely a token of a more fundamental objection to everything William's order stands for.

The novel consistently identifies the saint from Assisi with the characteristics of the cultural other: the mission of Francis's order was to make insiders of the outcasts (201–3); his ministry employed strategies of reversal. William summarizes Francis's accomplishment well: "'Francis taught people to look at things from another direction'" (478). William's position coincides with a recent view of the order that sees its worldly and profane spiritual strategies as a "carnivalized Catholicism." The "originality of Francis's religious genius" lay in his "attempt to identify the paradox of the carnival with the Christian paradox itself."[7] This characterization of the Franciscan order emphasizes its founder's liminal approach to life; Francis compelled "the friars to inhabit the fringes and the interstices of the social structure of his time." He denied the value of property, status, privilege, and material pleasure, promoting the idea of religion as a fraternity of horizontal relationships, not a hierarchical structure.[8] Francis deliberately located his order on the margins of the official culture, a position manifested as well in its commitment to vernacular language and culture and in its address to women as important members of its audience and significant participants in its spiritual message.[9]

Jorge's criticism of the saint who spoke with his "whole body" identifies an aspect of Franciscan communication particularly inimical to his own preference for redeeming the base through the lofty. He calls attention to the immediacy, spontaneity, and concreteness of Francis's thought and expression, a disposition that might be seen as the informing principle of what eventually became the order's primary contributions to philosophical empiricism.[10] William, with his emphasis on the truth of the individual, epitomizes this Franciscan tendency. Francis's idea of his rule as a practical model of living rather than an official document was in part responsible for the medi-

7. Carlo Ginzberg, "Folklore, magia, religione," in *Storia d'Italia*, vol. 1, *I caratteri generali* (Turin, 1972), p. 615, quoted in Maria Corti, "Models and Antimodels in Medieval Culture," *New Literary History* 10 (1979): 356. For a succinct account of the formation and development of the Franciscan order, see William R. Cook and Ronald B. Herzman, *The Medieval World View: An Introduction* (New York: Oxford University Press, 1983), pp. 294–315.

8. Victor Turner, *The Ritual Process: Structure and Anti-Structure* (1969; Ithaca: Cornell University Press, 1977), p. 145, and, in general, pp. 143–45. Fleming corroborates this view; see *An Introduction to the Franciscan Literature of the Middle Ages* (Chicago: Franciscan Herald Press, 1977), p. 17. See too the characterization of the Franciscans by Heiko Oberman, "The Shape of Late Medieval Thought," in *The Pursuit of Holiness in Late Medieval and Renaissance Religion*, ed. Charles Trinkhaus and Heiko Oberman (Leiden: Brill, 1972), p. 7.

9. Fleming, *Franciscan Literature*, pp. 15–22.

10. Francis's biographers describe his exploitation of the concrete sign. See the two lives of the saint by Thomas Celano, *St. Francis of Assisi*, trans. Placid Hermann O.F.M. (Chicago: Franciscan Herald Press, 1963), *First Life*, pp. 15–17, 48–49; *Second Life*, pp. 189, 244.

eval controversies over the interpretation of his original intentions. His shying away from abstraction, generalization, and univocal concepts defined an approach to language as well as life. Francis cultivated a "multivocal" symbolism; his language was highly personal and imagistic.[11]

This decoding of Franciscanism in *The Name of the Rose* broadens the historical base for Jorge and William's respective defenses of univocal and multivocal concepts of meaning and brings to fruition a difference implicit from the beginning in their opposing identities as monk and friar, Benedictine and Franciscan. This difference involves the social and institutional presence, the educational philosophies and methodologies, and the theological aims of the monastic and fraternal orders. It furnishes the medieval grounding of the modern theoretical positions with which William and Jorge can be identified.

II

"The Benedictines," remarks one historian, "did not cultivate talk." Though they did not embrace a strict rule of silence, they discouraged the use of speech for its own sake, whether for persuasion or amusement. In the sacralized universe to which monasticism laid claim, monks saw no need for proselytizing: their form of life gave witness "to a truth they considered established."[12]

In contrast, for the evangelical movement in which the Franciscans played no small part, verbal experience, and specifically preaching the word of God, were preeminent.[13] The intensely verbal nature of the fraternal religious experience and mission was well-suited to the urban society the friars served. It was a society whose members—merchants, bankers, lawyers, teach-

11. Turner, *Ritual Process*, pp. 141–42.

12. Lester K. Little, *Religious Poverty and the Profit Economy of Medieval Europe* (Ithaca: Cornell University Press, 1978), p. 198.

13. M.-D. Chenu, *Nature, Man, and Society in the Twelfth Century*, ed. and trans. Jerome Taylor and Lester K. Little (Chicago: University of Chicago Press, 1968), pp. 244–49.

ers—"did not make their living by praying, or by fighting, or by . . . working with their hands. They talked; they argued, they negotiated, they wrote; they entertained; above all, they tried to persuade other people." The friars appropriated the verbal modes of their urban environment: Francis was "a sort of street-corner or public-square" hawker of spiritual goods.[14] The Franciscans' manipulation of language displaced the ideally ordered speech of monastic psalmody and the peace of monastic silence, challenging the position Jorge asserts in his sermon on the apocalypse: that beyond praising and commenting on already revealed truth, "there is nothing to say."

This proliferation of talk was accompanied by other urban developments in which the friars played a central role. Not by accident, the harbingers of the new urban spirituality were also masters of the universities and schools where changing attitudes toward the substance and method of learning were beginning to influence practice.[15] In this new academic environment, as in the marketplace with which it shared a substantial fraternal population, the uses of language and the scope of human inquiry were broadened. This widening of intellectual endeavor was reflected in the heterogeneous composition of the urban institutions of learning and in the new goals they defined for themselves, which were responsive to the institutions' social presence.[16] Like the preachers of the word whose speech was defined in reaction to an increasingly ineffectual monastic silence, the masters of the urban schools frequently found themselves in conflict with the guardians of knowledge in the cloisters.

These developments in the intellectual culture of medieval Europe are frequently posed in terms of a dichotomy between monasticism and scholasticism. Monastic study involved the repeated reading of Scripture and its commentaries; it was itself a form of prayer. Scholastic education and thinking, in contrast,

14. Little, *Religious Poverty*, pp. 197, 199. Little compares the linguistic aspect of the friars' urban existence to monastic programs and the ideals of feudal society.

15. Chenu, *Nature, Man, and Society*, p. 251.

16. Jacques Le Goff, *Time, Work, and Culture in the Middle Ages*, trans. Arthur Goldhammer (Chicago: University of Chicago Press, 1980), pp. 122–49.

encouraged the speculative pursuit of new knowledge for its own sake.[17] The distinctive pedagogies of monastic and scholastic culture were imaged in their different approaches to the study of Scripture. The monastic *lectio divina* embroidered upon the scriptural text in its sequence of reading, meditation, and prayer; the scholastic *lectio* posed questions of the text and to the reader. The respective "roles of the reader" in these two forms of *lectio* are distinct: the monastic reader gathers and arranges authorities on the text; the scholastic employs the rational coherence of philosophy as a criterion, distinct from the authority of the revealed word, for the acquisition of truth.[18] Implicit in each type of reading is a distinctive view of the text and of theology. Monastic *lectio* asserted the fundamental priority of the revealed truth; the *sacra pagina* it studied was one constant in a sacralized world whose exegesis was "subordinated to an eschatological perspective sacred beyond the movements of time and the operation of causes on earth." The scholastic *quaestio*, in searching out causes and reasons, "risked treating scripture simply as another problem."[19] Emphasizing interpretation over the grounds of faith, it opened study to options and opinions and made the sacralized world and text of monastic contemplation an object of knowledge susceptible to the workings of a valorized method.[20]

These developments in the state of medieval learning in the twelfth and thirteenth centuries reverberate in the *Rose*'s portrait of fourteenth-century intellectual culture.[21] William is a

17. For general descriptions of the two educational ideologies and methods, see Jean Leclercq, *The Love of Learning and the Desire for God*, trans. Catharine Misrahi (1961; New York: Fordham University Press, 1974), pp. 1–9; David Knowles, *The Benedictines* (New York: Macmillan, 1930), pp. 13–16. For a discussion of the monastic/scholastic distinction that complements my approach here, see Brian Stock, *The Implications of Literacy: Written Language and Models of Interpretation in the Eleventh and Twelfth Centuries* (Princeton: Princeton University Press, 1983), chap. 4, "Language, Texts, and Reality," especially pp. 326–29, 403–10.

18. Leclercq, *Love of Learning*, p. 89; Chenu, *Nature, Man, and Society*, pp. 291, 300–301.

19. Chenu, *Nature, Man, and Society*, p. 306.

20. Ibid., pp. 294–95, 303–7.

21. Eco comments on this mingling of twelfth-, thirteenth-, and fourteenth-century history in his novel (*PS* 26).

scholar in the medieval sense of the word. A devotee and student of Occam, he exemplifies that new social category of masters (*magistri*), who, free of the ties of ecclesiastical feudalism, traveled about, living in cities and sometimes serving as advisors to princes. William's relationship with Adso is that of master and student; many of their exchanges are modeled after the scholastic *quaestio*, that dialectical method of inquiry which dominated the intellectual activity of the schools and universities.[22] Although Adso proves an able, eventually a very committed student of the new learning, his initial response to William bespeaks his monastic orientation: "In time I realized that what seemed [his] . . . lack of confidence was only curiosity, but at the beginning I knew little of this virtue, which I thought, rather, a passion of the covetous spirit. I believed instead that the rational spirit should not indulge such passion, but feed only on the Truth, which (I thought) one knows from the outset" (15). Adso offers here a more innocent version of Jorge's view of intellectual inquiry. For all his sinister qualities, Jorge in one important respect simply voices opinions that directly echo those of his historical medieval forebears, as the twelfth-century judgment of Rupert of Deutz illustrates: "Whatever can be thought up apart from sacred scripture or fabricated out of argumentation is unreasonable and therefore pertains in no way to the praise or acknowledgment of the omnipotence of God."[23]

Monastic and scholastic orientations toward language and knowledge thus gloss the opposing intellectual "styles" that William and Jorge bring to the central debate in *The Name of the Rose*. In the Middle Ages the terms of this debate were frequently qualified by shades of opinion and complex allegiances that in themselves constitute a substantial chapter in the history of philosophy and theology in the twelfth and thirteenth centuries. Scholastic practice may have distinguished itself from monastic study by its openness to contradiction and variety, but insofar as it sought to totalize knowledge through the rational construction of *summae*, it also consolidated Christian author-

22. Chenu, *Nature, Man, and Society*, pp. 273, 291–300.

23. Chenu (ibid., p. 272) quotes from Rupert's *De omnipotentia Dei* xxiii (*PL* 170:473). For other twelfth-century opinions on both sides of the debate, see pp. 310–11.

ity at a "moment when the Church began to enforce orthodoxy more rigorously than ever before," insisting that "everyone accept . . . not just the infallible pronouncements of popes and councils but every statement of orthodox theologians."[24]

The novel's portrait of fourteenth-century intellectual culture shows just this sort of ideological shading. Ubertino di Casale, though a former student of the Paris masters, wears the robes of the order whose theology is compatible with the anti-intellectual attitude of his Franciscan Spiritualism. Thus Ubertino both appreciates and censures William, who in his turn admires the spiritual science of Roger Bacon and the skepticism of Occam. William is the most important locus of this ideological shading, his complexity attesting to the way the novel shies away from reductiveness to achieve its portrait of medieval culture.

William's many individual personality quirks—he laughs when he is most serious and sounds most doubtful when most sure of himself—are clearly related to the Franciscan delight in paradox. His cautious assertion of the truth of individual things over universal laws marks his alliance with his order's predilection for the concrete. His sympathy with the aims of Francis's order and with the socially and politically outcast associates him with the "otherness" that Jorge execrates. Yet his is a difference that both embraces and moves beyond his Franciscan identity. In the novel it is Saint Francis, not William, who is a sign of the cultural other. The novel gives the detective a semiotic resonance of a wider and different range. William tempers his countercultural sympathies with the knowledge that Francis's intentions were inevitably and necessarily compromised by his having to seek official sanction for his endeavors (202). He understands how the dangerous certainty of a Jorge can also be nurtured within the bosom of Franciscanism itself, as Ubertino aptly illustrates. Friend to Emperor Louis and former inquisitor, Oxford-educated William has his own strong affiliations with the powers of the official culture he regularly criticizes.

With his eye set simultaneously on different worlds, William

24. John Boswell, *Christianity, Social Tolerance, and Homosexuality* (Chicago: University of Chicago Press, 1980), p. 330.

acts in the novel as a figure of mediation. It is precisely the role of mediator—between the representatives of Pope John and those of the Emperor and the Spiritual Franciscans—that William has come to the abbey to fulfill. Representing an order whose social role was mediation (204), he also functions as mediator on another, a philosophical, level, his arguments determined by his operative belief that signs "are the only things man has with which to orient himself in the world" (492). According to Jorge's typological categories, William may be the "Minorite clown," but he can more appropriately be considered a messenger between the center and the margin, hegemony and difference, official and unofficial culture. His cultural status is imaged in the way he moves freely in and out of the library and up and down the levels of the Aedificium, the novel's emblem of culture. Though he has his own role in the novel's pattern of oppositions, William also calls into question the very structuring of culture in these binary terms.

William brings into focus one of the novel's major points: theological beliefs, political sympathies, even attitudes toward books have to do less with the respective contents of any of these than with ways of life and methods of interpretation. An empiricist, a student of nature, a logician who deems logic useful but irrelevant because "there is no order in the universe" (492), William manifests a cautious pluralism and openness in his reading of signs. For instance, he assuages Adso's postcoital guilt by explaining that though Scripture may say woman is a source of temptation and a vessel of the devil, God nonetheless made her of noble stuff and gave her a vital role in the story of human redemption (252). Similarly, he counters Adso's assessment of the Koran as "a perverse book," with the assertion that it is a "book containing a wisdom different from ours" (315).

This mediate stance sets William in opposition not only to Jorge but to the blind monk's ideological cohorts—Gui, Ubertino, and the abbot, all of whom believe in certainty, in a truth that is fixed, total, and univocal. These seemingly disparate figures—Dominican, Franciscan, and Benedictine—form a kind of ideological backdrop against which William's point of view is defined. Gui, for instance, pursues the inquisitorial activities which William has renounced. His persecution of heretics is based on his mission as a "humble instrument of the truth" who knows how to "distinguish the viper of heresy wherever it may nest" (389). Ubertino exhibits a fanatical faith in his ability to know the difference between ardors born of pious and impious ends (58). He also shares with Jorge a contempt for the "pride of the intellect" (60) and for William's strength, the exercise of reason. The abbot shares Jorge's reactionary opposition to change (36) and, like Gui, claims to know by "rule" what a heretic is (153). His meditation on the "language" of gems, which is "'multiform . . . according to the sense of the selected interpretation,'" endorses "'authority, the most reliable commentator of all and the most invested with . . . sanctity'" (448).

Jorge, Gui, Ubertino, and the abbot all express anxiety about the proliferation of learning and the multiplicity of signs. Their reverence for traditional authority sets in high relief William's skepticism about tradition as a repository of truth. The novel's juxtaposition of these divergent views invokes a familiar medieval *topos*: the quarrel of the ancients and the moderns. Jorge and the abbot, even Adso at times, display an ideological nostalgia for the past in the face of the onslaught of the new. Early in the story Adso bewails the state of a world out of joint, paraphrasing a song from the *Carmina Burana*: "The young no longer want to study anything, learning is in decline, the whole world walks on its head" (15).[25] In contrast, master William is numbered among those scholars who from their earliest appearance were identified as the *moderni*; as a Franciscan, he is of the "new and strange" order that attracted the attention of lay society. His devotion to Occam associates him with a philosophical movement characterized as a *via moderna* in sharp opposition to the *via antiqua* of tradition.[26]

The novel images the dichotomy of ancient and modern not only in the quarrel of Benedictine and Franciscan, monastic and

25. Ernst Curtius discusses the song as an example of the "world upside down" motif; see *European Literature and the Latin Middle Ages*, trans. Willard Trask (1953; New York: Harper and Row, 1963), pp. 94–98. On the quarrel of the ancients and the moderns, see pp. 251–55. Chenu mentions the song (p. 317) in his discussion of "tradition and innovation" in the high Middle Ages; see *Nature, Man, and Society*, pp. 310–30.

26. Chenu, *Nature, Man, and Society*, pp. 316–17, 319; Gordon Leff, *The Dissolution of the Medieval Outlook* (New York: Harper and Row, 1976), p. 10.

scholastic views of learning but also in its opposing versions of the apocalyptic: the Spiritual Franciscans' "modern" apocalyptic anticipates the coming of Joachim's new era, whereas Jorge's older version awaits, not a new age, but doomsday. Adso contrasts the "audacity" of the modern Gothic style with the old Romanesque of the abbey, a style epitomized in the old apocalyptic imagery of its tympanum. And yet, the ancient abbey is not immune to modernity. Its abbot was trained as a scholastic; it is a venue for visiting radicals and common women.[27] The novel's entire structure of institutional, theological, and intellectual oppositions reflects the innovative (modern) challenges to traditional (ancient) orthodoxies that appeared in the twelfth through fourteenth centuries.[28]

The novel's polemical juxtaposition of past and present thus reflects actual historical movements, styles, and ideas. But like its representation of medieval themes and issues, its opposition of ancient and modern is also charged with contemporary significance, complicated in this instance by the subject of modernity itself. In *The Name of the Rose* the opposition of past and present, ancient and modern, inevitably suggests links between the novel's medieval modernity and our own. This deliberate opposition directs attention, then, not only to the novel's purposive representation of the Middle Ages but to the implications and viability of the terms through which that representation is accomplished.

III

In his essay "Poetics of the Open Work," Eco considers the relation of medieval and modern in order to draw distinctions

---

On the relation of nominalism and the *via moderna*, see William T. Courtnay, "Nominalism and Late Medieval Religion"; and on the Franciscans, see Heiko Oberman, "The Shape of Late Medieval Thought," both in Trinkhaus and Oberman, *Pursuit of Holiness*, pp. 52–53 and p. 12, respectively.

27. For these elaborations on the concept of ancient and modern in the novel I am indebted to Richard K. Emmerson.

28. On the problem of modernity in the Middle Ages and in relation to our own time, see Oberman, "Shape of Late Medieval Thought," pp. 3–25.

between different aesthetic experiences. He contrasts the conception of meaning inherent in the medieval theory of fourfold allegory to that embodied in modern, "open" works. Although the medieval theory of allegory offers a certain multiplicity of meaning, it also follows rules

> that entail a rigid univocality. The meaning of allegorical figures and emblems which the medieval reader is likely to encounter is already prescribed. . . . Any symbolism is objectively defined and organized into a system. Underpinning this poetics of the necessary and the univocal is an ordered cosmos, a hierarchy of essences and laws which . . . each individual must understand in the only possible way, the one determined by the creative *logos*. The order of a work of art in this period is a mirror of imperial and theocratic society. The laws governing textual interpretation are the laws of an authoritarian regime which guide the individual in his every action, prescribing the ends for him and offering him the means to attain them. (*RR* 51–52)

The modern work, in contrast, lies "open to constantly shifting responses and interpretive stances": "in it an ordered world based on universally acknowledged laws is being replaced by a world based on ambiguity" in which "directional centers are missing and . . . values and dogma are constantly being placed in question" (*RR* 53, 54). Whereas the medieval conception of a hierarchically ordered and ordained cosmos "reflects the syllogistic system, a logic of necessity, a deductive consciousness," the modern aesthetic is allied with the philosophical and scientific notion of a "field of possibilities," "a corresponding devolution of intellectual authority to personal decision, choice, and social context," and the emergence of multivalue logics that incorporate "*indeterminacy* as a valid stepping-stone in the cognitive process" (*RR* 57–58).

These notions of medieval and modern correspond to the distinctions we have observed in the *Rose*. Faith in an ordered cosmos of univocal significance unites figures as disparate as Jorge, Gui, Ubertino, and the abbot—it is what makes them "medieval." The abbot's explanation of the "marvelous language" of gems beautifully illustrates Eco's medieval aesthetic of prescriptive allegorical readings. At the height of his erotic passion,

Adso searches for the authoritative meanings of such an ordered cosmos: "The fact is that correct interpretation can be established only on the authority of the fathers, and in the case that torments me, I have no auctoritas to which my obedient mind can refer, and I burn in doubt" (248). In contrast, William's analysis of cause and effect, his "sense of the individual," and his appreciation for the constantly shifting relations between single entities illustrate the "perceptive ambiguities" and the dynamic potentiality of "cognitive positions" which Eco associates with the modern "open" work (*RR* 59).[29] These constructions of reality—closed and open, medieval and modern—bring into focus the medieval totalizing systems of meaning so prominent in the novel, which are played off against William's obvious modernity. Admittedly, his is a modernity impressively built on the solid foundation of the novel's medievalism, his ideological position emerging inevitably from his Occamism and Franciscanism, as well as from the configuration of historical details that shape his character.

It is clear that Eco intends these characterizations of medieval and modern as hermeneutic categories rather than as "true" and full descriptions of historical periods. Certainly, medieval aesthetics is not simply reducible to allegory, any more than modern aesthetics is sufficiently characterized by the word "ambiguity." Nor does the Middle Ages have a corner on readings prescribed by faith in an ordered cosmos. Eco has also looked at medieval allegory in terms of its internal workings, observing that what medieval Platonists deemed a "mazelike network of real properties, is in effect a mazelike network of *cultural* properties." Meanings were determined by a "typology of possible co-texts, so that the best interpretation is always the one recorded by some (intertextual) *auctoritas*" (*SP* 104). And Eco describes the process by which authority was constituted in the Middle Ages. When Augustine, for example, decided that an understanding of Scripture required knowledge of science, he authorized Christian writers to introduce "into the interpretive

29. Cf. Stephens, who also brings this essay to bear on the novel ("Ec[h]o in Fabula," pp. 51–53).

circle . . . all the knowledge of classical civilization, as it was inherited by the late Roman culture." Thus what came to be known as medieval "authority" and tradition issued directly from the early fathers' decision to salvage classical learning. Political and cultural powers work to establish the "rules for good interpretation" (*SP* 151).[30]

However they are chronologically or historically defined, then, the labels "medieval" and "modern" also designate attitudes toward experience and modes of interpretation. Eco observes elsewhere that such designations may be seen as "ideal categories," ways of operating (*PS* 66).[31] The meaning of the terms "medieval" and "modern" also resides in their relation to each other. Moderns have a way of becoming ancients, for "modernity, materially speaking, is a mobile value."[32] The mobility of modernity relates the medievalism of *The Name of the Rose* to central issues of contemporary critical theory.

IV

The "medieval" view of meaning I have attributed to Jorge, Gui, and the abbot corresponds to Derrida's description of the "idea of the book." Invoked to explain medieval metaphors for divine creation and for the "system of signified truth," the "idea of the book" is "the idea of a totality, finite or infinite, of the signifier" which is prior to the sign and itself signifies an eternal verity.[33] Though a metaphorics of writing and the book occurs

30. Eco remarks that the struggle by the "gatekeepers of orthodoxy" to impose their own interpretation grew out of the very plenitude of Scripture itself, which created the need for a theory of allegorical senses (*SP*, 149–50). Cf. Jesse Gellrich, *The Idea of the Book in the Middle Ages* (Ithaca: Cornell University Press, 1985), pp. 128–30.

31. He uses this phrase in a discussion of the postmodern. See also Jean-François Lyotard, *The Postmodern Condition: A Report on Knowledge*, trans. Geoff Bennington and Brian Massumi, Theory and History of Literature 10 (Minneapolis: University of Minnesota Press, 1984), p. 79.

32. Chenu, *Nature, Man, and Society*, pp. 319–20. On definitions of modernism in historical and typological terms, see Denis Donoghue, "The Promiscuous Cool of Postmodernism," *New York Times Book Review*, 22 June 1986.

33. Jacques Derrida, *Of Grammatology*, trans. Gayatri Chakravorty Spivak (Baltimore: Johns Hopkins University Press, 1976), pp. 15, 18.

throughout world literature, in the Middle Ages it was employed ubiquitously to indicate the two versions of God's writing—Scripture, the book of God's word, and nature, the book of his works.[34] The "idea of the book" posits the system of signification as a given; it provides the founding notion of the medieval disciplines and the model for the totalizing structures evidenced in the medieval ideas of the encyclopedia, mirror, and summa.[35]

The "idea of the book" pervades *The Name of the Rose*. It accounts for the novel's many implicit and explicit references to the actual books that articulated the medieval totalizing impulses and confidence in absolute meaning—the summae and encyclopedias, the bestiaries, lapidaries, and herbals that lend to the novel some of its most dense and decorative passages.[36] The "idea of the book" is also reflected in the abbot's discourse on the language of numbers and gems (444–48) and Adso's vision of the lush and ordered cosmos depicted on the tympanum of the abbey church, a vision inspired by John's Revelation, the book of Scripture that was itself said to be the totality of all others (40–45). The abbey's library evokes the medieval logocentric impulse, mirroring the structure of the world in its all-inclusive structure of knowledge.[37] The affiliation of the library with the medieval "idea of the book" is further reinforced, perhaps even inspired, by the medieval comparison of the totality of Scripture to the unity of a building (*aedificium*).[38]

34. The seminal source of commentary on the metaphorics of the book is Curtius, "The Book as Symbol," in *European Literature*, pp. 302–47. For the application of Derrida's ideas to medieval systems of meaning, see Gellrich, *Idea of the Book*, pp. 29–50.

35. Gellrich, *Idea of the Book*, p. 239; R. Howard Bloch, *Etymologies and Genealogies: A Literary Anthropology of the French Middle Ages* (Chicago: University of Chicago Press, 1983), pp. 19–20.

36. Eco discusses complementary medieval techniques of ordering the universe—the inventory, list, and catalog—in *AC*, 8–10.

37. For commentary on the chain of family resemblances associating the encyclopedia/library with the metaphorics of the book, see Eugenio Donato, "The Museum's Furnace: Notes toward a Contextual Reading of *Bouvard and Pécuchet*," in *Textual Strategies: Perspectives in Post-Structuralist Criticism*, ed. Josué V. Harari (Ithaca: Cornell University Press, 1979), pp. 213–38.

38. Hugh of St. Victor's description of the oppositions of the *aedificium* of sacred Scripture expresses the interpretive ideology I have identified with the hege-

The novel's most impressive evocation of the "idea of the book" is surely Adso's lyrical musing on the meaning of his lover, who becomes through his interpretation a "chapter in the great book of creation." But by the time he narrates his story, the confidence of his youthful allegorical reading yields to an aged monk's fear that his reading of nature's book was in fact the evasion of an excessive love. When his "joyous veneration" of creation fades, Adso remains in the more uncertain present in which he is unsure if the recording of his recollections is a "sinful succumbing to the terrestrial passion . . . a foolish attempt to elude the flow of time, and death" (281). He wonders if his relaxed contemplation of a divine text may be, not the highest form of reading, but rather the willful evasion of temporality. His question highlights the fragility of interpretations yielded by the signifying system that the idea of the book presents.

Like his reflections on the book of nature itself, Adso's interpretive dilemma as a whole corresponds to a central idea and procedure of recent theory: it juxtaposes stable systems of meaning to the idea of language constituted as a play of signifiers. Thus Derrida contrasts the "idea of the book" with "writing" (*écriture*); Barthes opposes "work" and "text"; Eco himself speaks of limited and unlimited semiosis.[39] These homologous oppositions distinguish a view of the linguistic sign as "sign-of" something—an origin, presence, or center—from a conception of language as a "system where the central signified, the original or transcendental signified, is never absolutely present outside a system of differences."[40] With their concern for the presence or

---

monic culture of the Middle Ages: "Divine Scripture is like a building. . . . The foundation is in the earth, and it does not always have smoothly fitted stones. The superstructure rises above the earth, and it demands a smoothly apportioned construction. Even so the Divine Page, in its literal sense, contains many things which seem both to be opposed to each other and, sometimes, to impart something which smacks of the absurd or the impossible. But the spiritual meaning admits no opposition; in it, many things can be different from one another, but none can be opposed" (*The Didascalicon of Hugh of St. Victor: A Medieval Guide to the Arts* 6.4, trans. Jerome Taylor [New York: Columbia University Press, 1961], p. 140).

39. See, for example, Derrida, *Of Grammatology*, pp. 6–26; Roland Barthes, "From Work to Text," in Harari, *Textual Strategies*, pp. 73–81; Eco, *TS, passim*.

40. The quotation is from Derrida's seminal essay, "Structure, Sign, and Play," in *The Languages of Criticism and the Sciences of Man: The Structuralist Con-*

absence of the sign's origin, these positions clarify the connection between language theory and philosophy: each is fundamentally occupied with ontological questions.

In recent years the act of locating that which the sign signifies in an independent structure of relations has frequently been identified with structuralism; the collapsing of the idea of the independent referent, its displacement by a sign constituted solely by its relation to other signs, is what is meant by deconstruction.[41] To be sure, these terms have accumulated an array of usages in the past two decades. Though they frequently, and productively, indicate methodologies of analysis, they more appropriately reflect philosophical positions, each construed in light of the other.

Briefly, deconstruction maintains that the history of Western metaphysics has been a series of substitutions that always postulate a stable center to which signs point, a fixed origin or metaphysical presence.[42] The grip of metaphysics on Western philosophy is evident in these names for putative fundamental categories—essence, existence, idea, being, substance, transcendentality, consciousness, man, God.[43] Even a secular philosophy such as structuralism assumes a model in which independent parts act in reciprocal relationship, and in which "meaning and signification are both transparent and already in place."[44] If

---

troversy, ed. Richard Macksey and Eugenio Donato (Baltimore: Johns Hopkins University Press, 1970), p. 249.

41. For a characterization of structuralism by its most famous proponent, see Claude Lévi-Strauss, *Tristes Tropiques,* trans. John Russell (New York: Atheneum, 1967), pp. 54–64, and *Structural Anthropology,* trans. Claire Jacobson and Brooke Grundfest Schoepf (Garden City, N.Y.: Doubleday, 1967), especially pp. 1–53. For a helpful overview of structuralism, see Edith Kurzweil, *The Age of Structuralism: Lévi-Strauss to Foucault* (New York: Columbia University Press, 1980), pp. 227–246. Derrida advances his critique of Lévi-Strauss in *Of Grammatology,* pp. 101–40.

42. Derrida, "Structure, Sign, and Play," p. 249; *Of Grammatology,* p. 3; and "The Supplement of Copula: Philosophy *before* Linguistics," in Harari, *Textual Strategies,* pp. 84–85.

43. See Derrida, "Structure, Sign, and Play," p. 249; and "Différance," in *Margins of Philosophy,* trans. Alan Bass (Chicago: University of Chicago Press, 1982), p. 6.

44. Robert Young, "Post-Structuralism: An Introduction," in *Untying the Text: A Post-Structuralist Reader* (Boston: Routledge and Kegan Paul, 1981), p. 3.

meaning is separable from the sign and prior to it, then a "science of presence" is inherent in the binary structure so favored by structuralism, and the sign's "longing for a center" generates a hierarchy of oppositions in which the intelligible is superior to the sensible, soul to body, and meaning to word.[45] In this sense modern linguistics can be seen as the final inheritor of Western philosophy, dispensing with overt grounding in religion but holding on to a metaphysics of presence that alone enables both linguistics and philosophy to make sense of themselves.[46]

This dialectic between transcendent and contingent polarities foregrounded in recent theory may furnish a "defining subtext" that can be found nearly everywhere.[47] Eco, for example, manifests his interest in this hermeneutic struggle throughout his criticism, primarily through an effort that succeeds in synthesizing the similarities underlying divergent theories on both sides of the debate. His *Theory of Semiotics*, for instance, has been called a "unified field theory of structuralism, post-structuralism, and semiology." In this work Eco follows Derrida's "critique of Lévi-Strauss's pursuit of a myth of origins," offering his notion of unlimited semiosis as a counter to the structuralist assertion of an independent and natural motivation for the sign.[48]

Eco engages the terms of the structuralism/deconstruction debate more pointedly in the earlier work from which the *Theory of Semiotics* was derived, *La struttura assente*.[49] Here Eco of-

45. Spivak, "Translator's Preface," *Of Grammatology*, pp. lviii, lxix.

46. Derrida states this position in various ways; see "Structure, Sign, and Play," p. 250, and "Supplement of Copula," pp. 82–83.

47. R. Howard Bloch, review of *Romanesque Signs: Early Medieval Narrative and Iconography*, by Stephen G. Nichols, Jr., *Speculum* 59 (1984): 423–24.

48. For this assessment of the *Theory of Semiotics*, see Michael McCanles, "Conventions of the Natural and the Naturalness of Conventions," *Diacritics* 7 (1977): 54–55; on the similarity of unlimited semiosis and Derridean deconstruction, see p. 62. McCanles thinks Eco fails in his effort to define a semiotics independent of an a priori natural code; see pp. 58–63.

49. As noted earlier, I have used the French edition of this work; my discussion here involves section D, especially pp. 321–87. See De Lauretis's account of section D of *La struttura assente* in *Umberto Eco*, pp. 29–33. On the whole, the *Theory of Semiotics*, as one would expect from the title, is less concerned with the philosophical resonance of its semiotic findings. The section of *La struttura assente* which I discuss here does not appear in the *Theory of Semiotics*.

fers a detailed critique of Lévi-Strauss's naturalizing of structure in the universal rules of the "human spirit." He advances the more Derridean position that denies an ontology to structure and sees the constitutive "difference" of the sign as the origin of all communication. In denying structure and affirming the continual play of language, this view calls into question the very idea of the code on which semiotics depends. Eco recognizes there is no easy reconciliation between these two tendencies, for this dialectic of presence and absence—this difference—is what enables all language (and all thought) (*SA* 373–84). But Eco is nonetheless committed to the social and historical bases through which people communicate. If there is no single structure or code, there are structures and codes that have a methodological usefulness, if not a metaphysical value. He maintains, in fact, that "structural models are only valuable if one *does not pose* the problem of the origin of communication" (*SA* 383). Structure is an "operative technique," a "fictive hypothesis"; "to the extent that it offers . . . useful tools for moving about the universe of social and historical relations," it satisfies, "at least in part, our endless desire and gives it limits with which the human animal is often content" (*SA* 387).

V

The Name of the Rose reveals its debt to recent theory in many individual details. The labyrinthine library realizes one of this theory's prominent metaphors for the decentered text. Adso's incessant querying of the relation of sign and thing, sign and sign, as well as his meditation on equivocal and univocal meanings and dissimilar similitudes, constitute an exploration of the *différance* that deconstructs the classic structure of the sign. At one point he even says: "Now I am tormented by the problem of difference itself" (196).[50] The novel's preoccupation with meta-

50. The English only suggests what the Italian "Ora sono afflitto dal problema stesso della differenze" (*Rosa* 199) more directly reveals. Adso invokes here the Derridean neologism "différance." Both the French verb "différer," from which the neologism was created, and the Italian "differire" carry the double meaning

phor and allegory also bears witness to this appropriation of the favored tropes of modern theory. Metaphor and allegory figure prominently in recent theory for the same reason that they have had a long and complex critical history: the nature and function of these tropes bear a crucial connection to the signifying capabilities of language and the structure of the sign.[51]

Eco clearly identifies the "medieval" aspects of modern theory when he compares the strategy of Lévi-Strauss's defense of universal structure to that of the medieval philologist who, "when faced with a discrepancy between diverse scriptural passages, or between these and the pages of an *auctoritas*, affirms that either he has not understood the text or that the discrepancy is an error of transcription. The single thing that is not admitted—by the foundations of a universal structural logic—is the 'real' possibility of a contradiction" (*SA* 348). More recently, Eco has invoked Chomsky, Jakobson, Lévi-Strauss, and Barthes to assert that "nothing is closer to the medieval intellectual game than structuralist logic."[52] Such identifications of contemporary theorists with "medieval" hermeneutic techniques adumbrate the

---

of "to differ" and "to defer." When Adso speaks about the "problem of difference" (e.g., 244–45), it is generally with the sense of what English communicates as "to be not identical, to be other or discernible." But even where the English "difference" limits Derrida's polysemic concept, the notion of *différance*'s "temporizing" is also present in the larger context of Adso's ruminations; see Derrida, "Différance," pp. 8–9.

51. For the discussion of metaphor in recent theory see Derrida, "Supplement of Copula," pp. 82–120, and "White Mythology: Metaphor in the Text of Philosophy," in *Margins of Philosophy*, pp. 209–71; Spivak, "Translator's Preface," *Of Grammatology*, pp. xxii–xxiv; Eco, *SP*, 87–129. On allegory, see Stephen Greenblatt, "Preface" to *Allegory and Representation*, English Institute Papers, n.s. 5 (Baltimore: Johns Hopkins University Press, 1981), pp. vii–xiii, and in that volume Joel Fineman, "The Structure of Allegorical Desire," pp. 26–60; Jesse Gellrich, "Deconstructing Allegory," *Genre* 18 (1985): 197–213; Maureen Quilligan, *The Language of Allegory: Defining the Genre* (Ithaca: Cornell University Press, 1979); Paul de Man, "The Rhetoric of Temporality," *Interpretation: Theory and Practice*, ed. Charles S. Singleton (Baltimore: Johns Hopkins University Press, 1969), pp. 173–209; J. Hillis Miller, "The Two Allegories," in *Allegory, Myth, and Symbol*, ed. Morton W. Bloomfield, Harvard English Studies 9 (Cambridge: Harvard University Press, 1981), pp. 355–70.

52. Eco, "Towards a New Middle Ages," in *On Signs*, ed. Marshall Blonsky (Baltimore: Johns Hopkins University Press, 1985), p. 500.

Rose's fullest appropriation of theoretical themes and procedures. By playing off the medievalism of an idea of centered structure and a metaphysics of the sign against the modernity of a deconstructionist view, the novel requires that we see its entire structure of binary relations in light of this theoretical opposition.

In the now classic formulation with which he concluded his early critique of Lévi-Strauss, Derrida spoke of the "two interpretations of interpretation."[53] In whatever theoretical terms we pose them—the "idea of the book" and *écriture*, structuralism and deconstruction—these code words for methods of interpretation provide the reference point for the hermeneutic and linguistic debate of *The Name of the Rose*. Adso steps in and out of an unstable interpretive realm in which his confidence in the sign's reference to a natural signified is regularly unmoored by his conflicting emotions. His semiotic education reaches its climax when he asks William: "'Then I can always and only speak of something that speaks to me of something else, and so on. But the final something, the true one—does that never exist?'"(317). William by no means offers a certain reply to Adso's question, but his commitment to an idea of the sign as signifying only other signs and his belief in the sign's usefulness, if not its "presence," attests to his sympathy with "difference." If Adso reads nature and experience as the writing in God's book, William is inclined to see them as *écriture*. Jorge's confidence in a transcendent signified and an order of truth makes him—by Derrida's and Eco's definition—a structuralist, while William reveals himself as a deconstructionist with his assertion that "'the only truth lies in learning to free ourselves from insane passion for the truth'" (491).

VI

The final episodes of *The Name of the Rose* illustrate how the novel medievalizes theory; how, in effect, theory is already

53. Derrida, "Structure, Sign, and Play," pp. 264–65.

medievalized. If the novel devotes much attention to underlining the distinction between William and Jorge, it also points up their necessary connection. Most simply, each achieves his desired end: William solves the mystery, and Jorge brings about the permanent suppression of Aristotle's book on comedy. In this conclusion Eco follows conventions of detective narrative, showing the complementarity of intellect and the mutual admiration of pursuer and pursued. Jorge accords to William this grudging praise: "'What a magnificent librarian you would have been'" (466); and Adso, witnessing their intellectual "high noon," sees in the two what they do not see in themselves:

> I realized, with a shudder, that at this moment these two men, arrayed in a mortal conflict, were admiring each other, as if each had acted only to win the other's applause. The thought crossed my mind that the artifices Berengar used to seduce Adelmo, and the simple and natural acts with which the girl had aroused my passion and my desire, were nothing compared with the cleverness and mad skill each used to conquer the other, nothing compared with the act of seduction going on before my eyes. (472–73)[54]

William is as ardent in his doubt as Jorge is in his belief. To paraphrase a statement he makes about Saint Francis (478), William is Jorge seen from the other direction. They are opposing terms of a binary relation which, like signs themselves, are only known through their difference. William's deconstruction can occur only through Jorge's metaphysics; the blind monk's medievalism enables the Franciscan's modernity.

The metaphysical complicity in which William and Jorge participate attends the novel's other opposing terms. Jorge even acknowledges the necessary relation between some of these terms when he tells William he does not fear the fervor of heretics because

> "we know them all and we know the root of their sins, which is also the root of our holiness. . . . Their presence is precious to us, it is in-

54. On William and Jorge as opponents in detective narrative and as representatives of opposing literary models, see Robert F. Yeager, "Fear of Writing, or Adso and the Poisoned Text," *SubStance* 14 (1985): 243–48.

scribed in the plan of God, because their sin prompts our virtue, their cursing encourages our hymn of praise, their undisciplined penance regulates our taste for sacrifice, their impiety makes our piety shine, just as the Prince of Darkness was necessary, with his rebellion and his desperation, to make the glory of God shine more radiantly, the beginning and end of all hope." (476)

Yet this structure of oppositions does not point in the direction of a narrowly conceived structuralist reading. Rather, it underscores the nature of *The Name of the Rose* as a novel that interrogates the concept of structure itself as it has been discussed and deconstructed by the linguists, philosophers, and theorists of our age as well as of the Middle Ages. In the novel this interrogation produces the same result as Eco's theoretical reflections on structure "pushed to extreme conclusions": it recovers "the deep core of all interrogation of the foundations of knowledge, of the definition of man's place in the world, of the very definition of the world" (*SA* 386).

The novel's pursuit of structure also follows the course that much recent theory considers inherent in the "violent hierarchy" of the sign's binary structure. Derrida, for instance, observes that one term of a philosophical opposition always "controls the other . . . [and] holds the superior position. To deconstruct the opposition is first to overthrow [*renverser*] the hierarchy."[55] The novel's structuring of its oppositions in political and polemical terms embodies this theoretical stance, as does its pervasive attention to reversal and transgression. One of the great achievements of *The Name of the Rose* is its seamless interweaving of the politics of binary structure with the ostensible personal, historical, and literary concerns of its several narratives.

The final exchange between William and Adso most fully realizes the novel's critique of the metaphysics and politics of binary structure. As the library goes up in flames, the Franciscan acknowledges that his success in detecting Jorge's culpability has required the very principles and assumptions of the philos-

55. Quoted from *Positions* (Paris, 1972), in Spivak, "Translator's Preface," *Of Grammatology*, pp. lxxvi–lxxvii.

ophy—the metaphysics—that Jorge stands for. He remarks that a false pattern led him to the mystery's truth: "'There was no plot . . . and I discovered it by mistake'" (491). When Adso counters this paradoxical statement with a catalog of the many "true" things his mentor had discovered while imagining an "erroneous order," William replies: "'The order that our mind imagines is like a net, or like a ladder, built to attain something. But afterward you must throw the ladder away, because you discover that, even if it was useful, it was meaningless. . . . The only truths that are useful are instruments to be thrown away'" (492). Just as Eco acknowledges structure as a useful but "fictive" hypothesis, so William deconstructs his logic while recognizing that it is only the idea of a center, of presence, that makes discourse possible.

The very possibility of discourse is in fact the subject of William and Adso's final conversation, as Adso articulates his difficulty in accepting William's assertion that "there is no order in the universe": "I dared, for the first and last time in my life, to express a theological conclusion: 'But how can a necessary being exist totally polluted with the possible? . . . Isn't affirming God's absolute omnipotence and His absolute freedom with regard to His own choices tantamount to demonstrating that God does not exist?'" Delivered without "any feeling in his feature," William's reply—"'How could a learned man go on communicating his learning if he answered yes to your question?'" —displays the same taste for the paradoxical that he has shown throughout the novel in similar moments of profoundly philosophical discussion. Adso interprets its double meaning: "'Do you mean . . . that there would be no possible and communicable learning any more if the very criterion of truth were lacking, or do you mean you could no longer communicate what you know because others would not allow you to?'"(493). Adso's question offers two possibilities: one philosophical, the other overtly political—both are dimensions of the signifying capabilities of language which the novel consistently explores in complementary terms. Adso's contemplation of a God of absolute omnipotence and absolute freedom may be tantamount to "demonstrating that God does not exist." But it is also tantamount to acknowledging a universe of infinite semiosis or a play (*jeu*) of language whose relation to the "criterion of truth" is inseparable from the grounds on which that truth is defined and communicated. Thus Adso also hints at the potential censorship that could obstruct the discourse of one who would communicate learning—if it were possible—without the standard of truth offered by the various myths of presence. With this question Adso thus reiterates the point toward which the novel's deconstruction of monastic love, Franciscan politics, and Aristotelian comedy has tended all along.

Adso's question also sets up his own approach to the hermeneutic battles played out throughout the novel—the subject of the next chapter. But his interpretive effort has a more immediate relevance to the novel's medievalizing of theory. It is highly appropriate that his assessment of the problems of meaning and interpretation epitomized by the mystery comes to rest in basic theological questions. His recasting of his epistemological concerns in this direction corresponds to deconstruction's commentary on the linguistic sign in terms of the "metaphysics" of its structure and its "transcendent" signified. As Derrida puts it: "The age of the sign is essentially theological."[56]

Adso's resort to theology thus clarifies the larger rationale for the medieval setting of *The Name of the Rose*. The Middle Ages provides a perfect arena in which to explore the terms and implications of recent theory, because it was a period in which theology and metaphysics not only informed the discussion of the sign but manifestly colored all aspects of life and all modes of discourse. If logocentrism is "the belief that the first and last things are the Logos, the Word, the Divine Mind, the infinite understanding of God, an infinitely creative subjectivity," then the Middle Ages represents the crowning moment of logocentric thought in the history of the West.[57]

We have seen how the central terms of the recent theoretical critique of the traditional conception of the sign are also preeminent in medieval theories of language. Ideas of presence, stable

56. Derrida, *Of Grammatology*, p. 14.
57. Spivak, "Translator's Preface," *Of Grammatology*, p. lxviii.

structure, and origin are central to the language theory of medieval commentators who expressed their confidence in absolute reference as well as of those who concentrated on the relations of signs to each other. These similarities between medieval and modern theory are a crucial component of the larger relationship of medieval and modern in *The Name of the Rose.* It is clear, then, that the novel's medievalism consists of much more than the simple recovery of a period in the history of Western culture. The "medieval" in the novel is in part a sign for a mode of interpretation, for a view of the structure of language, and for an attitude toward experience. In *The Name of the Rose* the Middle Ages is a grand metaphor—for the science of presence, for the metaphysical construction of the sign, for the very notion of structure. As the incarnation of all that is signaled by the concept of structure, the Middle Ages is a perfect trope for the allegory of theory in *The Name of the Rose.*

[6]

"Tolle et Lege"

The medievalism of *The Name of the Rose* raises important questions about the use and reading of history. If, as I have suggested, the novel employs the Middle Ages as a metaphor, the capacity of the medieval trope to signify something beyond the conventionally historical is nonetheless dependent upon the exacting authenticity of the novel's medieval historical details. Eco in fact has promoted a certain confusion about what is medieval, what modern, in his novel, claiming that "every now and then a critic or a reader writes to say that some character of mine declares things that are too modern, and in every one of these instances . . . I was actually quoting fourteenth-century texts. And there are other pages in which readers appreciated the exquisite medieval quality whereas I felt those pages are illegitimately modern" (*PS* 76–77). But the novel's modern embroiderings on the Middle Ages persuade us finally because they so logically manipulate historical events, ideas, and persons, a procedure that Eco himself explains: "If a character of mine, comparing two medieval ideas, produces a third, more modern, idea, he is doing exactly what culture did; and if nobody has ever written what he says, someone, however confusedly, should surely have begun to think it (perhaps without saying it, blocked by countless fears and by shame)" (*PS* 76). In these terms, to imagine Occamite William as a deconstructionist is not so very outrageous at all.

Such an identification, in fact, points to the way in which the novel's interplay of medieval and modern is most pronounced: its depiction of competing views of language and meaning that may be construed in both medieval and modern terms. Recently, the medieval discussion of signs has frequently been seen as "on a par with the strategies of signifying that have become commonplace in the wake of structuralism and especially in 'deconstruction.'" This view "sees medieval sign theory as inclining toward, if not prefiguring, modern concerns with arbitrary signs, deferred meaning, postponed ends and textual indeterminacy."[1] Though *The Name of the Rose* incorporates all of these contemporary concepts into its medieval story, Eco's intention is not simply to relocate deconstruction to the Middle Ages. The novel also explores in detail those medieval logocentric structures dedicated to stabilizing the sign in terms of origin and end.[2]

So the *Rose* does not simply call attention to precise correspondences between, or equate, medieval and modern views of the linguistic sign. Eco is far too sensitive to history to dispense with it in this way. When he jibes at theorists with no sense of history who foolishly believe that semiotics was invented "only yesterday by the sycophants of structuralism"; or when he cites Leibnitz's *De organo sive arte cognitandi* as evidence that some aspects of poststructuralist thought were "actually developed much earlier" (*SP* 23), he indicates that ideas of structure and deconstruction are also "mobile values."[3] His novel suggests

1. Jesse Gellrich, *The Idea of the Book in the Middle Ages* (Ithaca: Cornell University Press, 1985), pp. 21, 22. The point is not whether these modern deconstructors of the medieval sign are right or wrong but that medieval sign theory can be capacious enough to permit both a traditional and a poststructuralist reading. Augustine's theory is a case in point; cf. the views of Marcia Colish, *The Mirror of Language*, rev. ed. (1968; Lincoln: University of Nebraska Press, 1983), p. 41; and R. Howard Bloch, review of *Romanesque Signs: Early Medieval Narrative and Iconography*, by Stephen G. Nichols, Jr., *Speculum* 59 (1984): 424.

2. Gellrich, *Idea of the Book*, p. 21.

3. The first example is from the "Preface" to *Beato di Liebana*; quoted in Teresa De Lauretis, *Umberto Eco* (Florence: La nuova Italia, 1981), pp. 5–6.

that it is more appropriate, and more useful, to consider the hermeneutic options we have identified with medieval and modern as having always been and continuing to be available. Such a view may profitably result not only in the rehabilitation of the Middle Ages but in a new perspective on our own modernity.[4]

The more pressing question the novel poses, I believe, concerns the implications of the hermeneutic options themselves. If the novel allegorizes a debate between interpretive positions, it appears to come to a rather grim resolution. The novel's conclusion signals a dead end to the rival hermeneutics, as the premonitions of disaster in the series of random and premeditated deaths are fulfilled in the conflagration of library and abbey that the apocalyptic subtext has promised all along. The novel's sympathies may lie with William, but it also shows that even he is not immune to the fanatical fervor that characterizes Jorge's far less benign ideological position. Though generally directed toward good ends, William's devotion to knowledge and to books can also resemble the lust for which he excoriates Benno and Gui (395–96). His ill-timed attempt to seize the forbidden book from Jorge unwittingly implicates him in the destruction of the intellectual life he so deeply loves: he causes the tussle during which the fire in the library is ignited and very nearly brings about his own and Adso's death (481ff.). It is painfully ironic that William and Jorge's efforts to preserve knowledge, albeit in distinct ways, culminate in both a real and a symbolic deconstruction of culture and civilization in which there is nothing left to read.

Or, rather, almost nothing. For the *Rose* does not conclude with the apocalyptic conflagration of library and culture. Narrator Adso is, quite literally, left to pick up the pieces. Throughout the novel's hermeneutic debate, he is of a divided mind. His education by William requires that he shed the notions of linguistic and cosmic structure central to the monastic identity he seems to re-embrace at the end of the novel. Yet he punctuates his story with acknowledgments of the difference between his

4. Gellrich expresses a complementary view; see *Idea of the Book*, pp. 31, 253, 255.

past and his present thoughts. Finally, he offers his story itself, the uncertain product of an aged hand. This chapter looks at Adso's contribution to the dialogue of structure and decentering, medieval and modern, in *The Name of the Rose*. It considers how his narrative and the novel embody the theoretical issues they consistently address.

I

At the end of the novel Adso tells how, as a grown man, he returned to the ruins of the burned abbey, and, sifting through the rubble that was once the library, collected some fragments of parchment:

> Mine was a poor harvest, but I spent a whole day reaping it, as if from those disiecta membra of the library a message might reach me. . . . I collected every relic I could find . . . and afterward at Melk, I spent many, many hours trying to decipher those remains. . . . When I found, in time, other copies of those books, I studied them with love, as if destiny had left me this bequest, as if having identified the destroyed copy were a clear sign from heaven that said to me: Tolle et lege. At the end of my patient reconstruction, I had before me a kind of lesser library, a symbol of the greater, vanished one: a library made up of fragments, quotations, unfinished sentences, amputated stumps of books. The more I reread this list the more I am convinced it is the result of chance and contains no message. But these incomplete pages have accompanied me through all the life that has been left me to live since then; I have often consulted them like an oracle, and I have almost had the impression that what I have written on these pages, which you will now read, unknown reader, is only a cento, a figured hymn, an immense acrostic that says and repeats nothing but what those fragments have suggested to me, nor do I know whether thus far I have been speaking of them or they have spoken through my mouth. But whichever of the two possibilities may be correct, the more I repeat to myself the story that has emerged from them, the less I manage to understand whether in it there is a design that goes beyond the natural sequence of the events and the times that connect them. And it is a hard thing for this old monk, on the threshold of death, not to know whether the letter he has written contains some hidden meaning, or more than one, or many, or none at all. (500–501)

Adso reveals here the subtly shifting ideological contours of his doubt. At the same time that he wonders about the meaning of his story, he also intimates that his randomly gathered fragments may speak with the force of an oracle. He suggests that the narrative he has constructed from them shows the precise patterning of a "figured hymn" or an "immense acrostic," forms that medieval writers produced in the confidence that their words reflected a cosmic order.

Adso's juxtaposition of divine inspiration and pure chance as possible sources of his narrative once again raises the issue of two "interpretations of interpretation," his quandary over the origin and authority of his reconstructed text serving as a précis of what that story has been about. Affirming both centered, present meaning and the "play" of the text, Adso's remarks here clearly illustrate the difficulty of choosing "whichever of the two possibilities may be correct." His claim that his writing "is only a cento" is correct, nowhere more resonantly than in the passage just quoted. Adso's self-deprecating "only" diverts attention from what a cento inevitably communicates, what earlier in the novel he more respectfully recognized as the "imperceptible dialogue between one parchment and another, a living thing, a receptacle of powers not to be ruled by a human mind, a treasure of secrets emanated by many minds, surviving the death of those who had produced them or had been their conveyors" (286). Paradoxically, at the moment when he conveys his most modern sentiments—his uncertainty about whether his text "contains some hidden meaning, or more than one, or many, or none at all"—he is also most intertextually medieval.

Adso's gathered fragments here are a cento of quotations from some of the most influential texts of classical, medieval Latin, and vernacular culture. The "pages" ("fogli") consulted "like an oracle" allude to the leaves of the *Aeneid*'s Cumaean Sibyl on which were written prophecies (in Virgil's words "notas et nomina"—signs and names; 3.441–52). They presumably contained Apollo's truth only when arranged as the Sibyl ordered them; once scattered by the wind their message was irrevocably lost. The origin and fate of the sibylline leaves signal an important theme that emerges from the intertextuality of Adso's final words: the gathering or dispersion of textual fragments and the communication of a message that may be inspired or random.

The collocation of sibylline leaves and divine message evoked by Adso's gathering of the fragments is also reminiscent of *Paradiso* 33. Dante makes the windblown leaves a metaphor for the fragility of his vision of God, a vision that in the concluding lines of the *Comedy* he images as a book: "In its depth I saw ingathered, bound by love in one single volume, that which is dispersed in leaves throughout the universe" (ll. 85–87).[5] Unlike Adso's fragmentary text, Dante's heavenly gathering of dispersed leaves constitutes a single illuminated image of totality, fusion, and presence (ll. 88–105). But Dante knows that his language inevitably falls short of communicating this totality and presence; the perfection of the celestial book makes him acutely aware of the mortal, human limitations of his own text (ll. 106–8; ll. 121–23).[6]

The sense of an exalted spiritual vision that the Dantesque allusion lends to Adso's concluding meditation is matched by the far more humble but no less spiritual resonances of another text called to mind by his reverent scavenging among the remains of the library. Thomas of Celano's *First Life of St. Francis* relates that whenever the saint

5. *Divine Comedy: Paradiso*, ed. Charles S. Singleton (Princeton: Princeton University Press, 1975), pt. 1, pp. 376–77: "Nel suo profondo vidi che s'interna, / legato con amore in un volume, / cio che per l'universo si squaderna." Dante's use of the metaphorics of the book here and elsewhere in the *Comedy* is discussed by Ernst Curtius, *European Literature and the Latin Middle Ages*, trans. Willard Trask (1953; New York: Harper and Row, 1963), pp. 326–32. The relation of the sibylline and book imagery of *Paradiso* 33 to medieval codicology, the circulation of the *Comedy*, and Dante's intentions for the work are discussed by John Ahern, "Binding the Book: Hermeneutics and Manuscript Production in *Paradiso* 33," *PMLA* 97 (1982): 800–809 . The allusion to one of Dante's most famous uses of the metaphorics of the book at the end of the *Rose* is particularly striking, given the novel's invocation of *Inferno* 5 at its midpoint; see Chapter 2. My argument for a Dantesque allusion in this scene is supported by the location of Dante's vision of bound fragments of the celestial book—it is prepared for by his vision of the mystic rose of *Paradiso* 30–32.

6. See Gellrich's discussion of *Paradiso* 33 in *Idea of the Book*, pp. 157–66; and that of Susan Noakes, "The Double Misreading of Paolo and Francesca," *Philological Quarterly* 62 (1983): 235.

would find anything written, whether about God or about man, along the way, or in a house, or on the floor, he would pick it up with the greatest reverence and put it in a sacred or decent place, so that the name of the Lord would not remain there or anything else pertaining to it. One day when he was asked by a certain brother why he so diligently picked up writings even of pagans or writings in which there was no mention of the name of the Lord, he replied: "Son, because the letters are there out of which the most glorious name of the Lord God could be put together."[7]

Celano emphasizes Francis's linguistic consciousness—his reverence for the words of Scripture, indeed all language, as sacraments, "physical objects, precious elements of ink and parchment . . . consecrated by the articulation of their divine author."[8] Francis's gathering of fragments of writing illustrates a view of the word as divine presence which offers a striking counterpoint to Benedictine Adso's skepticism regarding the meaning of his own text.

The allusion to Celano is hardly out of place in a work that so thoroughly explores the implications of Franciscan ideology, particularly for linguistic and textual matters. Images of textual fragmentation abound in medieval literature by and about Franciscans. In *Paradiso* 12 Dante has Bonaventure speak of his order as a book whose individual leaves are the friars: "Nevertheless, I say, he who should search our volume leaf by leaf might still find a page where he would read, 'I am as I always was'" (ll. 121–23).[9] Quoting John 6:12, Bonaventure introduces his *Life of St. Francis*: "This, then, is my principal reason for undertaking this task, that I may *gather together* the accounts of his virtues, his actions and his words—like so many *fragments*, partly forgotten and partly scattered—although I cannot accomplish this fully, *so that they may not be lost* . . . when those who lived

7. Thomas of Celano, *St. Francis of Assisi*, trans. Placid Hermann O.F.M. (Chicago: Franciscan Herald Press, 1962), *First Life*, p. 73.

8. John Fleming, *An Introduction to the Franciscan Literature of the Middle Ages* (Chicago: Franciscan Herald Press, 1977), p. 23, and see also pp. 22–27.

9. "Ben dico, chi cercasse a foglio a foglio / nostro volume, ancor troveria carta / u'leggerebbe 'I' mi son quel chi'i' soglio'" (*Paradiso*, pt. 1, pp. 136–37).

with this servant of God die."[10] Particularly in William's absence, these instances of Franciscan fragment-gathering identify Adso's textual activity—and his text—as an inheritance of the tradition of the saint of Assisi.

Adso is identified with Francis in yet another way. His preoccupation with his text as chance fragments or oracular message is reminiscent of Francis's practice of *sortes*, "divination through random consultation of a scriptural passage," which attested to his belief in the "imperative power of the sacred text as a goad to immediate and radical action."[11] The resemblance between Adso's musings and the chance consultation of Scripture is even more directly invoked by his allusion to one of the most famous medieval accounts of conversion. In the *Confessions* (8.12), Augustine tells how he heard a child's voice chanting: "Tolle et lege" (Take up and read): "I interpreted this solely as a command given to me by God to open the book and read the first chapter I should come upon. For I had heard how Anthony had been admonished by a reading from the Gospel at which he chanced to be present, as if the words were addressed to him: 'Go, sell what you have, and give to the poor, and you shall have treasures in heaven . . .' and that by such portent he was immediately converted to you."[12]

Adso's interpretation of his randomly preserved textual fragments as "a clear sign from heaven that said to me: Tolle et lege" expresses his desire for a divine authorizing of their meaning. His clear association of his own bits of text with Augus-

10. *Bonaventure: The Soul's Journey into God, the Tree of Life, The Life of St. Francis*, trans. Ewert Cousins (New York: Paulist Press, 1978), pp. 182–83; italics in original. Bonaventure's quotation from Scripture, as well as his general technique of compiling his *Life* from earlier versions, simply reflects the authority and manner by which saints' lives were written, a process that made them centos; on the writing of saints' lives, see Fleming, *Franciscan Literature*, p. 37.

11. Fleming, *Franciscan Literature*, p. 25. For an example of Francis's practice of *sortes*, see Bonaventure's *Life*, pp. 200–201.

12. *The Confessions of St. Augustine*, trans. John Ryan (Garden City, N.Y.: Doubleday, 1960), p. 202. On the "tolle et lege" *topos* in classical and early Christian writing, see Pierre Courcelle, *Les Confessions de saint Augustine dans la tradition littéraire: Antécédents et postérité* (Paris: Etudes Augustiniennes, 1963), pp. 155–63.

tine's certainty about the import of a chance message takes on even greater significance in light of both the outcome of Augustine's *sortes* and the larger linguistic context in which it occurs. When Augustine finally heeds the command to "take and read," the text he reads is "'Not in rioting and drunkenness, not in chambering and impurities, not in strife and envying; but put you on the Lord Jesus Christ, and make not provision for the flesh in its concupiscences'" (Romans 13:13–14). It is a text that enables him to resolve the problem of sensuality which had stood in the way of his conversion (8.11), and this resolution obviates the need to read further, because "all the dark shadows of doubt fled away." Augustine's struggle with concupiscence, dispelled by a simple act of reading, recalls Adso's experience of carnal desire, though Adso arrives at no clear acceptance of the authority and finality of scriptural language, no permanent dissolution of his doubt, no comforting end to reading.[13] Yet Adso's allusion to the Augustine who "took and read" also directs attention to his story's more general kinship with the *Confessions* as an autobiography that is also a philosophy of language. Like Augustine's work, Adso's narrative "links his changing states of self-awareness and his comprehension of the outside world" to a linguistic epistemology.[14] In his reflections on language Adso shares with Augustine a final reference point in the relation of man and God. Like Augustine, too, he is drawn to the possibility of a redeemed rhetoric, yet he falls far short of embracing it because of the "shadow that the great darkness" casts on an aging world.[15]

Adso's allusion to Augustine's "tolle et lege" underscores both the preeminent theme and the intertextuality of the novel's final pages. For the injunction to "take and read" carries with it the idea that such directed reading need only be accomplished in order for the sought-after meaning to reveal itself. The meaning implicit in all of Adso's touchstones in the medi-

13. See Walter E. Stephens, "Ec[h]o in Fabula," *Diacritics* 13 (1983): 62.

14. Colish, *Mirror of Language*, p. 17.

15. On Augustine's conception of a redeemed rhetoric as formulated in the *Confessions*, see Colish, *Mirror of Language*, pp. 17–38; and Gellrich, *Idea of the Book*, pp. 116–22.

eval conversation about language is clear. The sibylline leaves, the pages of Dante's universe, Francis's textual fragments, and Augustine's Scripture all establish a common connection between actual or metaphoric texts and the experience of divinity. Classical prophecy, Christian visionary poetry, biography and autobiography thus provide Adso's meditation on his cento with a subtext that bespeaks the possibility that signs give access to a transcendent signified. The preoccupation of these texts with change, fragmentation, and dispersion only serves as a counterpoint, a human perspective on the totality and order of the signified that they all affirm.

Yet the force of Adso's musings runs in another direction, one that abandons "work" and "image" in favor of the mystic's rapture: "I shall soon enter this broad desert, perfectly level and boundless, where the truly pious heart succumbs in bliss. I shall sink into the divine shadow, in a dumb silence and an ineffable union, and in this sinking all equality and all inequality shall be lost, and in that abyss my spirit will lose itself, and will not know the equal or the unequal, or anything else: and all differences will be forgotten" (501). This hasty retreat from difference reiterates the terms by which the novel's discussion of language has proceeded all along. But Adso's desire for presence in a solitude and silence without signs by no means resolves the novel's treatment of problems of reading and meaning, any more than the allusions to medieval affirmations of a transcendent signified should be seen as something other than evidence of the inevitable "whispering of books among themselves." The mode of discourse that Adso chooses here to describe his wish for an end to discourse is perfectly consonant with the novel's monastic setting and its narrator's vocation; it is, in fact, its highest realization.[16]

16. The monastic propriety of the idiom and inclination of Adso's final musings has a bizarre and amusing counterpart in Jorge's eating of the poisoned book. It is obviously an allusion to Revelation 10:9–11, in which John eats the book; see Bernard McGinn, *The Calabrian Abbot: Joachim of Fiore in the History of Western Thought* (New York: Macmillan, 1985), chap. 5, "'Take the Book and Eat It': Joachim and the Apocalypse," pp. 145–60. Jorge's eating also illustrates the monastic recommendation to "chew" the reading of the scriptural

Despite monastic emphasis on the love of learning, the desire for God always took precedence. Monastic discipline sought a mystical communication with the ineffable, a truth outside language that was nevertheless the ultimate contact with the signified.[17] For the monastic writer, literature—indeed all uses of language—can only be secondary, offering an illustration of "the impotence of our condition . . . the inadequacy of what we say to represent what gives us our life."[18] In a sense, here was the ultimate dilemma for medieval Christian writers: they had been given the "acutely paradoxical . . . mission" of having to express the inexpressible in the only available language, one that is forever inadequate.[19]

II

The conclusion of *The Name of the Rose* thus articulates the same oppositions that structure its several narratives and mark its kinship with contemporary theory. For despite Adso's asserted preference for a silence beyond difference, his prolonged meditation on signs, seen as a whole, moves away from ideas of presence and centered structure toward the modern idea of the "text" that defers and plays with meaning through a metonymic logic in which "the activity of associations, contiguities, and cross-references coincides with a liberation of symbolic ener-

---

text, one prominent version of the *topos* of the read/eaten word, which "saturates the western discourse of literacy"; for this observation I am grateful to Mark Amsler, "Augustine's Scene of Reading" (paper delivered at the Twenty-first Annual Conference on Medieval Studies, Western Michigan University, 1986). See also Jean Leclercq's comments on monastic *ruminatio* in *The Love of Learning and the Desire for God*, trans. Catharine Misrahi (1961; New York: Fordham University Press, 1974), pp. 89–90.

17. Michael McCanles argues that Eco's own theory betrays an impulse similar to the one Adso expresses here. He compares Eco's position in the *Theory of Semiotics* to the negative theologies of Meister Eckhart and Nicholas of Cusa, according to which human words are able to reflect the divine only in propositions in which these words are negated; see "Conventions of the Natural and the Naturalness of Conventions," *Diacritics* 7 (1977): 62–63.

18. Leclercq, *Love of Learning*, p. 328.

19. Colish, *Mirror of Language*, p. 2.

gies."[20] Adso painfully experiences the deferral of the signified at every important juncture in the novel, nowhere more poignantly than when he says: "I leave this manuscript, I do not know for whom; I no longer know what it is about" (502). The experience of reading the novel is also preeminently one of deferral, for the metonymic logic of its "association, contiguities, and cross-references" directs attention not to the meaning of the work but to the very processes by which meanings are constituted.

The novel's solicitation of contemporary notions of textuality is epitomized in the Latin hexameter that also provides its title: "stat rosa pristina nomine, nomina nuda tenemus" ("The rose remains in name alone; we hold the naked names"). Eco has identified the source of the hexameter in the twelfth-century *De contemptu mundi* by the Benedictine Bernard of Morlay, noting the verse appears in the context of the *ubi sunt* theme: "But to the usual topos (the great of yesteryear, the once-famous cities, the lovely princesses: everything disappears into the void), Bernard adds that all these departed things leave (only, at least) pure names behind them" (*PS* 1).[21] He has also acknowledged that interpretations of the novel's title might well consider the frequent use of "rose" in medieval and modern discussions of the function of the linguistic sign, and he has reviewed the cultural and literary multivocality of the "rose" (*PS* 1, 3; *SP* 214). But such efforts to explain the novel's title and Latin hexameter come up short, not, Eco would maintain, because of his trickster-like inclinations, but because of the nature of language and reading: "The title rightly disoriented the reader, who was unable to choose just one interpretation; and even if he were to catch the possible nominalist readings of the concluding verse,

20. Roland Barthes, "From Work to Text," in *Textual Strategies: Perspectives in Post-Structuralist Criticism*, ed. Josué V. Harari (Ithaca: Cornell University Press, 1979), p. 76.

21. The poem appears in Thomas Wright, *Anglo-Latin Satirical Poets and Epigrammatists*, Rolls Series 59 (London, 1872), 2:3–102. An English translation by H. Preble, "The Scorn of the World," appeared in *American Journal of Theology* 10 (1906): 72–101, 286–308, 496–516. On the *De contemptu*, see John Boswell, *Christianity, Social Tolerance, and Homosexuality* (Chicago: University of Chicago Press, 1980), p. 277.

he would come to them only at the end, having previously made God only knows what other choices. A title must muddle the reader's ideas, not regiment them" (*PS* 3).

The ambiguous Latin hexameter itself implies this potential for disorienting the reader. Eco assesses Bernard of Morlay's remarks on "the name of the rose": "for the Benedictine what remains of the real (?) rose (if any) is precisely this evanescent, powerful, fascinating, magical name" (*PS* 83). Yet for all its implicit acknowledgment of an "idea of presence" that names may only signify, the verse's assertion that only names remain is at least remotely reminiscent of the Derridean position that "il n'y a pas de hors-texte." Thus the play of the novel's text extends even to its authoritative final sentence.

Yet I do not think that Eco means to suggest that the only meaning available to writer Adso and his readers is an unbounded textuality, an endless and undifferentiated play of text that, in communicating everything, ultimately communicates no more than the mystic's "ineffable union" in which "all equality and all inequality shall be lost." Adso may move about in a realm of interpretive confusion, asserting one mode, then undoing it the next moment, giving himself over to semiotic negation in a passage that also evokes Saint Francis's belief in the sacredness of even the most humble and fragmentary signs.[22] But his words and those he attributes to others are always situated, always bounded by ideological imperatives, by the declared aims of his narrative, by his implied addressee, and by the work in which they are presented.

The novel's final Latin quotation serves as an obvious instance of this situating of Adso's discourse. Whatever its ambivalence regarding distinct views of the linguistic sign, "stat rosa pristina nomine" is also a specific utterance within Adso's story that partakes of the particular monastic authority of his narrative. Borrowed from a Benedictine's world-weary reflections on a dying era, the verse speaks in the language and from the viewpoint of the Benedictine milieu in which an aging Adso feels comfortable. The quotation's Latinity allies it with what was

22. Cf. Stephens, "Ec[h]o in Fabula," p. 63.

identified earlier as the hegemonic side of medieval culture, which, significantly, is here accorded the novel's final word. The medieval "authorizing" of the verse from within Adso's narrative even has a counterpart in the contemporary reception of that narrative as a whole. To an audience for whom Bernard of Morlay's Latin is not easily accessible (and the novel does not translate it in the manner in which it sometimes paraphrases other Latin quotations), "stat rosa pristina nomine" is a code for elitist, high-brow culture. Probably more than anything else in the novel, the hexameter has fostered the perception that the *Rose* "means" something arcane and mysterious, after the fashion of both the Middle Ages and the obscure discourse of professors of semiotics.

The concluding paragraphs of Adso's narrative situate the potential for an endless textuality in yet another and different way. Adso's mystic reverie and his multivalent musings on his cento yield to the sensations of the material human body: "It is cold in the scriptorium, my thumb aches" (502). Though this simple acknowledgment of corporeality is itself verbal, Adso's turn from interest in the sign to preoccupation with the body is the last of a series of such gestures in his narrative. The novel's individual stories of love, politics, and laughter all enact this turn, as Adso's reflections on the sign's *différance* are displaced, respectively, by the sheer physicality of impassioned sexuality, the diseased, misshapen, tortured body of poverty and heresy, and the life-giving and death-ridden material body of human existence itself. In each instance it is Adso's experience of the young peasant girl—as his lover, as Gui's captured heretic, as the subject of his dream of the *Coena*—that elicits this consciousness of the body. As we have seen, the girl is appropriated in the novel by the various discourses that predominate in each of its distinct stories. As such, she provides an image of the sign's multivalence, of textuality itself. But through her Adso also comes to feel "the weight of the body of death," "the mortal human body, its sufferings and corruption" (249, 434), a form of knowledge that he seems to distinguish from all his verbal appropriations of her. This form of knowing is what he implies when, realizing she cannot escape being burned as a heretic, he laments that he "was not even allowed—as they did in the romances of chivalry I had read with my companions at Melk—to lament and call out the beloved's name. This was the only earthly love of my life, and I could not, then or ever after, call that love by name" (407). Despite his ignorance of "il nome dell'amata" (*Rosa* 409), his loss, his fear, and his pain are of and for something "earthly" that he nonetheless knows. If Adso's beloved, the unnamed "rose," is an image of textuality, her identification with materiality may also be seen as an acknowledgment, not of a transcendent signified, but of the body—from the experience of which names are constituted. It is the only form of presence available to us.[23]

Adso's grounding of textuality in the experience of the body at the penultimate moment of his narrative is analogous to the strategy of the entire novel. Though the *Rose* seems to be quite deliberately designed as an image of the deconstructionist's text, the "play" of this text is bounded by the historical object it represents. For all of its enactment of a metonymic textual logic marked by "associations, contiguities, and cross-references," the novel—largely through its meticulously detailed reconstruction of a material culture—also communicates the fact that there was a Middle Ages. Whatever the theoretical resonance of its medieval setting, the novel pays a loving tribute to a rich and fascinating historical era. The features of the *Rose* which have delighted readers well-versed in the Middle Ages—the plan of the abbey and its church, the decoration of the apocalyptic tympanum, the arrangement of the scriptorium, the contents of its books and the illuminations on their pages, the food, herbs, diseases, and instruments, especially William's precious spectacles—all attest to what William might describe as "the truth of the individual." They are the purest form of history. The novel's demonstrative textuality and the linguistic preoccupations of Adso's own story may make an innocent historicism impossible,

23. On the physical and textual meaning of the girl in the novel, see Teresa De Lauretis, who focuses on the importance of gender as the epitome of the problem of difference ("Gaudy Rose: Eco and Narcissism," *SubStance* 14 [1985]: 22–24, 26–27). De Lauretis considers the novel's principal oppositions in terms similar to those advanced here; see, for example, p. 25.

but *The Name of the Rose* does not retreat from the idea that the Middle Ages offers an object for study, provided we acknowledge that it is only in our individually constituted, ideologically determined versions of it that that object is available at all. History is real, even if historical questions are also hermeneutic questions.

III

In one of Adso and William's early discussions of heresy, Adso struggles to elicit from his master not only information but an unambiguous opinion. "'But who was right, who is wrong, who was wrong?'" he asks. When William provides the unsatisfying reply that "'They were all right in their way, and all were mistaken,'" Adso cannot contain himself: "'And you . . . why don't you take a position, why won't you tell me where the truth is?'" (204–5). The reader who has borne with the novel's protracted discussion of the rival hermeneutics might well echo Adso's questions, even while anticipating that he will receive no simple answer. If the novel does finally speak on behalf of a particular view of meaning, it is not of the either/or variety that Adso hopes to obtain. Rather, it is more of the both/and sort to which William is frequently inclined. Ultimately, the novel endorses an approach to interpretation that exposes the limitations of its own binary structures.

As Adso's meditation on his fragmentary text suggests, the novel's sympathy for the openness of textuality is bounded by the ideology of specific discourses, the presence of the corporeal body, and the existence of material and historical culture. But by insisting on these contexts of language, the novel does not simply effect a mediation between the prescriptive and playful versions of signification we have thus far considered in terms of such metaphoric oppositions as presence and absence, structure and deconstruction, medieval and modern. Rather, these ways of situating the discourses in the novel and the novel as discourse bring up a third, and different, position that is most effectively conveyed in the idea of the dialogic.

A concept originally advanced in twentieth-century linguistics to illustrate the locutionary situation of a particular kind of discourse, dialogism has been favored by Slavic linguists and theorists. It enjoys its current fashion primarily through the works of Mikhail Bakhtin. In recent theory the dialogic has become much more than a linguistic term; it is offered as a description of language itself. Dialogism presents an alternative to the hermeneutic rivals that have dominated language theory in this century. In contrast to both the personalist, stable view of centered meaning and the deconstructionist view that locates meaning in the structure of difference, dialogism "holds that meaning is rooted in the social, but the social conceived in a particular way." Meaning is possible "but only *indirectly* . . . in words I take and give back to the community according to the protocols it establishes. My voice can mean, but only with others: at times in chorus, but at the best of times in a dialogue."[24]

Dialogism is a useful concept for describing how language and discourse work. It can be understood in several senses: it describes "the natural state of being of language as such and a valorized category of certain discourses."[25] The dialogic nature of language involves a group of relationships—of the word to its addressee, to other discourses, to linguistic change, to its speaker. Any discourse participates simultaneously in all these relationships; it is always intended, always "ideologically saturated."[26] Discourse is always marked by the speaker whose appropriations of language are marked by the speaker's particular social and historical moment and specific situation. Yet speak-

24. Michael Holquist, "The Politics of Representation," in *Allegory and Representation*, ed. Stephen Greenblatt, English Institute Papers, n.s. 5 (Baltimore: Johns Hopkins University Press, 1981), pp. 164–65; see also pp. 166–67. For a challenge to this reading of dialogism, see Denis Donoghue, "Reading Bakhtin," *Raritan* 5 (1985): 107–19, a discussion of the implications for language theory and literary criticism of Bakhtin's use of this series of homologous oppositions (monologic/dialogic, centripetal/centrifugal, epic/novel, myth/heteroglossia).

25. Ken Hirschkop, "A Response to the Forum on Mikhail Bakhtin," *Critical Inquiry* 11 (1985): 674.

26. Mikhail Bakhtin, *The Dialogic Imagination: Four Essays*, ed. Michael Holquist, trans. Caryl Emerson and Michael Holquist (Austin: University of Texas Press, 1981), p. 271.

ers are themselves created through language; in linguistic situations they both act and are acted upon:

> There are no "neutral" words and forms—words and forms that can belong to "no one"; language has been completely taken over, shot through with intentions and accents. For any individual consciousness living in it, language is not an abstract system of normative forms but rather a concrete heteroglot conception of the world. All words have the "taste" of a profession, a genre, a tendency, a party, a particular work, a particular person, a generation, an age group, the day and hour. Each word tastes of the context and contexts in which it has lived its socially charged life; all words and forms are populated by intentions.[27]

The Name of the Rose is dialogic in the two senses of the term previously mentioned: it represents language as a dialogic phenomenon, and it realizes itself as a dialogic discourse. When, to communicate his erotic joy, Adso turns to "other inner words, heard in another time and in other places, spoken certainly for other ends," he illustrates the dialogism of his own utterance (244). The novel's concern for situating specific political discourses, its sense of the "ideological saturation" of words such as "heresy" and "holiness," its preoccupation with the individual intentions of a speaker such as Gui, its concern for the institutions that authorize such utterance—these are examples of the dialogic relationships in which all discourse inevitably participates. The Babel of languages by, or perhaps in spite of, which Salvatore communicates is an image of dialogic heteroglossia itself. The novel's consciousness of Adso's monastic idiom, its casting of the mystery plot in terms of questions of censorship, even its appropriations of the silence of holy men and poor peasant girls all contribute to its representation of the fundamentally dialogic nature of language. Its individual narratives are "saturated" with each other, the stories of love, heresy, and laughter speaking in a dialogic chorus. From the dialogic field of discursive relationships, the novel offers its extended meditation on the structure of the linguistic sign and its mode of signifying,

27. Ibid., p. 293.

and its consideration of the uses, intentions, and origins of utterance. Its interest in the generation of meaning is always tied to these questions: who speaks? to whom? under what conditions?

These dialogic features of language furnish the novel's prominent themes; they also contribute to its self-consciousness as an instance of discourse. A brilliant concatenation of medieval discourses, the *Rose* also epitomizes its own dialogic relation to the several discourses it exemplifies: detective fiction, historical novel, best-seller, novel of ideas. The most noteworthy of these dialogic relationships is that which the novel bears to the discourse of recent theory. We have already observed the novel's dialogue with theoretical metaphors: the metaphor of the text as labyrinth is literalized in the library's floor plan; the concept of marginality informs the description of an illuminated manuscript page; deconstruction's critique of the transcendent signified is incarnated in a portrait of an overtly "metaphysical" era. Even the poisonous secret of the murders has a theoretical resonance. When the herbalist Severinus notes that the Greeks used the word "pharmacon" for both poison and medicine (108), he calls to mind Derrida's explication of the word *pharmakon* as one of the "privileged words" that indicate the "double, contradictory, undecidable value" of the sign.[28] And the metaphors of recent textual theory are discernible even in the introduction to the novel, as the speaker describes his longing for the lost text and for an idea of the author as a stable originary entity.[29]

The novel's dialogue with theoretical discourse is also realized in the narrative's overarching appropriation of the theoretical trope of desire. "Desire" is the word used by deconstruction and

28. *Dissemination*, trans. Barbara Johnson (Chicago: University of Chicago Press, 1981), p. 221. See Johnson's comment (p. xxiv) on the importance of the translation of *pharmakon* to Derrida's reading of Plato's *Phaedrus*.

29. See, for example, Jerome McGann, *A Critique of Modern Textual Criticism* (Chicago: University of Chicago Press, 1983). Stephens also points out the introduction's allusion to textual theory through its mention of Mabillon, the founder of modern textual criticism, and the "Abbaye de la Source"; see "Ec[h]o in Fabula," pp. 63–64. De Lauretis comments on the novel's thematizing of critical terminology ("Gaudy Rose," p. 21).

psychoanalysis to indicate the movement by which meaning emerges from difference, deferral, and absence. The trope of desire epitomizes Adso's experience as lover and as reader of texts: in both roles he experiences loss and undergoes a linguistic crisis, seeking the presence of his beloved and of meaning. His eroticized reading literalizes the *jouissance* or bliss of the text "that imposes a state of loss, the text that discomforts . . . unsettles the reader's historical, cultural, psychological assumptions, the consistency of his tastes, values, memories, [and] brings to a crisis his relation with language."[30]

As such, Adso's situation is strikingly congruent with that of the autobiographical voice that introduces the "manuscript" of the novel.[31] The speaker (who appears to be male) tells how he translated a French version of Adso's work into large notebooks while traveling up the Danube with his "beloved." But the French book disappears when the beloved walks off with it "one tragic night" outside Salzburg: "And so I was left with a number of manuscript notebooks in my hand, and a great emptiness in my heart" (2). The dialogue with the circumstances of Adso's narrative goes further: each narrator constructs a story from "fragments"—"I had only my notes left," says the voice (3). Each is riddled with doubt. The beginning and ending of the novel thus proclaim it as a testament of desire: absence of the beloved and of an authorized, complete text occasion the desire that constructs Adso's narrative and *The Name of the Rose*.

The Name of the Rose achieves a dialogic relationship with theory that corresponds to Bakhtin's notion of the plural-voiced, hybrid, parodic text that crosses languages and discourses and recognizes their boundaries as "deliberately flexible and ambigu-

30. Roland Barthes, *The Pleasure of the Text*, trans. Richard Miller (New York: Hill and Wang, 1975), p. 14.

31. The voice is not identified in any way in the English version of the novel, though the inclusion of the date "January 5, 1980" makes it contemporary and hints at a connection with the "author." The Italian version of the novel establishes a connection with Eco more provocatively by naming one of his own works: the voice of the introduction mentions Temesvar's "On the Use of Mirrors in the Game of Chess" as a work "that I have already had occasion to cite (at second hand) in my *Apocalittici e integrati*" (*Rosa* 13). On the connection between the narrator and Adso, see De Lauretis, "Gaudy Rose," pp. 22–23.

ous."[32] To be sure, the novel's representation of theoretical discourse could be construed in light of other theoretical models as well. Eco's own notions of interacting codes, intertextuality, and unlimited semiosis correspond in many instances to dialogic conceptions of language and discourse. Indeed, it might be said that the term "dialogic" points toward the kind of discourse that is possible in the semiotic universe that Eco describes. The dialogue with theoretical discourse in *The Name of the Rose* deliberately engages a congeries of theories whose common ground is their foundation in notions of the structure and function of the sign. Eco's novel displays the same synthetic impulses as does his theory.

The Name of the Rose is a story about interpretation told from a perspective that puts into play various interpretive ideologies, a story whose medieval setting is perfectly congenial to, even encouraging of, such an endeavor.[33] The novel works finally not to advance the particulars of any one theory but to make evident the strategies and consequences of theoretical positions generally, to call attention to those acts that, in more normative kinds of critical discourse, theorists and critics—Eco among them—say we perform all the time, whenever we are motivated to "take and read."[34]

IV

This account of the *Rose*'s dialogue with contemporary theory leads us finally to assess the novel's status as discourse. Such an assessment has many elements to consider, for *The Name of the Rose* is a hybrid form of discourse: it is an international

32. Bakhtin, *Dialogic Imagination*, p. 308.

33. Not surprisingly, the novel's dialogic preoccupations further mark its kinship with the medieval past it so compellingly renders; see Paul Zumthor, *Speaking of the Middle Ages*, trans. Sarah White (Lincoln: University of Nebraska Press, 1986), p. 90; and Umberto Eco, "Towards a New Middle Ages," in *On Signs*, ed. Marshall Blonsky (Baltimore: Johns Hopkins University Press, 1985), p. 504.

34. This position largely agrees with that of Leonard G. Schulze, "An Ethics of Significance," *SubStance* 14 (1985): 88–89.

best-seller and a philosophical and theoretical work. Produced from within the academy, it has been the subject of analysis in scholarly journals and conferences, but it has also attained a cult status. These features of the novel's reception point toward larger issues. The first concerns its relationship as "literature" to the mode of discourse identified as "criticism." The second involves the reception of a high-brow novel of ideas by contemporary mass culture.

Theoretical activity of the past few decades has fostered the now familiar idea that, as linguistic signs refer only to other signs, there can be no essential difference between literature and criticism: "both modes are subsumed into 'writing' as such."[35] Thus we have seen the emergence of new modes of discourse in works by such writers as Barthes and Derrida, who renounce "the axis of truth in favour of a discourse neither critical or literary, yet in some respects both," hoping "to subvert their reintegration into academic criticism."[36]

Umberto Eco is no stranger to these new modes of experimentation. *The Name of the Rose* is simply his most detailed and ambitious effort in a series of works that "concretize" the semiotic imagination. His essay "On the Generation of Aesthetic Messages in an Edenic Language," his autobiographical preface to his *Beato di Liebana*, and his "Il marziano assento," which appeared in 1978 in the satiric monthly *Il male*, must also be mentioned here. These experiments underline "the continuity of cer-

35. Terry Eagleton, *Literary Theory: An Introduction* (Minneapolis: University of Minnesota Press, 1983), p. 139. For an early and now classic expression of this position, see Eugenio Donato, "The Two Languages of Criticism," in *The Languages of Criticism and the Sciences of Man: The Structuralist Controversy*, ed. Richard Macksey and Eugenio Donato (Baltimore: Johns Hopkins University Press, 1970), pp. 89–97.

36. William Ray, *Literary Meaning: From Phenomenology to Deconstruction* (Oxford: Blackwell, 1984), p. 209; for a discussion of these new discursive modes in the work of Barthes, see John O'Neill, "Breaking the Signs: Roland Barthes and the Literary Body," in *The Structural Allegory: Reconstructive Encounters with the New French Thought*, ed. John Fekete, Theory and History of Literature 11 (Minneapolis: University of Minnesota Press, 1984), pp. 195–96; on Derrida, see Geoffrey Hartman, *Saving the Text: Literature / Derrida / Philosophy* (Baltimore: Johns Hopkins University Press, 1981). For a positive assessment of the value of such experimentation, see Gregory L. Ulmer, *Applied Grammatology* (Baltimore: Johns Hopkins University Press, 1985).

tain imaginative and affective models in [Eco's] critical and theoretical writings with those explicitly narrative." Belonging to neither one genre nor the other, they are entities unto themselves that give "practical demonstrations of the function of semiosis, the contrivance of the open work, the manipulation of codes for aesthetic purposes, [and] invention as a modality in sign production."[37]

In their self-conscious departures from the conventions of authorship, these works bear witness to the breakdown of canonical definitions of literature and criticism. Through his novel Eco has taken considerable pains to refute the idea of the autonomous author, both in the framing device of its introduction and in the *Postscript*, an essay addressed to those who wished to know what the book "meant" but which is devoted entirely to dispelling any illusions about his "property rights" to meaning. Eco depersonalizes his relationship to the work, as well as that of its narrator, claiming, probably with a dig at modern criticism, that a novel "is a machine for generating interpretations" (*PS* 2). Perhaps Eco's disavowals of authorship are intended to recall the critical opinion that challenges that privileged position, advancing a different conception of "writing."[38] Yet at the same time they point up how difficult it is for readers to give up the idea of the author altogether, whatever recent theory may say about the play of meaning. Adso's desire for textual authority and for ordered meaning (like that of the narrator who introduces his story) offers a paradigm of the readerly function that creates the author. If the author is not the ultimate legislator of meaning, neither is the text an endless play of signs. As Eco says in a more straightforward statement elsewhere, author and reader are "textual strategies," metaphors that refer "to the discursive and interpretative processes that constitute social communication; the two do not represent the points of origin and arrival of a textual message but rather the nodes of intersection . . . of the various social discourses that traverse the text."[39]

37. De Lauretis, *Umberto Eco*, p. 79.

38. See, for example, Michel Foucault, "What Is an Author?" in Harari, *Textual Strategies*, p. 148.

39. De Lauretis, *Umberto Eco*, p. 3; this point is developed in her more recent essay, "Gaudy Rose," pp. 19–21.

The theoretical posturing evident in Eco's disavowals of authorial autonomy contributes to the status of *The Name of the Rose* as literary and critical discourse. Participating in the novel's larger representation of theoretical language and themes, these disavowals coincide with the novel's opening series of textual displacements to highlight the many manipulations of voice that the novel performs. Such manipulations embody the dialogic "saturation" of language in which there is no personal or ultimate word, while at the same time attesting to the "individualized . . . speech act" that performs them. They furnish an image of the "authentic environment of an utterance . . . [as] dialogized heteroglossia, anonymous and social as language, but simultaneously concrete, filled with specific content and accented as an individual utterance."[40] A writer will necessarily make use of these diverse, heteroglot languages for his own ends, refracting through them his own intentions: "the author does not speak in a given language . . . but . . . as it were, *through* language, a language . . . that he merely ventriloquates."[41]

Bakhtin's account of the modes of "ventriloquating" might serve as a description of the discursive maneuvers of *The Name of the Rose*, illuminating the relationships of its author to the "authorial" voice, of the narrator to the languages he employs, of the characters to the discourses represented in their language. For instance, the novel deploys the languages of medieval monk, scholastic, and peasant, and the real and symbolic intersection of Latin and vernacular. It enacts a dialogue with other texts, with the idioms and conventions of other genres, with past and present. This ventriloquating of other discourses relativizes "linguistic consciousness . . . of language borders . . . created by history and society." *The Name of the Rose* presents an image of the novel as "intentional and conscious hybrid": it organizes a "*system for bringing different languages in contact with one another*, a system having as its goal the illumination of one lan-

40. Bakhtin, *Dialogic Imagination*, p. 272, and, in general, pp. 269–301.

41. Ibid., p. 299. See Bakhtin's description of the modes of appropriation of "another's speech," pp. 303–66, especially the instances of "double-voiced discourse," pp. 324–31.

guage by means of another."[42] With this overall aim, the novel underscores its affinity with literary criticism and theory, which pursue similar goals.

In *The Name of the Rose,* the notion of ventriloquating another's speech also points toward the practical aim of the novel's linguistic displacements and refractions. Bakhtin's life as well as his theory are instructive in this context. His dialogic conception of hybrid constructions and his notion of "speech of another" provided him with an "authorial loophole" through which he was able to ventriloquate ideas that were politically distasteful to the Soviet system. To that end he not only appropriated the voices of other writers, publishing his work under others' names, but he adopted the codes of certain ideologies (e.g., Marxism, psychoanalysis) in order to speak his own views. Produced under conditions of censorship as well as under potential threats to his life, Bakhtin's works thus exemplify the "dialogic space" that they describe.[43]

Though in writing the *Rose* Eco was by no means threatened by the censorship and political repression against which Bakhtin labored, the mode and rationale of his novel's utterance nonetheless correspond to those offered by Bakhtin's work. Bakhtin manipulated his personae, spoke in parables and allegories, and converted a radical, materialist Orthodox Christianity into a linguistic and moral philosophy.[44] These techniques are strikingly pertinent to Eco's novel: its manipulations of authorial and narrative personae; its attention to allegory, metaphor, and other modes of verbal indirection; and its interest in the place of corporeal reality in a philosophy of language all mark its own dialo-

42. Ibid., pp. 323, 366, 361. Bakhtin's description of the devices through which the novel creates "the image of a language" reads almost like a theoretical blueprint for Eco's novel; see pp. 358–66. On Bakhtin's idea of the novel as an ideal type, see Robert Anchor, "Bakhtin's Truths of Laughter," *Clio* 14 (1985), 237–57.

43. Holquist, "Politics of Representation," pp. 168–81. Holquist likens Bakhtin's ventriloquating to the early Christians' use of parable and allegory to spread a message to which the dominant culture was ideologically inhospitable. Such modes of indirection are typical of Russian utterance and often produce an allegorical "Aesopic language" (pp. 174, 180).

44. Ibid., pp. 174–76.

gism. The novel's medieval setting enhances its dialogic tactics, because the incarnational emphases of medieval Christian philosophy, linguistics, and aesthetics provide a historical reference point for a more contemporary materialist view of language. In *The Name of the Rose* Eco "ventriloquates" through the ideological codes of fiction a philosophy and politics of language.

If Bakhtin's dialogic manipulations of his works were occasioned by his poverty, imprisonment, and the social conditions of language, is there a comparable rationale for Eco's "throwing of his voice" in *The Name of the Rose*? Certainly it was not to circumvent the immediate dangers of his political environment, though some have seen the novel as a fable of contemporary Italian politics and culture. Rather, through its ventriloquism the novel embodies the circumstances of all utterance, calling attention to the political basis of all speech. More specifically, the novel's dialogic manipulations of "another's speech" may also be seen in light of its own reception.

Though it seems inappropriate to consider Eco's much admired and successful novel as an object of overt censorship, it is important to recognize the degree to which it deals with that issue. The novel is about censorship, not just of Aristotle's lost book, but of a theory of language and interpretation. William's final words in the novel indirectly—and fittingly—address the subject of censorship: what is it possible and permissible to communicate? The narrator's introduction also raises the topic, but in a refracted discourse that seemingly forswears the relevance of its subject and thereby appears to dismiss questions of censorship:

> I transcribe my text with no concern for timeliness. In the years when I discovered the Abbé Vallet volume, there was a widespread conviction that one should write only out of a commitment to the present, in order to change the world. Now, after ten years or more, the man of letters (restored to his loftiest dignity) can happily write out of pure love of writing. And so I now feel free to tell, for sheer narrative pleasure, the story of Adso of Melk, and I am comforted and consoled in finding it immeasurably remote in time . . . gloriously lacking in any relevance for our day, atemporally alien to our hopes and our certainties. (5)

The context of the narrator's involvement with the book further complicates this disclaimer: "The scholarly discovery . . . entertained me while I was in Prague, waiting for a dear friend. Six days later Soviet troops invaded that unhappy city. I managed, not without adventure, to reach the Austrian border" (1). Though the narrator claims to be consoled by the "glorious lack" of relevance in his "atemporally alien" work, the highly charged political moment from which it emerges makes his words suspect.

Purporting to dispel all ties between "stories" and the "world," the *Rose*'s introductory disclaimer presents a microcosm of the large-scale displacement achieved in the novel's refraction of philosophy and theory as fiction. Its disavowal of politics and embrace of belles lettres for "pure narrative pleasure" is the quintessential ventriloquistic move. The very declaration of the purity of its intention is a model of indirection: its insistence on the irrelevance of the past to the present only underscores the possibility of the opposite; its delight in the uncommitted "man of letters" suggests that "tales of books" may also be tales of "everyday worries." These appropriations of voice thus obliquely affirm what they set out to deny.

By rendering the language of fiction, philosophy, and theory in all their discursive complexity, *The Name of the Rose* questions the autonomy of categories such as "literature" and "criticism" and directs attention instead to the linguistic and social arena in which these modes of speaking interact with all others. The novel's representation of medieval and modern worlds and languages constitutes a striking image of a prevailing version of the aim of critical activity: to affirm "the connection between texts and the existential actualities of human life, politics, societies, and events. The realities of power and authority—as well as the resistances offered by men, women, and social movements to institutions, authorities, and orthodoxies—are the realities that make texts possible, that deliver them to their readers, that solicit the attention of critics."[45] *The Name of the Rose* realizes a

45. Edward W. Said, "Secular Criticism," in *The World, the Text, and the Critic* (Cambridge: Harvard University Press, 1983), p. 5.

critical consciousness aware of the nature of language, the conditions of knowledge, and of its own cultural function. It thereby engages in the critical activity whose themes, terms, and issues it also represents.[46] The novel's most notable achievement is that it offers its criticism not in the normative discourse of critical inquiry but in the equally normative discourse of fiction.

V

The novel's relation to the normative discourses of fiction and theory is strongly connected to its reception by the literary and critical establishment and to its status as best-seller. One challenge to my argument for the novel's unique status as "fictional theory" maintains that the *Rose* fails as such because experimental conflations of literature and criticism will achieve their goals only if they can "resist subsumption within pre-existing generic classes." Because the *Rose* is a "traditional appropriation" of literary voice, a best-seller and—God forbid—a Book-of-the-Month Club selection, its success has occurred "at the cost of any subversive potential." According to this view, the *Rose* simply takes "refuge from the regress of criticism within the folds of literature—which presumably states its truth in a non-propositional mode that cannot be disproven," thereby reinforcing "the most traditional distinction of the canon, namely the difference between original work and critical work."[47]

These remarks are predicated on certain assumptions about both "literature" and "criticism" which make the latter the more rational mode of discourse whose statements are subject to logically determined criteria of truth and value. It would be

46. On this consciousness as the proper goals of criticism, see Edward W. Said, "Criticism between Culture and System," in *The World, the Text, and the Critic*, pp. 182–83; Robert Weimann, *Structure and Society in Literary History* (Baltimore: Johns Hopkins University Press, 1984), pp. 275–76; Eagleton, *Literary Theory*, pp. 205–6.

47. Quotations in this and the following paragraph are from Ray, *Literary Meaning*, pp. 209, 219.

fruitful, however, to keep in mind the degree to which recent theory has labored to divest itself of these assumptions. If, in fact, the aim of experiments in critical and literary discourse is to subvert their "reintegration into academic criticism," I can hardly think of a better sign of success than being chosen as a Book-of-the-Month Club selection, especially considering that some of the most "subversive" texts of recent years have served rather to widen even further the gap between academic and popular culture—a whole new generation of stuffed shirts in designer labels.

The actual subversion of academic discourse might not look all that subversive. The subject of "traditional appropriations" of literary voice is illuminated by Eco's description of the "postmodern reply to the modern," which recognizes "that the past, since it cannot really be destroyed, because its destruction leads to silence, must be revisited: but with irony, not innocently. . . . It is no longer possible to speak innocently" (*PS* 67). *The Name of the Rose* is a whole-scale ironic revisitation of the past, both through its subject and setting and through its appropriation of traditional literary forms—detective fiction and historical novel—which provide a compelling format for bringing theory into the marketplace. Though he probably did not predict the extraordinary success of his novel, Eco's choice of detective story was by no means innocent. He is no stranger to mass culture. His works have repeatedly bridged the gap between high-brow and low-brow—witness his interest in Woody Allen, "Peanuts," James Bond, Sherlock Holmes, comic books, and, more recently, his use of Superman, Bo Derek, and Disneyland as illustrations of contemporary cultural semiotics.[48]

Even with its appeal to popular taste, *The Name of the Rose* is still obviously not a book for everyone. I know a number of mass-market readers who have never made it, in Eco's words, to "the top of the hill." Yet I can think of no other work of comparable complexity which has reached as wide an audience as has the *Rose*. With its adaptation as a motion picture for an interna-

48. See Umberto Eco, *Travels in Hyper Reality*, trans. William Weaver (San Diego: Harcourt Brace Jovanovich, 1986). See Eco's comments on reconciling his work as a scholar and as an observer of popular culture, pp. ix–xii.

tional audience, *The Name of the Rose* made its full entry into the mass culture whose attention it captured shortly after its publication. The significance of this peculiar passage from one medium to another, from one kind of audience to another, is illuminated by Eco's own observations on popular literature. In his *Postscript* he notes that "the concept of amusement is historical" (60); it is related to changing conceptions of popular approval and value. Reminiscing about the early 1960s, he recalls how writers criticized successful "plot" novels as escapist and praised experimental works that were rejected by a mass audience. But within a few years several changes occurred: plot returned to the novel and people became accustomed to the techniques of the avant-garde; what had formerly been unacceptable was now "codified as entertaining" (*PS* 60–63). Quoting remarks he had made on changing criteria for experimental fiction in 1965, Eco observes

> "sterile, today, and foolish is the polemic of those who consider an experiment a failure because of the fact that it is accepted as normal. . . . We insist that the unacceptability of the message on the part of the recipient was a guarantee of value only in a specific historic moment. . . . I suspect that we will perhaps have to give up that *arrière-pensée* . . . whereby any external scandal caused by a work can be considered a guarantee of worth. The very dichotomy between order and disorder, between a work for popular consumption and a work for provocation, though it remains valid, should perhaps be re-examined from another point of view. . . . I believe it will be possible to find elements of revolution and contestation in works that apparently lend themselves to facile consumption, and it will also be possible to realize, on the contrary, that certain works, which seem provocative and still enrage the public, do not really contest anything. . . Just recently I met someone who, because he had liked a certain product *too much*, had relegated it to a zone of suspicion." (*PS* 63–64)

Amusement, Eco maintains, "seems to conflict with the more thoughtful ideas we believe we have about the novel" (*PS* 59).[49]

49. See also *PS* 65–72, and, for a similar assessment of the postmodern, see Jean-François Lyotard, *The Postmodern Condition: A Report on Knowledge*, trans. Geoff Bennington and Brian Massumi, Theory and History of Literature 10

Here Eco provides another instance of that refracted language which characterizes both the *Rose* and its *Postscript*, this time to locate the novel in the debate about "serious" and "facile" works. When Eco calls attention to the role of audience expectations in the reception of any work and to the changing nature of those expectations, he invokes a critical commonplace: conceptions of art change. Categories such as avant-garde and normative, high-brow and popular, are, like ancient and modern, mobile values. Not surprisingly, Eco's distinction between "serious" and "facile" works reiterates the familiar medieval dichotomy between *uti* and *frui*, which he mentions on the dust jacket of the Italian edition of his novel.[50] More important, in addressing the potential value of popular works that amuse, Eco in effect replays the basic terms of the *Rose*'s debate on laughter. His remarks on the strategies of popular, "amusing" fiction —are the high-brow and serious necessarily important? is the low-brow necessarily trivial?—could be posed in terms that relate directly to his novel: how can criticism amuse? what attraction can a theoretical work hold for mass culture? Thus the problematic genre and complex reception of *The Name of the Rose* themselves embody the intellectual and interpretive debate at the heart of the novel. Its preoccupations with the hermeneutics of laughter and with the tropes of comedy are its own hermeneutics.[51]

In terms of the relation between "literature" and "criticism," "popular" and "serious" work, it would be tempting to see *The Name of the Rose* as an instance of carnival, its best-seller status being but one way that it inverts the norms of serious academic discourse and of high culture, bearing a marginal relationship to both. According to this model, Eco's playful refractions

---

(Minneapolis: University of Minnesota Press, 1984), p. 79, and Fredric Jameson's "Foreword," p. xvi.

50. For comments on the novel's relation to high and low culture, see Stephens, "Ec[h]o in Fabula," p. 64; Robert F. Yeager, "Fear of Writing, or Adso and the Poisoned Text," *SubStance* 14 (1985): 40–43; Schulze, "An Ethics of Significance," p. 100.

51. Louis Mackey makes a similar point in a different way, suggesting that the novel is the lost book of Aristotle on comedy; see "The Name of the Book," *SubStance* 14 (1985): 30–39.

of language within his novel, his entire presentation of philosophy as fictional amusement, embody the interpretive enlightenment that William of Baskerville assigns to laughter. After the manner of carnivalesque reversal and corporeality, *The Name of the Rose* could thus be construed as Eco's own "baring of his rump" to the guardians and authorities of critical discourse. Like all such carnivalesque inversions, the novel could be deemed an "authorized transgression." It depends on the rules of critical discourse in order to make its point, accomplishing its questioning of canonical ideas of literature and criticism only by embracing the terms of the model it sets out to question.

But it is important to recall here that Eco is not optimistic about the potential for carnival to enact anything truly new or transgressive. Proposing that other modes of the comic may have "more critical power," he balances the fundamental conservatism of carnival with the potential of humor, which offers a different relationship between violation and rule. If carnivalesque comedy acts to affirm the norms it violates, humor lingers on the contradiction between violation and rule. As I have already noted—the point bears repeating here—carnivalesque comedy focuses on the violation itself; humor suggests the possibility that the rule is wrong:

> Humor acts as a form of social criticism. . . . Semiotically speaking, if comic (in a text) takes place at the level of *fabula* or of narrative structures, humor works in the interstices between narrative and discursive structures. . . . Humor does not pretend, like carnival, to lead us beyond our own limits. It gives us the feeling, or better, the picture of the structure of our own limits. It is never off limits, it undermines limits from inside. . . . When a real piece of humour [*sic*] appears, entertainment becomes avantgarde: a supreme philosophical game. We smile because we feel sad for having discovered, only for a moment, the truth. But at this moment we have become too wise to believe it. We feel quiet and peaceful, a little angry, with a shade of bitterness in our minds. Humor is a *cold* carnival. (FF 8)

Eco's account of humor enables us to take possession of the serious import of his amusing novel. *The Name of the Rose* enacts humor's metasemiotic critique of "cultural and intertextual frames." On the level of *fabula* and "in the interstices between narrative and discursive structures" it interrogates the relations between frames: the codes of fiction and criticism, of the work for popular consumption and for intellectual provocation are momentarily rendered unstable. It challenges these customary configurations of discourse, not by overturning them, but by letting them speak simultaneously.[52]

The theoretical models I have called upon here by no means exhaust the possibilities for appropriating *The Name of the Rose,* as fiction or as theory. These possibilities are as various as the novel's individual readers and their readings. The approach to interpretation and discourse which the novel demonstrates is capacious enough to embrace the complex circumstances of its own reception. The *Rose* medievalizes contemporary theory, showing all the while that theoretical issues have a history deeply embedded in the values and stories of Western culture. It offers itself as high-brow fiction for mass consumption.

My own reading has proceeded according to the interests and the strategies of academic discourse, literary and theoretical, because that is the realm in which I believe *The Name of the Rose* stakes its greatest claim. The novel embodies a form of textual experimentation that at the very least suggests possibilities for "breaking with the very ways literature, literary criticism and its supporting social values are defined."[53] Yet it may also be the case that we do not have criteria for judging the effectiveness of new modes of discourse whose intent is to subvert the means by which we designate "literature" and "criticism," that these criteria will take shape only as we experience them. Along with William of Baskerville we might properly look for the "truth of the individual." And we must also consider how the generic expectations of the academy might affect our judgment about these new modes of discourse. How will we recognize these modes? What will they look like?

52. This description of the novel as an embodiment of humor is entirely in keeping with Bakhtin's idea of dialogic parody; see *Dialogic Imagination,* pp. 51, 55, 311.

53. Eagleton, *Literary Theory,* p. 90.

In the face of these questions we would do well to follow one of the dialogic modes of "other speech" that the *Rose* so deftly explores and consider the parable—or the allegory—provided by William and Adso's hunt for the mysterious book. As they dig through a pile of the herbalist's books in search of the deadly volume, Adso comes upon the precious text. He shows its first pages to William, who dismisses him with "'No, that's Arabic, you idiot!'" a rebuke for which he later harshly reprimands himself. Adso may be forgiven his mistake, but the far better-educated William, forgetting that books may be anthologies of works in several different languages, misreads the signs at his fingertips and in the haste of the moment abandons the tools that would have enabled him to make the proper identification. Because of his readerly expectations and his human fallibility, he fails to realize that the book with its initial pages in Arabic was in fact the book he sought. All along, he had been looking for one in Greek.

Index

Library of Congress Cataloging-in-Publication Data

Coletti, Theresa, 1950–
Naming the rose.

Includes index.
1. Semiotics—History. 2. Eco, Umberto. I. Title.
P99.C56 1988 001.51 87-47872
ISBN 0-8014-2114-4